ASSASSINATION, ANARCHY, AND TERRORISM

A Sociological Analysis

Gerhard Falk

University Press of America,® Inc.
Lanham · Boulder · New York · Toronto · Plymouth, UK

Copyright © 2012 by
University Press of America,® Inc.
4501 Forbes Boulevard
Suite 200
Lanham, Maryland 20706
UPA Acquisitions Department (301) 459-3366

Estover Road
Plymouth PL6 7PY
United Kingdom

Library of Congress Control Number: 2011940017
ISBN: 978-0-7618-5756-3 (clothbound : alk. paper)
eISBN: 978-0-7618-5757-0

Dedication

This book is dedicated to the victims of assassinations and terrorism, and especially to the six million Jews who were murdered because of their religion.

CONTENTS

Acknowledgments   vii

A Brief History of Assassinations   ix

Chapter One: European Assassinations   1

Chapter Two: American Assassinations   35

Chapter Three: Asian Assassinations   59

Chapter Four: Latin American Assassinations   81

Chapter Five: African Assassinations   91

Chapter Six: Anarchy and Terrorism   99

Chapter Seven: American Terrorism   123

Chapter Eight: The Muslim Assault on Western Civilization   145

Chapter Nine: The Causes of Assassinations — Some Theories   165

Bibliography   183

Index   203

Acknowledgments

I am indebted to Clifford Falk for the extensive amount of time he spent proof-reading this book. In addition I thank him for the formatting and other work he expended in bringing this project to fruition.

I also thank Ursula A. Falk for proofreading this lengthy manuscript.

A Brief History of Assassinations

In 874 CE an Iraqi peasant, Hamdan ibn Ashrat, popularly known as Qarmat, became the leader of the Ismaili sect of Islam. Leaving a bloody list of conquests behind, the sect's doctrines and methods of killing indiscriminately inspired the Ismaeli of Alamut, or Eagle's Nest in northern Persia, now called Iran, to wage a campaign of terror and murder against all opponents of their faith. This campaign began about 1092, more than two hundred years after Qarmat started that sect.

In his spirit, the Ismaili Muslims organized a sect whose leader was to be absolutely obeyed. Living in a mountain fort, 10,000 feet above sea level, they were impregnable. Alamut became a center for a group of young men who used hashish, a hemp derivative, to give them hallucinations of various kinds, reputedly allowing them the courage to kill at their masters' word. The killers were called "hashasheen" in Arabic, from which the word "assassin" is derived.[1]

In the 2nd Epilogue to his great historical novel War and Peace, Leo Tolstoy (1828-1910) wrote an appendix in which he proposes that all of history is predestined, although we imagine that we have free will. Tolstoy wrote that Napoleon was mistaken when he believed he controlled events. According to Tolstoy, "great men" are only accepting responsibility for events which they do not really control but which control them. "Great men," said Tolstoy, are unable to recognize their own impotence in the face of historical occurrences which would have happened without Napoleon or any other individual. "In historical events," wrote Tolstoy," great men — so called — are but labels serving to give a name to the event, and like labels they have the least possible connection with the event itself. Every action of theirs that seems to them an act of their own free will, is in an historical sense not free at all, but in bondage to the whole course of previous history, and predestined from all eternity."[2]

If predestination were the only reason for the development of historical events, then it would be reasonable to conclude that the assassination of "heads of governments" and other politicians would make no difference in the course of events. Instead, predestination would take assassinations into account and history would proceed on its course of inevitable movements just the same.

Therefore, the assassination of heads of state should give us a clue as to the validity of Tolstoy's claims. While we cannot know for certain what might have happened if those assassinated had lived, it is reasonable to assume that the opportunity to continue on one's political path would have led to far different results than the consequences of assassination, particularly in those instances in which the successor of the assassinated politician conducted a policy utterly foreign to the victim.

Since the tyrant of Athens, Hipparchus, was assassinated in 514 BCE, over 700 political assassinations have taken place on all continents from China in Asia to the United States of America and all lands between.

The majority of these assassinations did not target heads of state, simply because there are so many other politicians. The motives for these murders are not always the same. Nevertheless, it is evident that there are many more assassinations in countries where a turnover of power by peaceful means is not available, as is the case in any dictatorship.

Zarbal Iqbal and Christopher Zorn published a study entitled "The Political Consequences of Assassination" in 2008. This is a truly rare effort on the part of social scientists to explore this issue. Their findings are that the assassination of a "repressive and autocratic leader" is much more likely to create political and or economic turmoil than the assassination of a leader in a country which enjoys a well accepted institutionalized mode of succession. Such assassinations may be called "targeted killings" in that the victim is named and well known and viewed as the sole cause of the dissatisfaction, leading to his murder.[3]

Four American presidents have been assassinated. In each instance these murders have led to widespread speculation concerning a "conspiracy" among unknown persons who are believed to be "behind" the murder. These conspiracy theories devolved particularly upon the three prominent victims of assassination in the 1960's, when John Kennedy, Martin Luther King, and Robert Kennedy were assassinated.[4]

In any case, assassinations of prominent politicians and particularly heads of state have had consequences in some instances which were of a major sort and made a real difference in the development of the society in which the assassination occurred. In other cases, there were no major changes in the policies of the government which endured such a murder. In fact, there are those who claim that assassination of political leaders usually fails in the sense that the policies of the victim will be continued by his successors. This is not to say that the accession of a different person to power did not make a difference of some kind in each case of assassination. That is true simply because no two people are the same. Nevertheless, differences in governing style are not the same as differences in policy. The former makes for little difference in outcome. Furthermore, there are a variety of motives for the assassination of politicians or those viewed as a threat by the killers.

TYPES OF ASSASSINATIONS

Tyrants have been assassinated for centuries. A tyrant is someone not elected who seizes power by means of force and remains in power only as long as someone else does not kill him. This kind of murder was quite common in ancient Greece, ancient Rome and numerous other city-states and countries. An example of this kind of assassination was the murder of Hipparchus in 514 BCE whose death led to the tyranny of his brother Hippias.[5]

We are here concerned, not with tyrants, but with political assassinations, which may not necessarily involve a head of state. Political murder can victimize people who appear to be in the way of the ambitions of any politician seeking power. Here we may distinguish "aristocratic" assassinations, which affect only a small group of people at the top of the power structure. For example, in 1876, the Italian anarchist, Errico Malatesta, told the International Working Men's Association, meeting in Berne, Switzerland, that "revolution consists more of deeds than of words."Putting words into action, Malatesta and others entered two Italian villages in 1877, seized the tax collector's safe, and distributed the money to the poor. This example led to numerous attacks on kings, queens, emperors and presidents, who were killed in Europe and America. The assassination of one of these oligarchs is replaced by another member of the power elite without much if any change in policies of living conditions. Besides tyrants and aristocrats, assassinations may also victimize revolutionaries who victimized many people, created disorder and misery, and provoked widespread hatred. This has been called "plebian" assassination.[6]

Assassinations for personal motives. The best example of this kind of murder was the killing of President James Garfield by Charles Guiteau, a disappointed office seeker.

Another type of assassination is for power. This is most common. The best examples of these assassinations were the incessant assassinations of Roman emperors, often by their own troops, leading finally to the disintegration of the empire. This not only would include Julius Caesar, killed in 44 BCE, but also the emperors Caligula, killed in 41 BCE, Domitian, assassinated in 96 CE, Caracalla, killed in 217 CE, Aurelian in 275 CE, Probus, killed in 282 CE, Valentinian II, killed in 392 CE, and Velantinian III, assassinated in 455 CE These assassinations continued in the Italian city-states. Then there were and are diplomatic assassinations. The Council of Ten in Venice organized many political assassinations, of which numerous European politicians became the victims.[7]

During the one thousand years of feudalism, ending with the 15th century, there were only two assassinations of heads of state. The reason for this abatement of assassinations was the church doctrine of the sacredness of human life and the belief that sovereigns had been installed by God and could not therefore be removed. Once these doctrines had been weakened by the Italian renaissance, political assassination became rampant, as rulers and their enemies killed each other routinely.[8]

The Italian fascists under Mussolini committed similar diplomatic murders, as did the German Nazis. Assassinations by reason of state are committed in the name of the state's security. It was Machiavelli who promoted this kind of killing, of which the killing of Wallenstein by the agents of Ferdinand II is only one example. More recently, the killing of Ernst Röhm, the boss of the German brown shirts, by Hitler, is a good example, as Hitler murdered one of his most ardent friends and supporters in order to placate the German generals.[9]

Then there is religious assassination. The Inquisition slaughtered thousands of Jews and some Muslims. It was motivated by religious fanaticism, as was the "Gunpowder Plot" of 1605, when Guy Fawkes, encouraged by the Jesuits, attempted to kill King James I and the whole British parliament. Finally, we have assassinations motivated by extreme nationalism. The killing of the German foreign minister, Rathenau, by German super-nationalists, together with the later assassinations of people who had no power but appeared unpatriotic or un-German by followers of Adolf Hitler, are excellent examples.[10]

Assassins of democratically elected political leaders usually claim that there is no difference between liberal democracy and dictatorships, as both reputedly are agents of "political repression." Yet, if caught, the same assassins who call democracy a form of tyranny demand every constitutional right the state has to offer. Those who believe such conspiracy theories are usually very few. In Italy, during the 1960s and 1970s, when most kidnappings and assassinations took place, only 3000 "combatants" committed all the terror and bloodshed known as "the armed resistance movement."

Those who commit acts of terror and murder seek to show the public that the government is impotent, leading to the spread of a public panic. The government is seen as "absolutely evil" by assassins of political leaders. These extremists usually claim that the government is the terrorists and that they are the counter-terrorists. Hence the claim that "the vote doesn't work but the rifle does." Such doctrinaire extremism is not interested in any facts or in reality. They generally believe that if they kill a head of state or other important person then the government will resort to repressive measures which in turn will provoke a revolutionary civil war. In addition, assassinations always lead to numerous conspiracy theories about secret worldwide "international reactionary plans."

All these beliefs which support political assassination show that murder begins in the mind and may well be based on beliefs which do not correspond to reality at all. Yet, "that which people believe is real is real in its consequences."

NOTES

1. Gerhard Falk. *Murder: An Analysis of Its Forms, Conditions and Causes,* (Jefferson, N.C., McFarland, Inc. Publishers, 1990), 95.

2. Leo Tolstoy, *War and Peace,* (London: Heineman, 1964), 657.

3. Zaryab Iqbal and Chirstopher Zorn, "The Political Consequences of Assassination," *Journal of Conflict Resolution,* vol. 52, no.3, (June 2008), 385-400.

4. Sheldon Appleton, "The Polls-Trends: Assassinations," *The Public Opinion Quarterly,* vol. 64,,no. 4, (Winter 2000), 490-522.

5. Mabel Lang, "The Murder of Hipparchus," *Historia: Zeitschrift fur Alte Geschichte,* vol. 3, no. 4, (1953), 396.

6. Oscar Jaszi, "The Stream of Political Murder," *American Journal of Economics and Sociology,* Vol. 3, no. 3, (April 1944), 335-355.

7. John J. Norwich, *A History of Venice,* (New York: Vintage Publishing, 1989).

8. Saul Padover, "Patterns of Assassination in Occupied Territory," *The Public Opinion Quarterly,* vol. 7, no. 4, (Winter 1943), 682.

9. Eleanor Hancock, *Ernst Roehm: Hitler's Chief of Staff,* (New York: Palgrave McMillan, 2008).

10. Ibid, 335-355.

Chapter One
European Assassinations

ANCIENT GREECE

The Assassination of Philip II of Macedonia (382 BCE – 336 BCE)

Philip became king of Macedonia in 359 BCE on the deaths of his father and two brothers. A skilled diplomat as well as a military innovator, he introduced the phalanx form of combat into the Macedonian army and thereby succeeded in conquering numerous adjacent towns, including areas then belonging to Athens. He also defeated the Illyrians and other ancient peoples in the Balkan hill country north of Macedonia. Philip conquered every important Greek city state, even to the Adriatic Sea. He attempted the siege of Byzanthium, later to become the capital of the Byzantine or late Roman Empire and called Constantinople. In 1453 it became Istanbul after the Turkish invasion.

In 336 BCE Philip was assassinated by one of his bodyguards as he entered a theater where the marriage of his daughter was to be celebrated. Historians have debated the motive for this assassination, which may have been instigated by Philip's son Alexander and his mother or inspired by other motives. In any event, that assassination led to the ascendancy of Alexander III to the throne of Macedonia, with dramatic and long lasting consequences for the entire ancient world.[1]

Alexander III is generally called "the Great" because he conquered a territory far greater than any territory ruled by one man before him. Before he died at the age of 33, he had subjected one million square miles, ranging from the Danube in the north and the Mediterranean in the west all the way to India in the east. Included in the empire was Egypt, Turkey, Syria, Judea, Gaza, Iraq, Iran and the Punjab area of India. This meant that Alexander had made himself master of an area one third the size of "the lower 48" states of the union.

Because Alexander did not live long, and his children were murdered, his generals divided the empire among them after Alexander died in 323 BCE.[2] The division of the Macedonian empire had far reaching consequences in European history. Although the empire was at first divided into four parts, two of the generals were unable to "hang on" to their kingdoms, so that only two empires evolved from Alexander's conquests. The Seleucid Empire in the east was founded by general Seleucus in 311 BCE. It included modern Lebanon, Syria, Iraq, Iran, Afghanistan, parts of Turkey, Armenia, Turkmenistan, Uzbekistan, and Tajikistan. (Stan means land, as in Uzbekistan or land of the Uzbeks).The southern Egyptian empire was founded by general Ptolemy in 305 BCE when he took the title of Pharaoh. Endless wars between the Ptolemaic dynasty in Egypt and the Seleucid dynasty finally located in Babylon (Syria) mark the nearly 250 years of their rule, until Rome defeated both and established themselves in all the former Greek territories by 64 BCE.

As the Seleucid Empire began to disintegrate because of numerous revolts against its rule, the Jews revolted against the Syrian — Greeks, as the Bible calls them, and established the Maccabean dynasty, which ruled Judea from 165 BCE until 70 CE, when Rome destroyed Jerusalem. The anniversary of the Maccabean dedication of the Temple in Jerusalem is to this day celebrated in every Jewish home. That celebration is called "Chanukah," the Hebrew word for dedication.[3]

Ptolemy I the Savior (367 BCE - 283 BCE) was a close friend of Alexander the Great and became the Pharaoh of Egypt by means of a number of assassinations and wars when Alexander died in 323 BCE. He died after forty years of constant war and is remembered as the founder of the great library at Alexandria. He wrote a history of Alexander's wars, which has been lost but served as the basis for subsequent histories of these campaigns. Ptolemy also sponsored the mathematician Euclid, whose Euclidian geometry is taught to this day.[4]

Fifteen generations of Ptolemies ruled Egypt from 323 BCE until the death of Cleopatra in 30 BCE. Then the Romans came and Egypt remained a province of that empire until the fall of Constantinople in 1453.

The Macedonian Greeks, together with the Seleucids and the Athenians, promoted the Hellenistic Age. While a good deal of attention is given Athens and its civilization, Hellenism is largely overlooked by popular histories. Yet, the two empires descending from the conquests of Alexander the Great left a considerable legacy behind. One was the Greek language, spoken all over the ancient world. The works of Aristotle and Plato, the writings of so many other Greek philosophers, and the New Testament were all written in Greek and understood. In fact, except for the tremendous influence of Judaism on the Western world, Greek civilization laid the foundations of European culture thereafter. This was true in politics, economics, law, and science, all of which were absorbed by the Romans and passed on to Western Europe. The Ptolemies also invented the use of money instead of barter and the organization of bureaucracy to serve the state. This system was used by the Roman emperors and passed on to the nation states which had been provinces of the Roman empire.[5]

The end of the Macedonian-Greek rule by Rome did not end Greek influence in the world. On the contrary, as Rome expanded its power, the numerous ethnic groups governed by Roman arms increased their influence, so that Greek and Jewish thought and literature, art and philosophy, mathematics and religion, became prominent in all of the Mediterranean provinces Rome dominated. To this day (2010) these influences govern the minds of men throughout the western world, although the Roman Empire has long since disappeared. The Hellenization (Hellas is the name of Greece in the Greek language) of Western civilization became the permanent inheritance of the entire occident.[6]

One may speculate forever whether the Greek culture would have become so influential if Philip II had not been assassinated. It is however by no means idle speculation that the short reign of his son Alexander transformed the western world. Alexander's campaigns diffused Greek culture throughout the Mediterranean world, so that the art, the architecture, and democracy became the inheritance of a large segment of mankind, together with Euclid's geometry and the Socratic method.

ROME

The Assassination of Julius Caesar

Although William Shakespeare (1564-1616) has furnished generations of English teachers with a livelihood, Shakespeare's description of Caesar is mostly fiction, suiting Shakespeare's imagination with little relevance to fact.

Of course, history is written in each epoch in a manner reflecting knowledge so far, added to the prejudices of the historian at the time. Nevertheless, it can be said with some confidence that ever since the historian Leopold von Ranke (1795-1886) demanded that history reflect "wie es eigentlich gewesen ist," or "as it truly occurred," a great deal of effort has been made to base historical biography on documents that reflect the facts and omits legend as far as possible.

It is well known that Edward Gibbon wrote a magnificent English prose in his famous study, The History of the Decline and Fall of the Roman Empire. It is also well known that Gibbon was unable to distinguish fact from fiction, so that he included numerous legends in his writings, legends which may have been old, even ancient, but nevertheless untrue.[7]

Therefore we are fortunate in that we can briefly reconstruct the life of Julius Caesar, whose assassination in 44 BCE had some major consequences, not only for Rome but for the western world thereafter.

Caesar was born Gaius Julius Caesar in 100 BCE in Rome, into the prestigious Julian family. Almost from birth he was embroiled in politics when, at a young age, he was appointed by his politician uncle to a minor position as priest in the ancient Roman religion. He married Cornelia in 84 BCE and fled from Rome two years later because the dictator Sulla had placed him on an "enemies" list. He returned at the age of 22, having been elected to the priestly Roman "pontificate." In 69 BCE Caesar was elected questor or judge. He then became governor of Spain and in 59 BCE he was elected consul and one year later he was appointed governor of Gaul, known today as France. From then, for seven years, Caesar led the armies of Rome to conquer all of Gaul, including everything west of the Rhine River.

Caesar became one of three consuls of Rome known as the triumvirs. The other two were Crassus and Pompey. After Crassus was killed in battle, Pompey was made sole consul, as Caesar was in Gaul until he crossed a small river, the Rubicon, with his troops, and chased Pompey out of Rome. Caesar then occupied Spain, and returned to Rome as dictator and consul. Having defeated Pompey at a battle in Greece, he returned to Rome as sole dictator after Pompey was assassinated in Egypt.

According to the constitution, all previous Roman dictators ruled only six months. Caesar made himself dictator for life because he had the army behind him. He was also made pontifex maximus, or head of the state religion, and used the title imperator. All these efforts to be absolute ruler of a country which was governed by a number of families and a senate led to Caesar's assassination, motivated by the fear of the senators that their privileges were threatened. Caesar was killed on the 15th or the Ides of March.[8]

Speculation concerning the outcome of Roman history if Caesar had lived is useless. We can, however, record that upon his assassination his adopted son, Octavian, ended the republic and established himself as an emperor and Rome as an empire.

Octavian (63 BCE – 14 CE)

When Caesar was murdered, his adopted son Octavian was 19 years old. He was in Greece at that time and returned to Italy, but not to Rome at once. Having entered Italy, he first contacted important politicians in Rome before coming home. He has been depicted as cautious and cool headed despite his young years. Arrived in Rome, he was legally pronounced the heir of Caesar.[9]

Nevertheless, Octavian shared power with Marcus Antonius and Marcus Aemilius Lepidus in a three man military dictatorship. This triumvirate did not last long. Lepidus was driven into exile in 36 BCE and Marc Antony committed suicide in 30 BCE after losing the battle of Actium a year earlier. Antony's death led to the suicide of his ally, the Queen of Egypt, Cleopatra, as well.[10]

Now, Octavian became the sole consul of Rome. Yet, he continued to support the Roman senate as the "true" ruling power in Rome. In fact, Octavian took several years to finally in 23 BCE establish himself as emperor because he was supported by the army, ever ready to attack the Senate if needed by Octavian. Octavian compelled the Senate to grant him numerous powers for life. He ruled by means of patronage, military power and financial success. Further, he called himself "son of God" on the grounds that the senate had recognized Julius Caesar as a god in 42 BCEE (after his death).

In January of 27 BCE the Senate gave Octavian the title of Augustus, derived from the Latin word augere, to increase, and used in English to this day as in "augment." This was a religious title so that Augustus could claim divinity.[11]

There can be little doubt that Caesar intended to make himself sole ruler of Rome for life. Nevertheless, his murder meant that it was his adopted son who carried out that ambition and succeeded in bringing about an empire larger than any that had been seen in the Western world. In 25 BCE when Rome was still a Republic (Res Publica, the public thing) Rome ruled about 1,061,000 square miles and had a population of approximately 57 million. By the year 50 CE. Roman rule had grown to cover 1.6 million square miles. At its greatest extent, the Roman empire included 1.9 million square miles with a population of 88 million in the year 117 CE.[12] The United States of America had over three hundred million people and 3.8 million square miles in 2009.

It is of course evident that before Casesar and Octavian converted the republic into a one man dictatorship and empire, Rome had already expanded far beyond Italy. Yet, the establishment of the empire under Augustus had numerous consequences associated with the sheer size of the empire in an age of poor communication. This led to the failure of the Romans to integrate so diverse a population ruled by them into a unified whole.

Consequently, Rome not only dispersed the Latin language all over Europe, but also absorbed into that language the numerous languages known to the peoples Rome ruled. The long range outcome of this dispersal is the use of 47 romance languages today, which may be described as the grandchildren of Latin. Five of these languages are national languages. They are Romanian, spoken by about 28 million people, almost all in Romania, Italian, spoken by approximately 60 million almost all in Italy, French, spoken by about 82 million worldwide, Portuguese, spoken by about 256 million in Portugal and Brazil, and Spanish, spoken by about 360 million in Spain and Latin America. The other 42 languages based on Latin are spoken by small minorities in either Romance speaking lands or in counties such as Dalmation, Corsican, Acadian, Romansch and Ladino.

English is also heavily influenced by Latin. About 28% of English words are directly descendent from Latin due to the invasion and settlement of the Romans in England in the first century and another 28% are of French origin due to the invasion of England by William the Conqueror and the French in 1066. Therefore, English is at least 56% of Latin descent.[13]

Therefore, one of the evident consequences of the assassination of Julius Caesar was and is the usage of the Latin based languages around the world.

The Assassination of Pompey (106 BCE – 48 BCE)

Roman history includes numerous assassinations of leading politicians which inevitably had consequences in addition to the assumption of power by the killers and their supporters. Julius Caesar was by no means the only political leader murdered by his rivals. Earlier, in 133 BCE, the senate murdered Tiberius Gracchus, a Roman "trinune." Later, eighteen Roman emperors were assassinated, beginning with Caligula in 41 CE and ending with Florianus in 276.

The victorious Roman general Pompey was assassinated in 48 BCE, four years before the murder of Julius Caesar. His death became most significant with reference to Jewish history and consequently the rise of Christianity as a world religion.

The "New Testament" includes the epistles or letters written by the apostles to the Jewish communities dispersed throughout the Roman Empire at that time. These letters were written to the Jewish communities in Rome, Corinth, Galatia, Ephesia, Phillippia, Thessalonia, Collosia and others. Evidently, Jews had dispersed into Greek and Latin speaking areas even before the destruction of the Temple in Jerusalem in 70 CE.

That destruction was provoked by the civil war within Israel concerning the dispute between two contenders for the throne of Israel. Josephus, in his Jewish Antiquities, wrote: "For this misfortune which befell Jerusalem Hyrcanus and Aristobulus were responsible, because of their dissension. For we lost our freedom and became subject to the Romans..." The result was that the Roman general Pompey was invited by both sides in that war of the Jews against one another to come into ancient Israel and settle the issue between Aristobulus and Hyrcanus, "each of whom asked him (Pompey) to come to his aid." As Josephus told it: "...but those of the other faction admitted Pompey's army and handed over to him the city and the palace." Pompey had come with his army in 63 BCE, destroyed parts of Jerusalem, entered the sacred Temple and, finding no statue or anything else in the "holiest of the holy," treated the Jewish temple with respect. Josephus describes the fall of the Temple in these words: "For Pompey and not a few of his men went into it and saw what it was unlawful for any but the high priest to see. But though the golden table was there and the sacred lampstand and the libation vessels and a great quantity of spices, and beside these in the treasury the sacred moneys amounting to two thousand talents, he (Pompey) touched none of these because of piety, and in this respect also he acted in a manner worthy of his virtuous character."[14]

The subsequent assassination of Pompey in Egypt meant not only that Pompey would never become emperor despite his great victories but that Israel became subject to far harsher treatment at the hands of the Roman occupiers than was the case when Pompey had first invaded Jerusalem. Thereafter, a succession of Roman governors and emperors made Jewish life most difficult in the

Jews' own country, particularly when the emperor Caligula demanded that his statue be set up in the Jewish temple and that he be worshipped as a god. The Jews revolted repeatedly while also fighting each other until Titus, then a Roman general and later emperor, burned the Temple in the year 70 CE and ended Jewish government in Israel until 1948, when the Jews once more proclaimed their independence in the land of their ancestors.[15]

One of the major reasons for the Jewish revolt against the Romans was the demand that the Jews recognize the emperor as a god. This demand had been enforced on the Roman population since Caesar was declared a god by the Roman senate and continued thereafter. Nothing is more obnoxious to Jews than the belief that a human is a god. This led to the revolt of the Jews in 70 CE and subsequently led to a further revolt against Rome in 132 CE, leading to the final defeat of the Jewish population in the Holy Land in 135 CE. Thereafter the dispersion of the Jews throughout the Roman Empire appeared to have become final as the emperor Hadrian forbade the Jews to ever settle in Jerusalem again and also prohibited the practice of Judaism.[16]

The dispersion of the Jews throughout the Roman provinces from Israel to Spain led to the success of Christianity and the success of that religion in literally conquering the ancient world around the Mediterranean. It is therefore evident that the assassination of Caesar and the earlier assassination of Pompey led to that dispersion and therefore the rise of Christianity. Christianity emerged as a world religion because it was founded by Jews. Christianity succeeded because millions of Jews fled into various Roman areas and there became Christians.

Of course, Christianity is by no means entirely of Jewish origin. Many beliefs held dear by Christians originated in Greece. Nevertheless, the dispersion of the Jews subsequent to the assassinations of both Pompey and Caesar was an essential element in the promotion of Christian beliefs.

RUSSIA

The Assassination of Czar Alexander II (1818-1881)

On March 13, 1881, Czar Alexander II of Russia was driving along the Catherine Canal in St. Petersburg when Nikolai Rysakov, a member of a revolutionary group called "People's Will," threw a grenade at him which did not touch him but wounded some of his bodyguards. As the Czar left his carriage and stood talking to the wounded bodyguards, a second assassin, Ignacy Hryniewiecki, tossed a second bomb between the feet of the Czar. This tore his stomach open, smashed his legs, and mutilated his face. He died an hour later.[17]

That assassination had major consequences for the Russian people, as the murdered Czar had instituted a number of important reforms which his son, Alexander III, would not continue. Instead repression of all liberal impulses in

Russia became the rule and as usual in Europe, the Jews were blamed for the murder of Alexander II, although they had nothing to do with this terrible act.

Although Alexander II was raised in St. Petersburg to view all dissent and criticism of authority as a serious crime, he became "the great reformer" after he succeeded his father to the throne of the Russian Empire in 1855. Six years after his accession to the throne, March 3, 1861, Alexander signed the emancipation law which gave the serfs in the empire their freedom, so that they could become independent communal proprietors on the land they farmed.

In addition, Alexander II reformed the Army and Navy, introduced a new judicial administration, fashioned a scheme of local self government, permitted elective assemblies in towns and rural areas, and made numerous other reforms. Nevertheless, those areas of the Russian empire inhabited by non-Russians in Poland, Lithuania and other non-Russian provinces were subject to constant agitation, leading to a number of uprisings which Alexander suppressed with exceptional brutality. Even the Polish language was prohibited, as was Lithuanian, Ukrainian, and other languages. No doubt, these repressions led to Alexander's murder, since the most liberal Czar in Russian history was also an oppressor.[18]

The consequences of Alexander's assassination led not only to the Russian revolution of 1917, but also promoted the migration of millions of Jews from Russia to the United States and elsewhere. In sum, the policies of Alexander III were repressive as, under the influence of his advisor, Konstantin Pobedonostsev, he rejected the reforms his father had achieved.

Konstantin Petrovitch Pobedonostsev was born in 1827. He became known to the royal family of Russia because, as a law professor, he had published a number of books on the law and was therefore asked to teach law to the royal family. Thereafter he was appointed chief prosecutor and tutor to the crown prince, Alexander III. Frightened by the changes brought about by the reform minded Czar Alexander II, Pobedonostsev used his influence on Alexander III to retard all reform efforts which came to nought on the assassination of Alexander II. It is most likely that the failure of Alexander III to continue the reforms of his father finally led to the revolution of 1917 and the assassination of the Romanov family in 1918.[19]

Pobedonostsev believed that power should be concentrated in the hands of the monarchy, that order and prosperity "is found at the top, in the person of the supreme authority," which was also viewed as the solution to any conflict. Pobedonostsev, an ardent believer in the Russian Ortodox dogma, also held "the Jews" responsible for any revolutions everywhere. He believed in a "Jewish conspiracy," a charge which religious haters from the Spanish Inquisition to the Muslims of the 21st century repeat again and again.

All these beliefs were taught to Alexander III when he was still "crown prince," so that he put them into policy once he became Czar. Pobedonostsev repressed all attempts to limit the power of the Czar, as had been achieved in

England. He supervised all plays, exhibitions and all literature to insure that nothing was said or shown that tended to dispute the authority of the government. He inspected libraries and read editorials of even the smallest circulation newspapers, which were heavily censored.

As chief prosecutor, Pobedonostsev hindered women's emancipation and prevented the reform of the marriage laws. Religion, too, was supervised and dissidents prosecuted. Lutherans and Uniates were fined and even imprisoned for using Lutheran or Uniate rites.

Pobedonostsev called the Russian people "a horde that lives in stone tents." His contempt for the Russian people was only surpassed by his hatred of the Jewish population, which mostly came under the control of Russia after the second and third partitions of Poland in 1793 and 1795.[20]

Russia is the world's largest country. It has 6,592,800 square miles, compared to 3.8 million square miles which comprise the United States. In 1897, 4.13% of the Russian population of 129 million, or 5,189,000, were Jewish.

Although Alexander II made Jewish life in Russia as miserable as it had been almost everywhere in the world, Alexander was nevertheless willing to relax some of the restrictions. These restrictions included that Jews could not hire Christian servants, could not own land, and could only travel in parts of his empire. On the accession of Alexander III and under the influence of Pobednostsev, Jews were labeled "Christ killers" and oppressors of Christians. Although the brutality of the Russians was later surpassed by German mass murders, the treatment of the Russian Jews under Alexander III and his son, Nicholas II (1868-1918), was indeed horrific.[21]

Jews were expelled from rural districts and from the interior of the country. Jewish women were forced to hold a "ticket" identifying them as prostitutes. Russian Jews, and those in Romania, were subject to special legislation, deprived of economic and educational opportunities, and subject to physical violence. These attacks were called "pogroms," meaning "to demolish," and occurred sporadically. The worst of these attacks came in 1903 in the town of Kishinev. Here 47 Jews were murdered and over 90 wounded at the instigation of the government of Nicholas II. Thereafter, massacres of Jews took place in eighty-four Russian towns, leading to the murder of 50,000. Jews were accused of "ritual murder" and other "crimes" which were inventions of the government and the church. All this and more led to the emigration of 1.7 million Russian Jews to the United States, while another 300,000 came from other European countries, so that between 1871 and 1914 more than two million Jews migrated to America.[22]

In 1882, one year after the assassination of Alexander II, Russian Jews, convinced that they had no future in their homeland, founded the town of Rishon-Le-Zion (The First in Zion) on the coastal plain of Judea. It marked the beginning of the return of the Jews to their ancient homeland and the establishment of an independent Jewish country, Israel, for the first time in 1,878 years.[23]

The Origins of the Russian Revolution

Russia has never been a free country. Yet, the reactionary policies of Alexander III and his successor and son, Nicholas II, led to the revolution of 1917 and the subsequent establishment of the communist state known as the Soviet Union. The Russian revolution began in the hope of creating a state based on the principle of liberty and equality as promoted by the American revolution of 1776 and the French revolution of 1789.

The revolution of 1917 had been provoked by the reactionary policies of Alexander III and the continuation of these policies by Nicholas II. That Czar and his aristocratic entourage had become utterly alienated from the Russian people, so that at the coronation of Nicholas, more than 2,000 people in the crowd witnessing the event were killed by the police, even as the imperial party danced at a ball sponsored by the French embassy.[24]

The resulting violence led Nicholas to resign on March 15, 1917, in favor of a cousin who refused the appointment. Subsequently, Alexander Kerensky organized a provisional government which lasted eight months and was then replaced by the Bolshevik (majority) government of Vladimir Ulyanov (Lenin), only to be replaced in turn by the brutal dictatorship of Stalin (Georgii Djugashvilii), which resembled the cruelties of Alexander III and Nicholas II. This means that the Russian revolution failed because it did not provide the Russian people with freedom but repeated under the label of communism the same tyranny that had always existed in Russia and exists there even in 2011 under the dictatorship of Vladimir Putin, a former head of the Stalinist secret police. This, then, is another consequence of the assassination of Alexander II, whose reforms might have given Russians an eventual free democracy.

FRANCE

The Assassination of Henry IV, King of France

The Edict of Nantes was issued by Henry IV in 1598. Henry IV was a Protestant by education and a Catholic by family ties. He practiced the Calvinist religion until he was confronted with the choice of remaining a Huguenot or ascending the throne of France after the assassination of Henry III. He chose the latter and became a Catholic. Then he was crowned King of France in 1594. Yet, his sentiments still favored the Protestants, so that in 1598, Henry IV issued the Edict of Nantes, which allowed Protestants the right to practice their religion. They were called "Huguenots" because the French could not pronounce "Eidesgenossen" in the German language used in Switzerland. That word means Comrades in the Oath, which Calvinists swore in their determination to renounce Catholic doctrine.

The Edict of Nantes, a city in western France at the Loire River, treated Protestants for the first time as equal French subjects, so as to bring about national unity. The edict reinstated the rights of Protestants and offered freedom of conscience to them, but not to Jews. The edict allowed Protestants to work in any field, or for the state. Protestants could now bring their grievances to the king. The most important consequence of the Edict of Nantes was the end of the religious wars which troubled France during the second half of the 16th century. The Edict reaffirmed Catholicism as the official religion of France.[25] When Henry was assassinated by François Ravaillac, a Catholic fanatic, in 1610, his widow Marie de Medicis became regent to her 9 year old son Louis XIII.[26]

Henry IV was "ahead of his time" in that he was willing to permit religious choice, at least for Protestants. He ended the religious wars that had plagued France for years. Yet, his murder led to the absolutism of his successors, particularly that of his grandson, Louis XIV, who undoubtedly provoked the events of the French revolution. Louis XIV ruled France from 1643 until his death in 1715, a period of seventy-two years. He called himself "the sun king." He revoked the Edict of Nantes in 1685 and fought five wars in an effort to create total uniformity in politics and religion in France. His successor Louis XV made no further concessions to the people of France, so that the repressions of Louis XIV continued into the reign of Louis XVI and, therefore, the French Revolution of 1789.[27]

It is evident that if Henry IV had lived, his reforms would have continued and therefore the decline in the power of the French kings would have resembled the English experience, which gradually reduced the monarchy to a ceremonial enterprise without political power. Because Henry IV was assassinated, repression continued, leading to the terror and bloody revolution of 1789 and the killing of Louis XVI and his wife, Marie Antoinette.

The Assassination of Jean Jaures (1859-1914)

On July 31, 1914, the French socialist leader Jean Jaures was shot and killed by Raoul Villain, who fired two bullets through a restaurant window. The next day, on August 1, 1914 France announced general mobilization against Germany as the First World War began.[28]

Villain, like so many other killers, believed that he had wasted his life, that he had no achievements, and that he wanted to do something that would give him publicity. He wanted to be remembered and in that he succeeded. Villain was a member of an organization called "The League of Young Friends of Alsace-Lorraine." This referred to the occupation of Alsace and Lorraine, two provinces of France at the Rhine River which Germany annexed after Prussia defeated the French in 1871. That defeat had profound consequences in France. It led to the notorious "Dreyfus Affair," in which a Jewish member of the

French general staff was falsely accused of collaborating with the Prussians. Although Dreyfus was eventually rehabilitated, he had spent years in a hideous prison on Devil's Island. The Dreyfus conviction and the subsequent recognition that the army had falsified documents to get the Jew convicted led to years of acrimony between supporters of the army and their opponents. Army supporters wanted a war of revenge against Germany so as to recover the lost provinces, but Jaures and the socialists made every effort to prevent such a war.[29]

Jaures was a member of the French parliament, where he held eloquent speeches seeking to avoid another war. He also wrote journal and newspaper articles against war. He sought the unification of all working class citizens of all countries, as proclaimed by his predecessor Karl Marx. This led to open calls for his assassination by newspapers and by members of parliament as well as government officials and soldiers.[30]

We can speculate that if the policies of Jaures had succeeded, the First and Second World Wars may have been avoided since the second war was the consequence of the first. Had Jaures lived, so much misery might have been avoided. Yet, on the day of Jaures' assassination, Germany and Austria were warning of the imminence of war between them and Serbia, because the Archduke of Austria, Franz Ferdinand, had been assassinated in Serbia on June 28, 1914. The great slaughter which followed and extended to the 2nd World War far outweighed the meaning of the assassination of the archduke. Yet that was not foreseen by those who went to war that fateful August.

AUSTRIA

The Assassination of Franz Ferdinand, Archduke of Austria

No assassination during the past century has received as much attention in the popular media as the murder of the Archduke of Austria, Franz Ferdinand, at Sarajevo, the capital of Bosnia-Herzegovina, on June 28, 1914. Ferdinand's wife, Sophie, Duchess of Hohenberg, was killed with her husband by Gavrilo Princip and his accomplices, Nedelyko Chabrinovich and Trifko Grabezh.[31]

This assassination was undoubtedly one of the contributing factors in precipitating the First World War, although so many other conditions also contributed to this horror that it would be foolish to view these murders as the only reason for so much carnage.

Franz Ferdinand was the nephew of the emperor of Austria and king of Hungary, Franz Joseph. He was the intended successor to his uncle, because the son of Franz Joseph, Crown Prince Rudolf, had died in 1899. The emperor had no other sons. Therefore, Franz Ferdinand was to become the next emperor and was called "Archduke" from the Greek "archein," to rule.

The assassination of the archduke was the product of a conspiracy organized by a number of Serbian government officials who supplied the killers with arms and with access to their eventual victims. These officials had organized a "National Defense" society, which was active in distributing propaganda against the "Dual Monarchy" of Austria-Hungary. This society was organized in 1908 after the annexation of Bosnia-Herzegovina by Austria. The Serbs felt threatened by the Austrian Empire and sought to unite all Serbs, as many lived in the Austro-Hungarian empire, particularly in Bosnia. Consequently, a second society of Serb nationalists was organized by some Serbian army officers. This society was commonly called "the black hand." This group was mainly responsible for giving the assassins the weapons they used.[32]

It was therefore not only Princip who shot at the archduke. Prior to this successful assassination, two other would be assassins threw bombs at Franz Ferdinand, but did not succeed in killing him. It is therefore astonishing that even after these efforts at murdering him earlier the same day, neither he nor his hosts made any real effort to protect him from further attempts.

There are many who believe that this assassination was "the cause" of the First World War while others dismiss the assassination altogether as a cause of that war. The fact is that there had been a great deal of tension between Serbia and Austria-Hungary, so that the assassination was by no means the only cause of the war. Nevertheless, it is entirely possible that no such war would have occurred if the assassination had not taken place.

Among the precipitating causes of the First World War, other than the assassination, were the increased concern of the German emperor and others over the mounting armaments acquired by Russia, the belief by the Germans that England would not enter a European war, that Germany had increased the number of its naval ships, that Germany was willing to make war on Russia knowing that Russia would never allow a fellow Slav country, i.e. Serbia, to be defeated or permit Serbia to lose its independence, and finally, that Austria, at the urging of Germany, presented the Serbian government with an utterly unacceptable ultimatum. That ultimatum led both France and Britain to believe that the demands made on Serbia were designed to establish Austrian and German control over the Balkans. Moreover, the Germans believed that they could easily defeat both Russia and France and therefore rejected all compromises proposed by England. Finally, the Germans and their allies never suspected that the United States would eventually enter the war against them. All told, therefore, the responsibility for the war rested on Germany.[33]

There is no doubt that the Second World War was the direct consequence of the First World War. Hitler, an Austrian, made it clear that he sought to revenge the defeat of Germany by attacking Poland in 1939 and overrunning France in 1940. To the extent that the assassination of the archduke influenced the decision to make war in 1914, Princip and his conspirators unleashed the most horrendous nightmare Europe and the world have ever known.

The Assassination of Engelbert Dollfuss (1892-1934)

On July 25, 1934, Austrian Nazis overthrew the Austrian government by force. They stormed the office of the chancellor, Engelbert Dollfuss, and shot him in the chest and killed him as he drowned in his own blood. The Nazis had entered his office as Dollfuss tried to escape by a back door. Here he was met by Otto Planetta, who shot him twice. In addition to the chest wound, Dollfuss was shot in the spine, making him instantly paralyzed. Dollfuss pleaded for a doctor and a priest but the killers ignored his demands. He died three hours after being shot.

Dollfuss became chancellor of Austria in 1932. In October of that year he took advantage of a 1917 Austrian law called THE WAR ECONOMY ENA-BLING ACT OF 1917, which allowed him to govern without parliament, so that he had become the dictator of the country. In March of 1933, the three presidents of the Austrian parliament all resigned and Dollfuss became absolute boss of Austria. In June of 1933, Dollfuss, now absolute dictator of Austria, prohibited the Nazi party, as he sought to insure the independence of his country. In February of 1934 Dollfuss bombarded workers in Linz, Steyr, and Vienna, because they had attempted an "armed rebellion" against him. Eight workers died. Dollfuss then banned all political parties in Austria except his Patriotic Front. Dollfuss then appointed an extremely wealthy member of the Austrian nobility, Ernst Starhemberg, as vice chancellor. He suspended the constitution and substituted one that would guarantee his permanent dictatorship. Dollfuss allied himself with the Italian dictator Benito Mussolini as a counterweight against Hitler's Germany. In view of subsequent events, it is worth speculation as to what might have been had Mussolini understood his own interests.[34]

GERMANY

The Assassination of Walther Rathenau (1867-1922)

"On June 22, 1922, Germany's first (and only) Jewish foreign minister, Walther Rathenau, was shot and murdered..."[35] That murder may seem to have been caused by the two men who shot Rathenau in the street of Berlin, inspired by what was later called "Nazi" ideology.

Such a view contradicts that hatred of Jews is endemic in Germany and that in 2011, 66 years after the Holocaust, the mass murder of six million Jews has not changed the view of Jews by the German population. A survey by the British Broadcasting Co. in April of 2008 indicates that Germans viewed Jews least favorably among all Europeans, who, in any event, have a low opinion of Jews and anything Jewish. In May of 2008 the German television network ZDF polled Germans concerning Jews and found that 53% have a negative view of Jews and 83% of Germans do not want to help Israel in any manner. Furthermore, large numbers of Germans deny the Holocaust and claim that the allied bombing of their country was a greater atrocity than the mass murder of Jews.[36]

A recent survey of German sentiments toward Jews and Israel by *Die Zeit*, a major German publication, revealed that the largest proportion of Germans side with the terrorist organizations Hamas and Hezbollah against Israel and pretend that Israel is the greatest threat to peace in the world today. Iran, China, and the Darfur holocaust are meaningless to Germans. Only the few Arab dead in Gaza disturb the Germans, as they try to rid themselves of the guilt of their Nazi past by claiming that Israel is today's Nazi state.[37]

Therefore it is best to view the German hatred of Jews as part of the German culture. This means that one cannot expect Germans to speak a language other than German, drive on the left side of the street when they have always driven on the right side, eat walrus blubber for dinner, or treat Jews as fellow humans. Therefore, the assassination of Rathenau in 1922 was an indication and forerunner of the mass killings of Jews to come eleven years later.

Those murders were of course the work of the Nazi party in conjunction with their allies in Germany and all countries occupied by Germany during the Second World War, where the population was only too happy to murder their fellow Jewish citizens. That raises the question whether the murder of Rathenau led directly to the gas chambers of 1941-1945.

Before he was assassinated, Rathenau was making decided progress in bringing relief to the Germans from the allied reparations demands. Since one of the most strident demands by Hitler and his followers was the defeat of the Treaty of Versailles, which included these huge reparations, it is evident that had Rathenau lived, he would most assuredly have been able to convince the allies to reduce the German tax burden. The Allies demanded that Germany pay $33 billion in reparations. When that money was not forthcoming, the allies invaded the Ruhr area in 1923 to collect coal instead of cash, as Germany was "broke." The Ruhr invasion led to widespread support for the Nazi ideology and hastened Hitler's attainment of power.[38]

The assassination of Rathenau had additional meaning. It proved to the Germans that their government was too weak to defend democracy and that violence wins. The German government was unable to counter the lies that had made the assassination possible and popular. In fact, the German government in 1922 failed to prevent the rise to power of the type of German who committed the murder of Rathenau.[39]

The entire Nazi ideology was founded on the premise that power would be allowed to govern at the point of a gun and that violence wins. Therefore the assassination of Rathenau proved that this view was sound and real. By killing the only Jew ever to hold a high government post in Germany, the bigots demonstrated their power and the failure of democracy to attract a majority of the electorate.

In sum, the murder of Rathenau confirmed the anti-Jewish culture of Germany, promoted dictatorship, increased pressure for Germany to pay "reparations," negated the tendency of some Germans to turn their country into a democracy, and exposed the German government as weak and irrelevant. Finally, the assassination of Rathenau provided later generations with an example of how Germans ought to deal with those who are different.

The Assassination of Ernst vom Rath (1909-1939)

On November 7, 1938, Herschel Grynszpan shot and killed Ernst Eduard vom Rath inside the German embassy in Paris, France. Vom Rath was a minor official in the embassy. However, his assassination led to one of the most horrible events in German history and foreshadowed the Holocaust.

Grynszpan was born in Hannover, Germany in 1921. He was the son of Polish immigrants who had come to Germany with many other Polish Jews to escape the constant harassment they faced in their native land. Of course, these Polish Jews did not know that things were even worse for them in Germany.

In 1936, Herschel moved to France and stayed with an uncle in Paris. He was only 15 at the time. Since he had come illegally, Grynszpan was not allowed to stay in France but was ordered to leave. Yet, he had no place to go. He could not return to Nazi Germany, nor would any country on earth allow a stateless Jew to enter (Since the return of the Jews to Israel, that cannot happen again). Then, on October 26 of 1938, Herschel learned that his entire family had been deported to Poland, as were all of the eight thousand Polish born Jews living in Germany. The Jews were driven across the Polish border with whips and bayonets. They had no food and no water. Many died and others were severely wounded by the German troopers. Having no place to stay, without a country and without a family, without money and without friends, Grynszpan decided to avenge the cruel treatment of his father and at the same time solve his own problems. Therefore he killed vom Rath.[40]

On November 9-10, 1938 the Germans used the murder of vom Rath to conduct a widespread attack on all Jews living in Germany and Austria. This attack has been labeled Kristallnacht, or Crystal Night, because the outcome was the distribution of glass and broken furniture on the streets of Germany and Austria as German mobs invaded Jewish homes and stores and threw the furniture through the windows into the streets. Domestic terror against Jews was by no means new in Germany. This was particularly true in small towns, where neighbors knew each other and Jews were an easy target for the Christian majority.[41]

German mobs attacked German Jews in the streets and entered their homes. They burned down every synagogue in Germany and Austria and killed somewhat more than 100 Jews outright. Although such murders are insignificant by the standards of the Holocaust yet to come, this was undoubtedly the most violent attack on the German Jewish population since the Middle Ages. Over 30,000 Jews were arrested and hauled into concentration camps. "Ordinary Germans, without provocation or encouragement, participated in the brutalities."[42]

Germans generally approved of these savage outbursts and hastened to attend rallies at which Nazi officials held vitriolic speeches blaming the Jewish victims for the destruction of "Kritallnacht." While there were those who publicly objected to the scattering of broken furniture and glass into the streets or found the public exhibition of violence distasteful, no one sympathized with their Jewish neighbors, but on the contrary expressed satisfaction with the persecutions they had witnessed. It must be added that after November 9-10, 1938, everyone in Germany knew about the brutal treatment of the Jewish population there, so that the postwar excuses by almost all Germans that they knew nothing about this cannot be believed, even by themselves.

The Assassination of Kurt Eisner (1857-1919)

Kurt Eisner was murdered on the street in Munich (München), the capital of Bavaria, in Germany on February 21, 1919. Eisner, who may have been the descendant of Polish Jews named Kosmanovsky, was the only prime minister of The Free State of Bavaria (Bayern). That state was and is the largest state in the German Federal Republic. Before November 7, 1918, Bavaria, governed by the Wittelsbach family, was the largest kingdom in the German empire. On that date, Eisner forced the king of Bavaria to resign. Then he proclaimed the creation of the Free State of Bavaria, of which he became the prime minister. Eisner's rule was short lived. Three months and two weeks after coming to power, he was murdered by the 22-year-old Anton Graf von Arco auf Valley. Graf is German for Baron. Commonly known as Anton Arco, this descendant of German nobility was also the grandson of the Jewish Oppenheimer banking family on his mother's side. Therefore, Anton was rejected for membership in German nationalist organizations, such as the Thule Society, devoted to the destruction of Jews. Evidently, Arco wanted to prove to his detractors that he was not Jewish or at least hated Jews. Subsequently, Arco was imprisoned for a few years but was finally pardoned and given a medal by Hitler.[43]

Kurt Eisner was born in Berlin in 1867. A journalist, he was a member of the Social Democrat party and fought for democracy in Germany, using his position as editor of a Nuremberg newspaper to advance his views. Later he became a free journalist in Munich. During the First World War, he was convicted of treason because he organized a strike of munitions workers. This led to imprisonment for nine months, after which he overthrew the Wittelsbach monarchy. His party having been defeated in the 1919 elections, he walked toward the

Parliament to present his resignation when he was shot in the back and died on the spot. Eisner had discarded his religion and believed that socialism would be the salvation of Germans and Jews in particular.[44]

The consequences of Eisner's death were anarchy in Bavaria and the rise of the Nazi party, culminating in the accession of Hitler to power in 1933. Now communists, socialists, and Nazis fought in the streets of Munich. A communist dictatorship was briefly in power but was brutally suppressed by the German army, with the result that Bavaria became the headquarters of most conspirators against the German republic established after the resignation of Emperor William II in 1918. Among all of these parties which fought for power in Bavaria, Hitler's National Socialist German Worker's Party became most successful because it engaged in radical Jew baiting. Since Eisner was Jewish, the population of Bavaria was easily led to believe that a Jewish conspiracy was responsible for all the ills of Germany, including the taxes needed to pay war reparations to the Allies, inflation, unemployment, and all kinds of ills. Of course, hatred of Jews had been the heritage of Christians for 1900 years, so that Hitler's appeal on these grounds was easily attained. Hitler shouted what others believed, so that he was undoubtedly the voice of Germany.[45]

The Assassination of Ernst Röhm (1887-1934)

On July 2, 1934, Ernst Röhm, commander of the SA or Storm Division in Hitler's Germany, was assassinated as he waited in a cell in the Stadelheim prison near Munich (München). Röhm had been arrested by Hitler personally on June 30, 1934, while he was on vacation at the resort of Bad Wiessee. Hitler had called Röhm the day before and asked him to assemble all the leaders of the SA. All were imprisoned the next day on charges of treason. This was of course a fabrication, since Röhm had been Hitler's best friend and ally since 1920 when he organized the SA or Sturm Abteilung.[46]

The real reason for the assassination of Röhm was Hitler's ambition. In 1934, the president of Germany, Field Marshall Paul von Hindenburg, was 86 years old and ailing. It was evident that Hindenburg would soon depart. Hitler wanted to become President of Germany and combine that office with that of chancellor so as to assume total power and control. He did succeed in this only because the army and the wealthy industrialists supported his ambition. The price Hitler had to pay for this support was the emasculation of the SA. The Sturm Abteilung had 2.9 million members in 1934, and was larger than the German army, which was limited in size by the Treaty of Versailles. Moreover, Röhm actively lobbied Hitler to absorb the army into the SA and make him, Röhm, minister of defense. Furthermore, Röhm believed that Germany should become a socialist country, as promised by the name of Hitler's party, the National Socialist German Worker's Party (Nazi is the abbreviation of the German word Nazional, as in Nazionalsozialistiche Deutsche Arbeiterpartei). The wealthy German industrialists who had paid Hitler's way, and without whom he could not become president, threatened to withdraw their support if socialism were introduced. Fearing his ambition would be frustrated, Hitler had Röhm and numerous other SA "big wigs" assassinated. The SA was reduced in size and its power severely curtailed. On the death of Hindenburg on August 2, 1934, Hitler named himself president and chancellor of Germany, labeled himself Führer (leader) and began Germany's descent into the abyss.[47]

The Assassination of Reinhard Heydrich (1904-1942)

On May 27, 1942, the German "protector" of Moravia and Bohemia, as the Nazi government called Czechoslovakia, was assassinated in a suburb of Prague by Josef Gabcik and Jan Kubis, two paratroopers, one Czech and the other Slovak. Gabcik tried to shoot Heydrich, a brutal killer of thousands of Jews and other "undesirables," but Gabcik's gun jammed. Kubis then threw a specially made bomb at Hedyrich's open car but the bomb hit the rear wheel and did not explode in the car. Both Heydrich and his driver jumped out of the car with drawn pistols, even as the bomb exploded outside the car, wounding Heydrich severely. The two assassins escaped as Heydrich collapsed on the street. Heydrich died on June 4, 1942. Even before the death of Heydrich, Hitler ordered the murder of at least 10,000 Czechs. This was carried out not only by the random killing of Czech citizens, but in particular by the slaughter of all the inhabitants of the village of Lidice, in which all the inhabitants were murdered in revenge for the death of Heydrich. After the slaughter, the village was burned down and all traces of the village were wiped out.[48]

Reinhard Heydrich was the deputy to the leader of the SS (Sturm Staffel or Storm Contingent) which planned the extermination of all European Jews at the Wannsee Conference on January 20, 1942. Heydrich asked 14 heads of departments of the German government to attend so that they could plan "the final solution of the Jewish problem."[49]

Thirty-four Deaths and the Red Army Faction

From the late 1960's until 1998, a group of angry Germans conducted numerous attacks on "the establishment" as they saw it. Included in these attacks were 34 murders of politicians, industrialists and members of the judiciary who were seen as oppressors and "Nazis" by the membership of the Red Army Faction (Rote Armee Fraktion).

These violent revolutionaries developed from the student protests of the 1960's which focused on the war in Vietnam but also included demands for women's rights, the end of "racism" and more consideration for the fate of the poor. Bomb attacks, arson and physical assault were the first methods used by the RAF.[50]

In 1970, two women, Ulrike Meinhof and Gudrun Esslin, founded the RAF, together with Andreas Baader and Horst Mahler. Their first murder occurred on the 22nd of October, 1971, when two RAF members, Horst Mahler and Irmgard Möller, shot and killed Norbert Schmidt, a 33 year old police officer. A second police officer was murdered by the RAF on the 22nd of December 1971. Several bombings were committed by the RAF in 1972 but no further murders were instigated by the RAF until April 24, 1975, when two German embassy administrators were assassinated in Stockholm, Sweden. Then, on May 7, 1976, police Officer Fritz Sippel was murdered by the RAF. Considerable publicity was provoked by these killings. Yet, the assassination of the chief federal prosecutor Siegfried Buback, his driver and a passenger in his car, became a sensation in Germany and in Europe.

Shortly after 9.a.m. on April 7, 1977, Siegfried Buback's dark blue Mercedes car was stopped at a red light in Karlsruhe. A motorcycle pulled up to his chauffer driven car as the motorcycle passenger fired 15 bullets into Buback and his driver as well as the passenger, all of whom died from their wounds.[51]

Less than three months later, the director of the Dresdner bank was murdered in his home. Dresden is a German city. On July 30, 1977, Susanne Albrecht, goddaughter of the banker Jurgen Ponto, visited him with Brigitte Mohnhaupt and Christian Klar. Ponto admitted them to his home, as he knew Albrecht very well. Albrecht gave Pontto a bouquet of red roses and was admitted to the living room, where she and her accomplices tried to kidnap him. When he resisted, they shot him dead and then fled in a getaway car driven by another member of the Roter Morgen terrorist group.[52]

Hanns Martin Schleyer was assassinated by the Red Army Faction on October 18, 1977. Schleyer was the very embodiment of German capitalism as President of the Confederation of German Employers' Association and President of German Industries. He was also a convinced Nazi, having joined the National Socialist German Workers Party early in 1933 as soon as Hitler became dictator. From there he advanced to membership and officer in the SS (Sturm Staffel or Storm Contingent), the murderous special "elite" force which was in charge of killing concentration camp prisoners. It is by no means surprising that a man with such a background became a top industrialist in postwar Germany. In fact, almost all the leadership in Germany from 1949 until they reached old age was composed of former Nazis.

On September 5, 1977, Schleyer was on his way from his office to his home in a chauffeur driven Mercedes. Behind him, three bodyguards were riding in another car. He was guarded by two guards at each of his two homes in addition to the three who covered his travels. During the drive home, a yellow Mercedes suddenly blocked Schleyer's way, having come into a one way street the wrong way. On the left of Schleyer's car a woman with a baby carriage blocked the way. Then five people came out of a nearby parked car and began shooting into the second Schleyer car, killing the bodyguards and the driver. Schleyer was then dragged out of his car and pushed into a small bus, accompanied by three women and three men. Schleyer was held for 44 days and was then killed on October 18, 1973.[53]

IRELAND

The Assassination of Louis Mountbatten

On August 27, 1979, Louis Mountbatten (Battenberg) was assassinated when a 50 pound bomb exploded on his fishing boat in Donegal Bay off the coast of Ireland. Mountbatten was a "lord" and the great grandson of Queen Victoria. He entered the British navy at a young age and, because he was "royalty," rose quickly in the British Navy until he became supreme commander of allied forces in Burma during the Second World War. He later was appointed chief of the United Kingdom defense staff and held other honorary titles.

The Irish Republican Army took "credit" for the assassination, claiming that Mountbatten had been responsible for far worse as last viceroy of India and other commands he had occupied. Killed with Mountbatten were Mountbatten's 14-year-old grandson, Nicholas, his grandmother, Lady Brabourne, and a 15-year-old "boat hand," Paul Maxwell. Three additional members of Mountbatten's party were injured but survived.

The bomb had been planted on Mountbatten's boat by Thomas McMahon, who was convicted of these killings and given a life sentence. Nevertheless, he was released in 1998.[54]

Since the Battle of the Boyne in 1690, when the Protestants defeated the Catholics, there had been sporadic fighting between the Irish of both religions. This culminated in the War of Independence from 1919 to 1921. In 1921 Ireland was partioned into the Irish Free State and Ulster, or Northern Ireland, which remained part of England.[55]

These arrangements satisfied some politicians but led to resistance on the part of both Catholics and Protestants in Northern Ireland. Approximately 42% of the Northern Irish population was and is Catholic, about 53% are Protestants and 5% are members of small minorities or have no religion. In 1966, the Irish Republican Army of Catholics and the Protestant Ulster Volunteer Force organized to protect the interests of each group. Believing that they were under siege by the Catholics in Northern Ireland and in view of the almost all Catholic Republic of Ireland, the PUV declared war on the IRA and assassinated John Patrick Scullion, a store owner in West Belfast, on June 11, 1966. Catholic barman Peter Ward was murdered in Belfast by the PUV on June 26, 1966. More assassinations followed. Then, in 1967, Catholics, imitating the Civil Rights marches in the United States, marched for civil rights in Northern Ireland, with the result that Protestants now organized marches. The Royal Ulster Constabulary attacked Catholic marchers, leading to the 1969 riots in which eight peope people were killed, 750 injured and several streets in Catholic neighborhoods were burned to the ground.[56]

By 1972 the fighting in Northern Ireland became intense as the Provisional IRA killed about 100 soldiers, wounded another 500 and carried out about 1,300 bombings, killing numerous civilians. The Provisionals announced they would continue bombings and killings until they achieved a united Ireland. Various political maneuvers did not contain the violence, so that on August 27, 1979, not only Lord Mountbatten and his boating companions were killed by a remote controlled bomb, but on that day eighteen soldiers were also killed by remote controlled bombs.[57]

The Brighton Hotel bombing on October 12, 1984, led to the assassination of five people, including Anthony Berry, a Conservative Member of Parliament and the wife of another politician and several hotel employees. The occasion was a gathering of members of parliament, who were staying at the hotel for a conference.[58]

The killing continued, so that in 1993 more Catholic civilians were killed by Protestants than IRA members, with the result that Protestants and Catholics killed each other in record numbers. The violence continued into 1996, including the bombing of Manchester, England, and the assassination of Stephen Restorick, a British soldier, in 1997. The Irish National Liberation Army, a Catholic organization, assassinated the leader of the Loyalist Volunteer Force, Billy Wright, in December of 1997, and in 1998 an IRA bomb killed 29 civilians.

Since then, the killings have continued despite the power sharing agreement of May 2007. That agreement was signed by the major parties to the conflict. However, splinter groups have continued the murders, so that on March 9, 2009, Stephen Carroll, a police officer and father of three children in Craigavon, was killed by shooting him in the head while sitting in his patrol car.[59]

The Assassination of Rosemary Nelson

On March 16, 1999, a bomb exploded under the hood of a car driven by Rosemary Nelson, a lawyer, who represented Catholics in Lurgan, County Armagh, as she drove from her home. She suffered fatal stomach injuries. She left behind a husband and three children.

Nelson had represented the residents of a Catholic housing project. A group calling themselves "The Red Hand Defenders" took "credit" for the killing, which was the third such murder committed by them in Northern Ireland. The purpose was to derail the peace accords signed in April of 1998 with an effective date of April 2, 1999. The Red Hand Defenders placed pipe bombs into Protestant homes and burned down Catholic churches.[60]

Subsequent to the assassination of Nelson, a number of public inquiries were conducted but did not succeed in identifying the killers, but led to speculation that the assassination was carried out by agents of the "Royal Ulster Constabulary." Nelson was evidently seen as "an enemy of the state" by the police and given no protection despite several warnings that she might be assassinated in a manner reminiscent of the killing of innumerable other citizens of northern Ireland. It is significant that this killing occurred after both Protestants and Catholics agreed to the "Good Friday Accords" in April of 1998. Those accords were negotiated by the American Senator George Mitchell and provide for a power sharing National Assembly designated to cooperate with the governments of the Irish Republic and England.[61]

Despite these agreements, violence has continued in Northern Ireland. In March 2009, just three days after two British soldiers were shot to death, a fourth police officer was shot by the so-called "Continuity Irish Republican Army." The chances are good that this violence will gradually disappear from Northern Ireland or Ulster.

ENGLAND

The Assassination of King Edmund I (921-946)

Edmund was 25 years old when he was stabbed to death by a robber named Liofa, who had been exiled earlier. He was murdered at the royal villa of Pucklechurch in Gloucestershire. Edmund was by no means king of England, as that country was perpetually engaged in warfare between rival "kings" or chieftains ruling counties or somewhat larger areas. Edmund had inherited the throne from his father, known as Edward the Elder, in 940. He governed Northern Mercia while his rival, Olaf Cuaran, ruled Northumbria. Numerous battles followed, directed both at domestic and Danish and Norwegian raiders.

Over the centuries, Edmund was elevated to "saintly" standing, as it was said of him that he was "humble," gave considerable sums to the poor, and had numerous other extraordinary qualities. In view of his short life and the distance of a millennium it is more than likely that the picture of Edmund is a distortion influenced by wishful thinking, ancestor worship, and a slavish need to enhance royalty. This need to attribute virtues to royal persons may be found in all societies, which employ such distinctions, but is also found in the American democracy, leading sycophants to call the American president "Mr. President" rather than using his name.

Because the Battle of Hastings of 1066 ended the royal infighting in England and made the Normans rulers of England, the assassination of Edmund had little effect on English history, largely shaped by the merger of the Anglo-Saxon and the French influence thereafter. This merger is of course visible to anyone speaking the English language, which is at least fifty percent of Latin and French origin.[62]

Spencer Perceval (1762-1812)

Spencer Perceval was the only British prime minister to be assassinated. He died on the evening of May 11, 1812, when John Bellingham shot him in the lobby of the House of Commons. Perceval belonged to the British aristocracy. His mother was a baroness and the granddaughter of the Earl of Northampton. His father had been first lord of the admiralty and advisor to two kings. Perceval was educated at an exclusive school called Harrow and later at Trinity College. Perceval's brother was labeled "Third Earl of Edmond." Perceval had an ordinary political career. He had been Solicitor General and Attorney General and Chancellor of the Exchequer (treasury). He became prime minister in 1809.

John Bellingham (1769-1812) killed Perceval because he believed that the British government had done nothing to help him while he was unjustly imprisoned in Russia. After failing in business several times, Bellingham went to Archangel, Russia, in 1800 as an agent for an import-export business. He returned to England two years later and then went to Archangel once more in 1804. As he was about to leave for Britain in November of that year, he was arrested and imprisoned on the grounds of not paying his debts. Debtors' prisons no longer exist but were quite common in the nineteenth century. His accuser was an English shipowner who believed that Bellingham had anonymously revealed the owner had sabotaged his own ship in order to collect insurance. Having been released from prison in 1809, he returned to England and killed the prime minister three years later. It took him three years to carry out this assassination because he spent those years petitioning the British government for compensation for his imprisonment. His last attempt to get compensation occurred on April 18, 1812, when he was refused by the Foreign Office. Thereupon he decided to buy a gun and rectify his situation. He argued at his trial that Perceval had placed himself above the law by refusing him compensation and that he, Bellingham, had a right to kill Perceval lest the prime minister destroy all liberty by ruling according to his whim.[63]

Bellingham was hanged on May 18, 1812. While murder is seldom justified, the assassination of Perceval demonstrated how governments seldom care about those they govern. This was not only true in 19th century England but continues to be true in 21st century America.

ITALY

The Assassination of Umberto I, King of Italy (1844-1900)

On July 29, 1900, Gaetano Bresci, a silk weaver, shot and killed the king of Italy. Umberto had just distributed some medals to several athletes. As he left the platform on which the athletes had been rewarded, the king entered his carriage when Bresci fired four shots from a revolver, of which three hit the king in the chest and killed him instantly.[64]

Bresci was arrested and sent to prison, where he died within a year under suspicious circumstances. At his trial he argued that he wanted to avenge the people killed by General Fiorenzo Bava-Beccaris, who commanded the murder of hundreds of demonstrators who protested a lack of food in Milan in 1898. Some of the demonstrators had found some shelter in a monastery, whose friars were feeding a group of beggars. Bava-Beccaria ordered the firing of canons into the walls of the monastery, leading to the death of 118 and the wounding of 450 beggars and friars. King Umberto I had ordered Bava-Beccaris to force the demonstrators out of Milan but did nothing to alleviate their hunger. After the killings, the king decorated General Bava-Beccaris for this "military action." This led Gaetano Bresci to decide that the king should die. Bresci was living in Paterson, New Jersey at the time of the Milan riots. He was weaving in a mill but spent his spare time working on an Italian newspaper.[65]

The Assassination of Giacomo Matteotti (1885-1924)

It is the judgment of historians that the assassination of Matteotti signaled the beginning of the Mussulini fascist dictatorship in Italy. Matteotti was murdered after the publication of his book *The Fascisti Exposed: A Year of Fascist Domination*. Matteotti was a member of the Italian Chamber of Deputies and there gave two lengthy speeches denouncing the Fascist party and Benito Mussolini, then prime minister but not yet dictator. He alleged that the Fascists committed voter fraud and used violence to gain votes. He was kidnapped and murdered eleven days later. He was seized, bundled into a car and stabbed to death. Then his body was tossed into the road.

Only three of the five kidnappers and murderers were arrested. They were convicted of both crimes but released by King Victor Emmanuel III. Over the years some historians have claimed that Mussolini was not involved in this assassination, while others have argued that Mussolini ordered the killing of Matteotti because Matteotti had evidence that Mussolini had sold exclusive rights to all Italian oil reserves to Sinclair Oil, an American company.[66]

The Assassination of Carlo Rosselli (1899-1937)

Matteotti was not the only victim of assassination ordered by Mussolini or at least committed by his followers. Together with his brothers, Aldo and Nello, Carlo served at the front during the First World War. After Aldo was killed, the brothers Carlo and Nello could have claimed exemption from the fighting because sons of a widow whose one son had been killed allowed them the right to be discharged from the service. They nevertheless served as junior officers until the end of the war.

When Benito Mussolini became the dictator of Italy, Carlo Roselli devoted all of his time to oppose the dictatorship. Because of his anti-fascist writings and speeches, Roselli was exiled to the island of Lipari, from which he escaped in 1929. He was able to reach Paris, where he joined other anti-fascists in exile.[67]

There, on the 9th of June 1937, Carlo and his brother Nello were murdered when they attempted to assist the driver of a car that appeared to be disabled on a road in a forest. They left their car and walked toward the "disabled" car when they were attacked by a gang of knife wielding killers. Both were stabbed and shot to death. The murders had been ordered and paid for by Galeazzo Ciano, Mussolini's son-in-law and foreign minister.[68]

The Assassination of Aldo Moro (1916-1978)

On May 9, 1978, the prime minister of Italy, Aldo Moro, was murdered by terrorists who had kidnapped him fifty-four days earlier. Moro's body was found in the trunk of a car in central Rome.

During the weeks of Moro's captivity, Giulio Andreotti was prime minister. Because Andreotti refused to negotiate with the captors and eventual killers of Moro, many Italians have subscribed to a conspiracy theory, particularly because Andreotti was also accused of ordering the killing of a journalist who was investigating the cover up of the Moro murder. Because the Italian police and secret service were unable or unwilling to rescue Moro, most Italians believe that Andreotti and others wanted him dead.[69]

The murder was committed by a gang who called themselves "the Red Brigade." This "brigade" was devoted to the communist cause. They viewed the murder of Moro as a practical plan in line with the "propaganda of the deed" slogan formulated in Switzerland a century earlier. The killer of Moro, Mario Moretti, said later that the murder was part of a plan for a Marxist revolution, which he claimed had broad support among the Italian public. It was of course Karl Marx who had always argued that revolutionary ideas exist only where there is a revolutionary class and that "...ideas are nothing more than the ideal expressions of the dominant material relations."[70]

The assassination of Aldo Moro is the subject of a book by Richard Drake called *The Aldo Moro Murder Case*. Drake concludes that the Marxist "Red Brigade" who killed Moro believed that this murder would lead to the collapse of the capitalist system and lead to a Marxist-Leninist revolution.[71]

YUGOSLAVIA

The Assassination of Alexander I of Yugoslavia (1888-1934)

Alexander Karagorgevic was shot to death on October 9, 1934, as he was being driven through the streets of Marseille, France in the company of the French foreign minister, Louis Barthou. The assassin was Vlado Chernozemski, a member of the Internal Macedonian Revolutionary Organization. Chernozemski also killed the driver of Alexander's car. Chernozemski was immediately cut down by a mounted policeman and then beaten to death by a crowd. Barthou was also shot. The killing of Barthou has been a matter of dispute for years and cannot be resolved. It is possible that Barthou was shot by Chernozemski. A French policeman may also have shot him by accident. In any event, he died in the afternoon of October 9 from a wound, which appeared to be minor.

Vlado Chernozemzki was a Bulgarian who had changed his name. In 1922, he joined the Macedonian revolutionaries. The same year, he killed the leader of the Bulgarian Communist party, Dimo Hadjidimov. Although sentenced to death, he was released in 1928 and then murdered another member of the Internal Macedonian Revolutionary Organization.[72]

It was no accident that a Bulgarian would kill Alexander in the name of Macedonian independence. At the time of the assassination, Macedonia was part of Yugoslavia. In earlier years, Bulgaria had repeatedly demanded that Macedonia be a part of Bulgaria on the grounds that the Christian population of Macedonia was mainly Bulgarian. Further, the Macedonians during the Turkish regime fled to Bulgaria, not to Serbia. The San Stefano Treaty between Russia and Turkey allotted Macedonia to Bulgaria in 1878. All of these reasons and more inspired the killer of Alexander, as Macedonia had been incorporated into Yugoslavia.[73]

The murder of Alexander appeared to favor the disintegration of Yugoslavia into several states. This was the aim of Ante Pavelich, the boss of the Ustasa, a Croatian party that sought the independence of Croatia and the establishment of a Nazi style dictatorship there. This did not happen as the Croatian people made no move to leave the Yugoslav confederacy. It was not until 1941 that Croatia became "independent" on the invasion of the country by Germany, who adopted the German "racial laws" and who became the puppets of Hitler.[74]

THE NETHERLANDS

The Assassinations of Pim Fortuyn and Theo Van Gogh

Religious bigotry led to the assassinations of two Dutch citizens within two years. On May 6, 2002, Wilhelmus Simon Petrus Fortuyn, a Dutch politician, was shot to death in a parking lot in Hilversum. Fortuyn had just given an interview, as he was running for office in an election to take place nine days later. His killer, Volkert van der Graf, said in court that he killed Fortuyn "to protect Muslims." Fortuyn was a Roman Catholic who spoke out against militant Islam in view of the increase of Muslims in the Netherlands, reaching one million out of a total population of 17 million. He said that the emergence in Rotterdam, Amsterdam, and den Hague of Muslim ghettos endangered the country's liberal traditions and the rule of democracy. He also objected to 40,000 immigrants entering the country each year. Fortuyn never participated in any demonstration or other action against Muslims but was killed because of his opinions.[75]

On November 2, 2004, the Dutch film director Theo van Gogh was assassinated in broad daylight on the street in central Amsterdam. Van Gogh saw the attacker, Mohammed Bouyeri, facing him with a gun and shouted "don't do it." But the Muslim jihadist was undeterred and callously shot van Gogh in front of a number of onlookers. Van Gogh, despite his injuries, stumbled to the other side of the street. Bouyeri followed him and stabbed and shot him again. He then slit van Gogh's throat with a butcher knife in the manner of a Halal slaughter, almost cutting off the victim's head. By then the police had arrived and shot the killer in the leg.

It turned out that Bouyeri was a member of the terrorist Hamas gang as well as several other similar organizations. He expressed great hatred for all things Western and demanded that everyone accept Islam. Bouyeri had pinned a note on his victim's body to the effect that all non-believers in Islam were going to meet similar fates.[76]

Mohammed Bouyeri was born in the Netherlands, the son of Moroccan immigrants. He became a community organizer and terrorist who had been arrested before for violent conduct. His hatred of van Gogh stemmed from van Gogh making a movie concerning the treatment of women in Muslim societies. The movie, *Submission*, shows abuse of Muslim women by their husbands. Van Gogh had a TV talk show and wrote a newspaper column in which he insulted Christians, Jews, and Muslims. Bouyeri also left a letter in his apartment naming Dutch politicians he intended to kill.[77]

At his trial, which resulted in a sentence of life imprisonment without the possibility of parole, Bouyeri said that "I was motivated by the law that commands me to cut off the head of anyone who insults Allah and his prophet."[78]

SPAIN

Since 1870, five Spanish prime ministers have been assassinated. They were Juan Prim, assassinated in 1870 by a mentally unstable assassin without any political motive, Antonio Canovas del Castillo, killed in 1897, Jose Canalejas, assassinated in 1912, Eduardo Dato Iradier, assassinated in 1921, and Luis Carrero Blanco in 1973. In addition, the former Prime Minister Ernest Lluch Martin was assassinated in 2000. Further, a number of political assassinations related to the Basque separatist movement have made Spain a dangerous country for those seeking to hold office.

The assassination of Antonio Canovas in 1897 was the consequence of the dictatorial policies he conducted during his six terms as prime minister. Canovas became prime minister first on December 31, 1874. He remained in office until September 12, 1875 but returned on the 2nd of December that year. This time he remained prime minister until March 7, 1879. His third term extended from December 9, 1879 to February 8, 1881, his fourth term began January 18, 1884, his fifth term began July 5, 1890 and ended December 11, 1892, and his sixth term began March 23, 1895 and lasted until he was killed on August 8, 1897. Therefore, Canovas was prime minister of Spain for nearly 22 years, including the overthrow of the monarchy in 1868 and its restoration in 1874. Canovas had been active in politics before becoming prime minister in that he held a number of appointed offices since 1854.[79]

During Canovas' rule, a ten year war had broken out in Cuba when the Cuban people attempted to gain independence from Spain. Using a large Spanish army, Canovas succeeded in the defeat of the revolutionary efforts by the Cubans. The Spanish held on to the island past Canovas' lifetime, although Spain made numerous concessions to the rebels.

At home, Canovas controlled the press, wrote a "constitution" in 1876 which defined religious freedom in the most narrow terms, eliminated the right of trial by jury, and eliminated numerous freedoms which had been guaranteed under the constitution of 1869.[80]

In 1896, a bomb was thrown at a Corpus Christi procession in Barcelona. This led the government to arrest 87 individuals, of whom 71 were declared innocent while others were executed or sent to prison for life. Nevertheless, the 71 innocents were ordered by Canovas to live in the West African Spanish colony of Rio de Oro. These sentences led Mechele Angiolillo to travel from Italy to Spain. He located Canovas at the thermal bath resort of Santa Agueda, where he shot him dead. Angiolillo made no attempt to flee. He freely admitted the assassination and was promptly killed himself. [81]

NOTES

1. D.M. Lewis, "The Fourth Century BC" in: The Cambridge Ancient History, vol. 6 (1994), 374.

2. Richard Stoneman, *Alexander the Great,* (London; Routledge, 2004), 2.

3. Bert van der Spek, "New Evidence from the Babylonian Astronomical Diaries Concerning Seleucid and Arsacid History," *Archiv fur Orientforschung,* vol. 44/45 (1997-1998), 167-175.

4. Peter Green, *Alexander to Actium: The Historical Evolution of the Hellenistic Age,* (Berkeley, The University of California Press, 1990), 13-14.

5. Michale Rostovtzeff, "The Foundations of Social and Economic Life in Egypt in Hellenistic Times,"*The Journal of Egyptian Archeology, vol.*6., no. 3, (July 1920), 161-128.

6. Charles Edson, "Imperium Macedonicum: The Seleucid Empire and the Literary Evidence," *Classical Philology,* vol. 53,,no. 3, (July 1958), 153-170.

7. Edward Gibbon, *The History of the Decline and Fall of the Roman Empire,* (New York: Twayne Publishers, 1963).

8. Luciano Canfora, *Julius Ceasar: The Life and Times of the People's Dictator,* (Berkeley: The University of California Press, 2007).

9. Mark Toher, "Octavian's Arrival in Rome," *Classical Quarterly, vol.*54, no. 1. (2004), 174.

10. G. W. Bowersock, "The Pontificate of Augustus," in: Kurt A Raaflaub and Mark Toner, *Between Republic and Empire: Interpretations of Augustus and His Principate,* (Berkeley, University of California Press, (1990), 380-394.

11. Walter Eder, "Augustus and the Power of Tradition," *in: The Cambridge Companion to the Age of Augustus,* (Cambrdige, Mass, *Cambridge Companions to the Ancient World,* (New York: Cambridge University Press, 2005), 13-32.

12. Charles Scarre, *The Penguin Atlas of Ancient Rome,* (London: Penguin Books, 1995), 5.

13. Raymond G. Gordon, Jr. *Ethnologue: Languages of the World, 15th Edition,* (Dallas, Texas: SIL International, 2000).

14. Josephus, *Jewish Antiquities,* Ralph Marcus, translator, (Cambridge, Mass: Harvard University Press, 1986), 485.

15. Solomon Grayzel, *A History of the Jews,* (Philadelphia: The Jewish Publication Society of America, 1947), 168-174.

16. Ibid, 184.

17. Bernard Pares, *A History of Russia,* (New York: Alfred A. Knopf, 1956), 403.

18. Wharton Barker, "The Secret of Russia's Friendship," *The Independent* (March 24, 1904), 647.

19. Alexandr Jurevich Polunov, "Konstantin Petrovich Pobedonostsev – Man and Politician," *Russian Studies in History,* vol. 39, no. 4, (Spring 2001), 8-32.

20. Ibid, 31.

21. Cecil Roth, *A History of the Jews,* (New York: Schocken Books, 1963), 354-355.

22. Geoffrey Wigoder , editor, *The Standard Jewish Encyclopedia,* 7th Edition, (New York: Facts on File, 1992), 942.

23. Cecil Roth, *A History,* 370.

24. Jesse D. Clarkson, *A History of Russia*, (New York: Random House, 1961), 360.

25. Ruth Kleinman, "Changing Interpretations of the Edict of Nantes," *French Historical Studies*, vol.10, no. 4, (Autumn 1978), 541-571.

26. Andrew Perregree, *Europe in the Sixteenth Century*, (Oxford, England, Blackwell Publishers, 2002). 48.

27. Eric Nelson, *The Jesuits and the Monarchy: Catholic Reform and Political Authority in France, (1590-1615)*, (New York: Ashgate Publishing, 2005).

28. Harvey Goldberg, *The Life of Jean Jaures*, (Madison: University of Wisconsin Press, 1962), 472.

29. Ibid, 471.

30. Ibid, 459.

31. Richard Belfield, *The Assassination Business: A History of State Sponsored Murder*, (New York: Carroll and Graf, Publishers, 2005), 237.

32. David MacKenzie, *Black Hand on Trial, Eastern European Monographs*, (New York: Columbia University Press, 1995), 391.

33. Bernadotte E. Schmitt, "July 1914: Thirty Years After," *The Journal of Modern History*, vol. 16, no.3, (1944), 204.

34. A.D. Harvey, "Austria's Diminutive Dictator," *History Today*, vol. 59, no. 7, (July 2009), 41-47.

35. Carole Fink, "The Murder of Walther Rathenau," *Judaism*, Summer 1995), 1.

36. Brad MacDonald, "Can Israel Trust Germany?" *The Trumpet*, vol. 19, no. 7, (August 2008), 1.

37. Leon de Winter, "Besessen vom Leid" *Die Zeit*, (April 2, 2009), 11.

38. Carole Fink, "The Murder of Walther Rathenau," *Judaism*, (Summer 1995)

39. Arnold Brecht, "Walther Rathenau and the German People," *The Journal of Politics*, vol. 10, no. 1, (February 1948), 40.

40. Michael Marrus, "The Strange Story of Herschel Grynszpan," *American Scholar*, vol. 57, no 1, Winter 1988), 69-79.

41. Daniel Jonah Goldhagen, *Hitler's Willing Executioners*, (New York: Alfred A. Knopf, 1996), 99.

42. Ibid, 101.

43. Gavriel Rosenfeld, "Monuments and the Policies of Memory: Commemorating Kurt Eisner and the Bavaria Revolution, 1918-1919." *Central European History*, vol. 30, no.2, (1997), 227.

44. Carl Landauer, "The Bavarian Problem in the Weimar Republic, 1918-1923," *The Journal of Modern History*, vol. 16, no.2, (June 1944), 98-99.

45. Ibid, 100-110.

46. Joachim Fest, *Hitler*, (New York: Vintage Books, 1975), 473-487.

47. Lothar Machtan, *The Hidden Hitler*, Basic Books, 2002), 107.

48. Milan Hauner, "Terrorism and heroism: the assassination of Reinhard Heydrich," *World Policy Journal*, vol. 24, no.2 (Summer 2007) : 85.

49. Steven Lehrer, *Wannsee House and the Holocaust*, (Jefferson, N.C. Mc Farldand, Publishers, 2000), 143.

50. Charity Scribner, "Buildings on Fire: The Situationist International and the Red Army Faction," *Grey Room*, Winter 2007), 30-55.

51. *Spiegel* Staff: "Germany Revisits RAF Terrorism Verdict," *Der Spiegel*, April 23, 2007), 1.

52. John Schmeidel, "My Enemy's Enemy," *Intelligence and National Security,* vol. 8, no.4, (October 1993), 59-72.

53. Lutz Hochmeister, *Schleyer: Eine Deutsche Geschichte,* (C.H. Beck Verlag, 2004).

54. No Author, "English Lord Assassinated in Terrorist Attack While Vacationing Aboard a Fishing Boat," *The New York Times,* (August 27, 1979), 1.

55. Mike Cronin, *A History of Ireland,* (New York: Palgrave Publishing, 2002).

56. Peter Taylor, *Loyalists: War and Peace in Northern Ireland,* (New York: TV Books, 1999), 59-60.

57. Ibid, 163.

58. Taylor, 188-190.

59. Eamon Quinn and John F. Burns, "After Killings Linked to I.R.A. Factions, Northern Ireland Defends Its Fragile Peace," *The New York Times,* (March 11, 2009), A6.

60. Warren Hoge, "Renegade Protestants Kill Lawyer in Ulster," *The New York Times,* (March 16, 1999), 1.

61. Warren Hoge, "An Irish Accord: Irish Talks Produce An Accord to Stop Decades of Blooished," *The New York Times,* (April 11, 1998), 1.

62. No author, "The Assassination of the Prime Minister: John Bellingham and the Murder of Spencer Perceval," *Contemporary Review,* vol. 290, no. 1691, (Winter 2008), 527.

63. John Bellingham, "Trial and execution of John Bellingham for the willful murder of the Right Hon. Spencer Perceval in the Lobby of the House of Commons," *Bristol Selected Pamphlets,* http://www.jstror. org. stable/60241852

64. No author, "Propaganda by the Deed," *Workers Solidarity,* No. 55, ()ctober 1998)

65. Emma Goldman, *Living My Life,* (New York: A. Knopf, 1934), Chapter 22.

66. Mauro Canali, "The Matteotti murder and the origin of Mussolini's totalitarian Fascist regime in Italy," *Journal of Modern Italian Studies,* vol14, no. 2, (2009), 143-167.

67. Stanislao G. Pugliese, "Death in Exile: The Assassinaiton of Carlo Roselli," *Journal of Contemporary History,* vol. 32, no. 3, (1997), 305.

68. Ibid, 312.

69. Allessandra Stanley, "Rome Journal: Agony Lingers, 20 Years After the Moro Killing," *The New York Times,* (May 9, 1998), A4.

70. Karl Marx, *The German Ideology,* (Amherst, NY: Prometheus Press, 1998), 61.

71. Richard Drake, *The Aldo Moro Murder Case,*(Cambridge, MA: Harvard University Press, 1995).

72. Joseph Rothschild, *The Communist Party of Bulgaria: Origins and Development,* (New York: Columbia University Press, 1959), 277-278.

73. A Bulgarian diplomat, "Bulgaria's Claims on Land She No Defends," *The New York Times,* (August 22, 1916), 8.

74. Allen Roberts, *The Turning Point: The Assassination of Louis Barthou and King Alexander I of Yugoslavia,* (New York: St. Martin's Press, 1970), 130-135.

75. Ambrose Evans-Pritchard, 'Fortuyn killed to 'protect' Muslims," *Telegraph,* March 28, 2003), 1

76. Janet Parker, "Murder in Broad Daylight," *The New Criminologist,* (June 30, 2005), 1.

77. Manfred Gerstenfel, "Radical Islam in the Netherlands: A Case Study of a Failed European Policy, " *Jerusalem Center for Public Affairs,* vol. 4, no. 14, (January 2005), 2.

78. No author, "Dutch court sentences van Gogh killer to life," *The New York Times,* (July 26, 2005), 1.

79. Stanley Karnow, "Antonio Canovas" in *Our Image: America's Empire in the Philippines,* (New York: Random House, 1989).

80. Earl R. Beck, "The Martinez Campos Government of 1879: Spain's Last Chance in Cuba," *The Hispanic American Historical Review,* vol.56, no.2, (May 1976), 275.

81. No author, "Angiolillo dies bravely," *The New York Times,* (August 22, 1897), 5

Chapter Two
American Assassinations

CANADA

The Iroquois word Canada means settlement. It was first used by French explorers in the 16th century concerning a few villages then located in Upper Canada and inhabited by Native Americans. Later, the word was applied to all settlements of Europeans in that region and was finally adopted as the name of the entire country. Canada, like the United States, has a territory comprising about 3.8 million square miles. The population of Canada is about 34 million.

Canada is a parliamentary democracy. The head of government is the prime minister. There is no president because the Queen of England, Elizabeth II, is the ceremonial head of state. On July 1, 1867 Canada became an independent country within the British Commonwealth of Nations when the British Parliament passed the British North America Acts.[1]

The Assassination of D'Arcy McGee (1825-1868)

Thomas D'Arcy McGee was shot to death on the street in Ottawa on April 7, 1868. The assassination was attributed to Patrick James Whelan, an Irish immigrant, who was believed to be a Fenian. A Fenian is a follower or member of the Irish Republican Army. The name is derived from Fionn MacCummhaill, a nineteenth century advocate of Irish independence. Whelan was hanged for committing this murder, although there has been a great deal of controversy concerning Whelan's guilt.

Thomas McGee has been called the founder of the Canadian nation. McGee was a journalist who started his career when at age 17 he moved from his native Ireland to the U.S.A. and became a reporter on a Boston newspaper. He returned to Ireland where he also worked as a journalist, but was forced to return to the United States because he was wanted by the British for his activities on behalf of Irish independence. Embroiled in Irish politics in the United States, he concluded that he could do more for the Irish cause by moving to Canada. There he edited a Montreal newspaper, The New Era, which promoted the unity of all

Canadians without reference to ethnic origin. He also wrote poems and history books and appeared as an effective public speaker. In 1857, McGee was elected to the Canadian parliament. This permitted him to gain wide publicity for his idea of confederation of the several Canadian provinces. This idea became popular when Canadians became worried about the American Union Army, which was powerful and appeared to seek an invasion of Canada.

McGee used his popularity and speaking ability to denounce the Fenians, i.e. the Irish Republican Army. These activities led to the view that he was "a traitor to Ireland." He was expelled from the Montreal St. Patrick's Society. Threats were made against his life and he was refused a cabinet post in the first Canadian parliament.

McGee was killed by a .32 caliber bullet in April of 1868. The police assumed that Patrick Whelan was the killer because they found a fully loaded .32 caliber handgun in his pocket. The trial of Whelan plainly violated the Canadian constitution in that the Prime Minister, John A. MacDonald, sat next to the presiding judge, William Buell Richards, in a clear violation of the principle of the separation of powers. By the time Whelan's appeal reached the Ontario Court of Appeals, Richards had been appointed to that court. Richards ruled against Whelan in a case he had himself heard in the lower court. This was a clear violation of Whelan's rights.

A play, Blood on the Moon, by Pierre Brault, deals with the conviction of Whelan. No definite evidence that Whelan murdered McGee has ever been produced. It is for this reason that a number of conspiracy theories concerning the murder of McGee continue to this day.[2]

THE UNITED STATES OF AMERICA

The United States has been the scene of numerous assassinations over the 235 years of our history. These assassinations of prominent people were motivated by political considerations as well as religious beliefs, racial animosities, and private grievances. Over fifty such assassinations can be identified, beginning with the killing of Joseph Smith, the founder of the Church of Jesus Christ of Latter Day Saints. We cannot discuss all of these assassinations but begin with 1844; the year Smith and his brother Hyrum were murdered in the jail at Carthage, Hancock County, Illinois.

The Assassination of Joseph Smith (1805-1844)

Joseph Smith was assassinated inside the Carthage, Illinois jail by a "mob" of Christians who hated and feared the Mormons, as the followers of Smith were called. Smith had volunteered to stay in jail together with his brother after he was promised protection by Governor Ford. Smith had been abandoned by some of his early followers because he preached plural marriage and propositioned the wives of two of his friends. He was then indicted in Illinois for engaging in polygamy, although he claimed to have only one wife. Smith was also accused of telling men that they had the right to marry ten virgins and of denying the trinity. Therefore, an angry mob killed Smith for his beliefs.[3]

Joseph Smith was a native of Vermont who grew up on a farm in Western New York near Palmyra. In 1827, Smith announced that an angel had shown him a set of golden plates that described how Jesus had visited the native Americans, whom he regarded as the lost tribes of Israel. In 1830, Smith published *The Book of Mormon* and organized the Church of Jesus Christ. He then moved to Kirtland, Ohio, and from there moved to Missouri. There a Mormon war developed as the Christians in Missouri drove the Mormons out in 1838. Therefore, Smith and his followers moved to Nauvoo, Illinois. Smith is regarded by his followers as a prophet and his writings are viewed as holy books on par with the Bible.[4]

Smith married about thirty women, a practice which triggered the enmity of many Americans. Therefore, the Mormons continued their voyages west under the leadership of Brigham Young, until in 1847 they founded Salt Lake City in Utah, which became their permanent home.[5]

The Assassination of Abraham Lincoln (1809-1865)

The murder of Lincoln by John Wilkes Booth has been described again and again in books, journals, movies, speeches and all other forms of communication. How Booth entered the balcony where Lincoln was watching the play "Our American Cousin," how he shot Lincoln in the back of the head, how he jumped to the stage while shouting "Hic Semper Tyrranis" or "This always to tyrants," how he was shot down in a barn in Maryland and how those accused of the conspiracy to kill Lincoln were executed, including innocent bystanders who had no part in the conspiracy.[6]

These stories concerning Lincoln's death together with his rise from birth in a log cabin to President have made Abraham Lincoln an American idol, worshipped in a manner described by sociologists as a civil religion. It was the Swiss philosopher Jean Jacques Rousseau who first used the phrase "civil religion" in his 1763 book *The Social Contract*. Since then, the civil religion draws upon such civil events as Independence Day, documents such as the U.S. Constitution and the Declaration of Independence, songs such as God Bless America and civil saints such as George Washington and Abraham Lincoln.[7]

It is doubtful that Lincoln would have attained the position of American sainthood had he not been assassinated. In life, Lincoln had many enemies who sought his death and who finally achieved that end. These enemies were mostly Southerners. Yet, there were also northerners and even British who disliked and hated Lincoln and who viewed his assassination with satisfaction. It is therefore necessary to minimize the deification of Lincoln so as to understand the reasons for his assassination.

During the Civil War, also called The War Between the States, Southerners viewed Lincoln as their most vociferous enemy. They evidently had good reason to think so as they believed that Lincoln provoked the war and that he was the cause of all their suffering. Seventy years later the author Charles W. Ramsdell wrote that Lincoln deliberately provoked the south into attacking Fort Sumter so that the south would receive the blame for a war that Lincoln wanted.[8] This view was also shared by a good number of English citizens. Lincoln was viewed as a military conqueror like Attila the Hun or Hitler.[9]

During the war, hatred of Lincoln was universal in the south, where threats against his life were frequent. A newspaper in Mississippi published an offer to pay $100,000 for "the miserable traitor's head." On hearing of his assassination, Southerners generally applauded the deed and many thought of it as at least some good news amidst the misery of hearing of Lee's surrender.[10]

Lincoln was also accused of subverting the Constitution by suppressing civil liberties, limiting the rights and powers of the states, and using the war as a means of bringing about racial equality. Some Democrats claimed that Lincoln represented a greater danger to the American people than all other causes combined.[11]

Lincoln was compared to the Roman emperor Nerox "who fiddled while Rome burned" and those who voted for him were accused by even northern newspapers of being traitors and murderers. Lincoln was attacked as a fool in Congress as even some Republicans opposed his re-nomination. Therefore, some viewed the assassination of Lincoln as a blessing.[12]

The hostility toward Lincoln was not limited to southerners. Much came from his party and from the British press. Many Englishmen were very much interested in the outcome of the American civil war. The British were largely of the opinion that Lincoln sought to impose a dictatorship on the United States and that he made war on the south so as to promote his personal ambitions. The London Times wrote that Lincoln sought to impose a military despotism.[13]

Even years after the end of the civil war, criticism of Lincoln continued. As late as 1932 the historian Harry Elmer Barnes wrote that Booth's shot made all the difference between a hero and a discredited politician.[14]

Likewise, Lincoln haters continued their criticism into the 20th century, as he was posthumously attacked for mocking Christianity, selling liquor, telling "off color" jokes and treating women with disrespect. Later, southerners sought to remove pro-northern history books out of southern schools. The retired president of the College of William and Mary, Lyon Gardiner Tyler, published a magazine in the 1930's called Tyler's Quarterly, which constantly attacked Lincoln and accused him of demolishing the union and destroying one million lives.[15]

In 1931, Edgar Lee Masters published Lincoln the Man in which Lincoln was accused of crushing free government and was maligned in a string of invectives. In 1959 Russell Hoover Quinn published a book calling Lincoln the country's "first dictator" and accusing Lincoln of "maiming the U.S. Constitution." Further such evaluations continued into the 1950's and into the 1980s.[16]

The Assassination of James A. Garfield (1831-1881)

Garfield was the 20th President of the United States. He had been a general in the Union army during the Civil War and was elected to the presidency after serving in the House of Representatives for one term. He was shot in the back by Charles J. Guiteau while walking in a Washington D.C. railroad station on July 2, 1881. At that time he had been in office only four months. He lived another two months and died on September 19 of that year. His was therefore the second shortest administration in U.S. history. Like Grant, Hayes, Harrison, and McKinley, Garfield became president by "waving the bloody shirt" as he campaigned on the basis of his Civil War record. Because Garfield was in office such a short time, he left no presidential achievements behind.[17]

It was his vice president, Chester A. Arthur (1829-1886), who unexpectedly made a difference during his administration. Arthur was called "the father of the civil service" in that he was instrumental in promoting the Civil Service Reform Act. During his presidency the first immigration law, the Chinese exclusion act, was passed by congress. His administration also saw the first ever diplomatic relations with Korea and the establishment of the Greenwich Meridian at a conference held in Washington in 1894.[18]

Garfield, like so many politicians, placed his personal ambitions above all other considerations. He betrayed his friends and exploited women to gain his ends. He even undermined the career of his most important benefactor, General William S. Rosecrans, because it suited his ambitions. Garfield ignored his debts to others and made numerous enemies on his way to the White House. One of these was Charles Guiteau.[19]

Guiteau was a religious fanatic who suffered from delusions of grandeur. Born in 1841, he ended up on the gallows in 1882 for the murder of James Garfield. To the end he claimed that he had done a good deed in shooting the president.

There can be little doubt that Guiteau was insane in the legal sense of that word in that he literally did not know "right from wrong." A present diagnosis might have called him schizophrenic. In fact, during his trial for murder some physicians testified that they viewed Guiteau as suffering from a "mental disease," although that testimony did not impress the jury. Yet, his history of making threats of physical violence, demanding to be appointed ambassador to

France, trying to attack his sister with an ax, and other bizarre forms of conduct indicated his failure to know reality.[20]

It is remarkable that the assassination of Lincoln did not lead to any effort to protect subsequent presidents of the United States from an equal fate. Garfield walked about Washington without any protection, although his murder took place only sixteen years after Lincoln was shot. Likewise, William McKinley became an easy target for yet another assassin in 1901.

The Assassination of David Hennessey (1858-1890)

David Hennessey was the police chief of New Orleans when he was assassinated on the street on October 15, 1890. That murder led numerous citizens to the immediate conclusion that Hennessey had been murdered by the Italian "Mafia" and that all Italian immigrants were somehow implicated in his murder.

For some years before 1890, many Italians and Sicilians had immigrated to New Orleans. Some of these immigrants were indeed associated with organized crime, as it was then understood. These criminal gangs preyed almost entirely on Italian immigrants but also engaged in the killing of rivals in the Italian-American community. It was therefore the avowed purpose of Chief Hennessey to wipe out the criminal gangs in his city. This earned him the enmity of various criminals in New Orleans so that he claimed shortly before he died of his wounds that "the Dagos did it." The word "Dago" is a derisive word for natives of Italy stemming from the Spanish name "Diego". The killing of Hennessey was given wide publicity in the newspapers of the day accompanied by a rise in anti-Italian sentiment that finally turned violent.[21]

Nineteen men with Italian names were tried for the murder of Hennessey between February 16 and March 13, 1891. The trial resulted in "not guilty" verdicts. Thereupon some angry citizens, inflamed by the newspapers accusations that the jury had been bribed, rushed through the streets shouting "kill the Dagos." Some 150 men then rushed the jail where the defendants were still available and hung eleven of them from lampposts to the cheers of the citizens. The Italian government threatened to send the Italian navy to attack the United States and avenge the lynchings. Nothing came of this except that the United States paid Italy $25,000. A trial was held of some of those who had participated in the lynchings, but the jury found all defendants not guilty.[22]

In 1977, Richard Gambino published a book entitled *Vendetta: A True Story of the Worst Lynching in America.*

The Assassination of William McKinley (1843-1901)

The assassination of the 25th President of the United States was easily achieved because he had no protection despite the murder of Garfield in 1881 and the killing of Lincoln in 1865. McKinley was shot by Leon Czolgosz on September 7, 1901 while attending the Pan-American Exposition in Buffalo, New York. McKinley was visiting the Temple of Music, where he shook hands with any visitor present to greet him. Among these was Czolgosz, who carried a pistol wrapped in a handkerchief. Standing directly in front of McKinley, Czolgosz fired twice, wounding the president in his stomach, pancreas and kidney. The bullets finally lodged in his back. McKinley died on September 14, 1901 from gangrene surrounding his wounds.[23]

William McKinley was a Civil War veteran. He served in the House of Representatives several times in nonconsecutive terms. In 1892 he was elected governor of Ohio. He took office as president on March 4, 1897. His vice-president was Theodore Roosevelt. During his presidency, Hawaii was annexed to the United States and the Chinese Exclusion Act extended to the migration of Chinese from Hawaii to the mainland. McKinley's name was attached to the McKinley Tariff.

The major consequence of the McKinley assassination was the succession of Theodore Roosevelt (1858-1919). Roosevelt brought to the presidency a wealthy New Yorker unlike the "log cabin" presidents who had been elected since the days of Andrew Jackson. Roosevelt was the youngest president ever to take office. He became known as a "trust buster," as the driving force behind the building of the Panama Canal, the mediator who settled the Russian-Japanese War, and the promoter of the food and drug laws of the United States. He too was shot by an anarchist but was not seriously wounded.[24]

Leon Czolgosz, the son of Polish immigrants, was born in Alpena, Michigan in 1873. At age 16 he became a glass worker in Detroit and later worked as a steelworker. Fired for participating in a strike, he became an anarchist, particularly after he witnessed a number of violent confrontations between labor and management. He read extensively about anarchy in socialist literature despite having voted Republican several times. He was convinced that American society was unjust, that the rich exploited the poor, and that he needed to do what Gaetano Bresci had done when he killed king Umberto I of Italy, that is, shock and galvanize the anarchist movement. Czlogosz refused to speak to his court appointed attorneys who argued that he was insane. This did not impress the jury. He was found guilty and electrocuted in October of 1901. Later reviews of Czolgosz's life and conduct concluded that he was insane in the legal sense. It is of course difficult to come to any reliable conclusions concerning anyone's emotional state "ex post facto."Several songs and plays have been produced concerning the assassination of McKinley.[25]

The assassination of McKinley had some unforeseen consequences for those who considered themselves anarchists and published material supporting that view. This expression is derived from the Greek an - archon meaning no ruler. Anarchists believe that there ought to be no government and that everything should be done to bring about a state in which all government is abolished.

A few of those who share these beliefs commit violence. Those of the vast majority publish journals and newspapers, hold speeches and try to persuade others to their views. There are today (2011) some anarchist groups, particularly in our Western states, as there always have been. Their influence was always minimal. Nevertheless, after the assassination of President McKinley, the newspapers and politicians of the day claimed that a vast anarchist conspiracy was responsible for the president's death and that it was essential that all anarchists be deported. It was believed that anarchists were inevitably immigrants and therefore dangerous for the citizens of this country. Since Czolgosz had a Polish name because his parents were immigrants, this seemed to confirm the hysteria around anarchists. Yet Leon Czolgosz was born in the United States, a fact hardly mentioned by the media.[26]

These beliefs were enhanced by the arrival in the United States of Johann Most, who came from England in 1882 and promptly formed the International Worker's People's Association, together with numerous publications advocating anarchy. Fear of anarchists bordered on hysteria and led to the arrest of a number of suspected supporters of anarchy in this country. Johann Most in particular was jailed for "inciting a riot," although there was no evidence to that effect. On appeal of convictions stemming from these efforts to suppress freedom of speech and of the press, the Supreme Court often held with the police and courts seeking to give away constitutional guarantees in favor of fear concerning anarchy.[27]

In view of the McKinley assassination, anarchists became subject to abuse of all kinds, including violence. Socialists, even if not anarchists, were also subject to such abuse, even as newspapers suggested that anarchists be sent to some Pacific island. Congress participated in this mass hysteria but could not succeed in passing a bill and making it into law.[28]

The hysteria concerning foreign anarchists led to an effort to secure passage of an immigrant exclusion law to the effect that not only those advocating the violent overthrow of the government be excluded from the U.S. but that this law also apply to people who were members of a group holding these views. When infighting made it impossible for Congress to pass such laws, the State of New York and other states enacted such laws themselves. These laws, however contrary to constitutional guarantees, were upheld by the Supreme Court.[29]

In time the anarchist hysteria was forgotten, as other issues satisfied the publics need to enjoy conspiracy theories of all kinds. Communism, sexual predators, terrorists, and a host of other groups each temporarily satisfied the need for enemies and conspirators, driving every one of these groups into oblivion as the next target emerged.

The Assassination of Antonin Cermak (1873-1933)

Cermak was shot in the lung by Giuseppe Zangara on February 15, 1933 while shaking hands with President-elect Franklin D. Roosevelt. Roosevelt was inaugurated in March of that year. Both men met at Bayfront Park in Miami, Florida by accident in that Roosevelt greeted numerous Miami citizens from his car. Cermak happened to be present as Zangara shot at Roosevelt, hoping to kill him, but hit five other people instead. The murder of Cermak resulted in the usual conspiracy theories concerning organized crime, the "lace curtain" Irish, the black community, and others.

Indeed, Cermak had numerous political enemies, as he organized a political "machine" in Chicago. In 1931, Cermak had succeeded "Big Bill" Thompson, a Republican, as mayor. Thompson was the last Republican to hold the office of mayor of Chicago to this day (2011). He too ran a "machine," which finally failed when numerous "ethnics" decided to vote for the Czech immigrant Cermak instead.[30]

Zangara had come to the United States from his native Italy in 1923. He was only five feet tall and weighted 105 pounds. He lived alone and worked as a bricklayer. Constantly plagued by pain stemming from severe stomach ulcers, he imagined that his pain could be alleviated if he killed the president. Originally he sought to kill Herbert Hoover. However, when Hoover was defeated by Roosevelt, Zangara traveled to Miami, where Roosevelt was scheduled to hold a speech.

Then, shortly before Roosevelt left, Cermak approached Roosevelt's car and as he did so, Zangara climbed on a chair and began shooting. This was despite a large contingent of police present to guard Roosevelt.

Before and during his trial Zangara told police and the court that he meant to kill Roosevelt because he hated all rulers and hoped to get relief from his stomach pain by killing Roosevelt. Zangara was electrocuted after revealing repeatedly that he wanted to die, as his life was a disaster. He had been forced to work as a day laborer by his father after his mother died. He had never gone to school, had no family after arriving in the United States, and was so plagued by illness and pain that he saw no purpose in living any longer. He had hoped to be shot by the police who surrounded Roosevelt but failed to commit "suicide by cop."[31]

The Assassination of Huey Long (1893-1935)

On September 8, 1935, Senator Huey Long of Louisiana was shot in the Capitol building of Louisiana at Baton Rouge. He died two days later. Although legend has attributed the death of Long to a Dr. Carl Weiss, researchers who exhumed the body of Long discovered that he was killed by the bullets of his bodyguards, who believed that Dr. Weiss had a gun. The bodyguards fired 61 bullets into Weiss, killing him instantly. One or more bullets hit Long.

After Long fell, it was discovered that he had a bloody nose and a swollen lip. In 1991, Professor James E. Starrs of George Washington University was granted permission to exhume the body of Long and to perform an autopsy. This effort proved inconclusive except that Starrs and his team of specialists reported that their examination "cast considerable doubt" on the assertion that Long was killed by Dr. Weiss.[32]

Huey Long was a lawyer and politician who was governor of Louisiana from 1928 to 1932, when he entered the U.S. Senate. By advocating a "Share the Wealth" program, he became immensely popular both in his home state and throughout the country. A dynamic speaker, he succeeded in becoming a "boss" who controlled the legislature and all appointments to political office. In 1929, he was impeached by the legislature, an effort which failed as Long bribed some members with cash and state jobs.

In 1932, Long entered the senate of the United States. Although he now spent much time in Washington, D.C., he returned to his home state frequently in order to control the state with a view of running for President against Franklin D. Roosevelt in 1936. This was a real possibility in view of the Great Depression, which had cost millions their livelihood. Long's proposals were popular not only because the phrase "share the wealth" appealed to so many of the poor, but also because he attacked Standard Oil and other corporations while advocating public works programs to solve the economic crisis.[33]

Economic downturns frequently produce charismatic leaders who speak well and claim to have simple solutions to complicated problems. Few people understand how the economy works nor do very many want to hear such explanations. People who are out of work or whose business has failed want immediate solutions to their problems. This permits demagogues like Long in the 1930's and President Obama in 2011 to claim that their programs will solve all problems at once and to use "strong arm" tactics to enforce their wishes. Included in these political maneuvers are the usual anti-Jewish conspiracy theories, which Long supported.

The Assassination of Carlo Tresca (1879-1943)

It is difficult to find any victim of assassination who had more enemies than Carlo Tresca, who was gunned down on a street in New York City on January 11, 1943. Tresca was crossing Fifth Avenue on foot when a black Ford pulled up beside him. A short man, carrying a gun, jumped out of the car and shot Tresca in the back and head. Tresca died instantly. The killer was Carmine Galante, a "made" member of the Costa Nostra (our thing), at that time a name for several crime families in New York.

Tresca had hoped to study law in Italy but his family did not have the money to send him to law school. In part he sought a legal career because he was motivated by hatred of injustice. Forced to leave Italy for fear of imprisonment for having "radical" views, he came to the United States in 1904 and entered the profession of journalism. He worked on several Italian-American newspapers and finally founded his own newspaper in which he denounced the Italian dictator Benito Mussolini, the German dictator Hitler, organized crime or the Cosa Nostra, and the communist party.

Tresca had been a union organizer who was involved in the strikes called by the Industrial Workers of the World. These strikes by the textile workers in Lawrence, Massachusetts, garment workers in New York City, the Paterson, New Jersey silk strike and the Mesabi Range, Minnesota miners strike, were supported by Tresca and his newspaper. In that same publication Tresca attacked Joseph Stalin and the communist dictatorship and criticized the Mafia and particularly Frank Costello, who at that time was the Capo de tutti Capi or Boss of all the Bosses in New York organized crime.

The Assassination of John F. Kennedy (1917-1963)

So much has been written and said about the murder of President Kennedy in 1963 that whole libraries could be filled with comments and theories about that gruesome event. Suffice it to say that John Kennedy was killed by shots fired from the Texas Book Depository in Dallas and that Lee Harvey Oswald fired those shots.

According to the Report of the President's Commission on the Assassination of President John F. Kennedy, Lee Harvey Oswald acted alone when he murdered Kennedy. The Commission held that no foreign government, nor organized crime nor anyone other than Oswald was responsible for the killing of the president. Popularly known as the Warren Report because it was chaired by Earl Warren, former governor of California, the report denies all of the conspiracy theories surrounding the fourth murder of an American president. Abraham Lincoln, James Garfield and William McKinley were the previous victims of presidential murder.[34]

In 1978, fifteen years after the assassination of President Kennedy, the House of Representatives asked a "Select Committee" to investigate the assassination again. The House report held that President Kennedy was probably assassinated as a result of a conspiracy but that the committee could not identify the conspirators.[35]

The belief in a conspiracy surrounding the Kennedy assassination was greatly influenced by the subsequent murder of Oswald by Jack Ruby, who shot

Oswald to death in the corridor of the Dallas Police Headquarters. This meant that no trial of Oswald was possible, although Oswald had not only killed Kennedy but also killed a Dallas policeman, J.D. Tippit. The reason for killing Tippit is also a matter of speculation because Oswald was never tried for either murder.[36]

Ruby was the operator of a nightclub in Dallas. He had been arrested a number of times for minor offenses but was also known as an explosive man who acted as his own "bouncer" and who may have had ties to organized crime. Ruby was a native of Chicago. He later moved to Dallas. There are some who allege that Ruby had ties to organized crime and was associated with the Italian "mafia." Others have denied this. Conspiracy theorists like to claim that Italian gangsters wanted to kill Kennedy because he and his brother, the attorney general, had convicted a number of professional gangsters, even though "the mob" had secured a Kennedy victory in the 1960 presidential election by all kinds of fraud. The theory holds that Ruby, who was dying of cancer, killed Oswald on behalf of his Mafiosi friends and thereby made their involvement invisible.[37]

Another conspiracy theory holds that Oswald acted on behalf of the Cuban dictator Fidel Castro. This theory is based on the fact that Oswald did live in Cuba after his return from Soviet Russia. These facts lead theorists to conclude that the Russian government recommended Oswald to Castro as a potential killer. Castro sought to revenge himself on Kennedy because Kennedy had sent a number of Cuban exiles to Cuba in 1961 with instructions to kill Castro. Furthermore, the U.S. government made a deal with organized crime practitioners, also designed to kill Castro. The belief that Castro killed Kennedy was shared by former President Lyndon Johnson.[38]

There are in addition numerous other conspiracy theories that seem remote and unjustified but continue to occupy movies, magazines, books and other media, although no proof of any such theories has been forthcoming.

John Kennedy was the son of privilege. Born in Brookline, Massachusetts in 1917, Kennedy was raised in a large Catholic family of Irish descent. His wealthy father sent him to private schools and Harvard College, graduating in 1940. He traveled widely in Europe with his parents and later with friends, and entered the U.S. Navy in 1941. He was injured severely after his PT boat was rammed by a Japanese destroyer in the Solomon Islands. He received several citations for bravery and returned to the United States a war hero.

This permitted him to enter politics, as he was elected to the House of Representatives in 1947. He remained there until 1953 when he was elected Senator from Massachussetts. He was elected President in 1960. In 1953, Kennedy married Jaqueline Bouvier, with whom he had four children.

Throughout his presidency, the Kennedys viewed themselves as royalty and persuaded the media to treat them as such. Accustomed to vast wealth and the obsequious conduct of sycophants, Kennedy, despite his "liberal" rhetoric, lived in a world known only to few Americans and divorced from the concerns of those who elected him.[39]

The Assassination of Martin Luther King (1929-1968)

On April 4, 1968, when King was 39 years old, James Earl Ray shot him while he was standing on the balcony of a motel in Memphis, Tennessee. That assassination led to more than 100 riots across the United States as Afro-Americans viewed King's death as motivated by racial hatred. In view of the sporadic shooting, looting and fighting that succeeded the news of the murder, the governor of Tennessee, Buford Ellington, ordered the National Guard to secure Memphis.[40]

King was a Baptist minister who led the 1955 Montgomery, Alabama bus boycott. He also organized the Southern Christian Leadership Conference and the 1963 March on Washington, D.C. In 1964 King was awarded the Nobel Peace Prize. In 1986 Congress established the Martin Luther King, Jr. Day as a U.S. national holiday.

King was born as Michael King. His name was changed by his father in honor of the German Protestant Martin Luther after the family had traveled in Germany. At age fifteen, King entered Morehouse College, graduating with a degree in sociology in 1948. Subsequently he earned a degree in divinity and a Doctor of Philosophy from Boston University with a dissertation that had been "plagiarized" or stolen.[41]

King's papers were donated to Stanford University by his widow, Coretta Scott. This led to the discovery by the librarians at Stanford University that Kings had not only used the dissertation of Jack Boozer, but that he had also plagiarized other authors in his earlier writings and in his speeches. A panel of scholars concluded that "plagiarism" was his long established practice."[42]

King came to the attention of the nation because he promoted the 1955 bus boycott in Montgomery after a fifteen year old girl, Claudette Colvin, refused to give up her bus seat to a white man in compliance with Alabama's "Jim Crow" laws. When Rosa Parks was arrested for the same conduct, she became the heroine of the civil rights movement as led by King. Colvin was and is ignored. In 1961, a group of civil rights activists organized in Albany, Georgia to end segregation all over the United States. King participated and was arrested and jailed after leading peaceful demonstrations against lunch counter segregation and other forms of bigotry and discrimination.[43]

On March 9, 1965, King led a march from Selma, Alabama to Montgomery, the Alabama state capital. This march ended peacefully after a previous march on March 7, 1965 led to violence on the part of the "white" population and the police. That date has since then been labeled "bloody Sunday," as protesters were beaten and police dogs attacked them. Subsequently King led a march on the 9th of March, which remained peaceful and demonstrated the nonviolent protest methods used in earlier years by Gandhi in India.[44]

King spoke out against the war in Viet Nam on the grounds that it cost more and more money and resources which could have been spent on President Lyndon Johnson's announced "war on poverty." He accused the United States armed forces of having killed a million North Vietnamese, "mostly children." King also advocated a redistribution of wealth in the United States, a policy which President Obama has attempted to put into effect in 2011. All these views and speeches led a number of the media to denounce King as a traitor and friend of the enemy in North Viet Nam.[45]

Kings's opinions gave him numerous enemies. Therefore a number of conspiracy theories developed which claimed, among other theories, that James Earl Ray did not act alone but was an agent of the U.S. government, that a Lloyd Jowers was the real killer, that King's retinue included "saboteurs" who were secret agents of the F.B.I. and provided Ray with an escape route and with the money to flee the scene, etc. etc.[46]

After his arrest at an airport in London, England, James Earl Ray confessed that he killed Martin Luther King. He was sentenced to 99 years in prison. In view of his confession, no trial was held, so that conspiracy theorists were able to constantly demand a trial so that "the truth" would be revealed. Coretta Scott King, Martin's widow, demanded such a trial as did many others. Ray insisted that he confessed under threats and pressure and that the rifle, with his fingerprints found near the scene of the murder, was not his.[47]

In 1998, Memphis District Attorney William Gibbons issued a 12 page report on the King assassination. A seven month investigation led Gibbons to the conclusion that he "remains absolutely convinced of James Earl Ray's guilt in the murder of Dr. King." This report did not satisfy the conspiracy theorists, including the King family. Because no trial was ever held, the motives of Ray cannot be discerned. Ray died of liver disease in 1998.[48]

Martin Luther King, like Abraham Lincoln before him, has become an American icon. References to King are part of the civil religion in the United States, so that any criticism of King is viewed as a semi-sacrilege. This is particularly true because a legal holiday is devoted to him, creating legends and a mythology that clouds his life in mystery similar to the lives of saints. Whatever his successes, there can be little doubt that the movement he led contributed greatly to the election of Barack Obama to the presidency in 2008 and the subsequent effort to enshrine Obama as well in a cloak of untouchable righteousness.

The Assassination of Robert F. Kennedy (1925-1968)

The murder of Martin Luther King had occurred only two months before the then United States senator from New York, Robert F. Kennedy, was shot to death in the kitchen of the Ambassador Hotel in Los Angeles, California. The killer was Sirhan Sirhan, a Palestinian immigrant motivated by religious hate.

Although warned by an F.B.I. agent not to walk through the kitchen, Kennedy entered a crowded kitchen pathway and was wounded severely by Saran's .22-caliber revolver. Kennedy died the next day at the Good Samaritan Hospital in Los Angeles.[49]

Kennedy was a candidate for the Democratic nomination for president of the United States when he died. In March of 1968 President Johnson had announced that he would not seek another term as president. This led Robert Kennedy to campaign for the office his brother had held before he was assassinated. Robert F. Kennedy became senator from New York in 1965 and therefore had reason to believe he could be elected president.[50]

The son of privilege, Kennedy catapulted from one appointed office to another in record time. Kennedy had eleven children. In view of his financial resources this did not prevent him from holding various government positions, which did not pay enough to normally support 13 people.

Kennedy, as attorney general, participated actively in the civil rights movement, which allowed him to gather numerous votes for the position of senator from New York, which has traditionally favored the cause of minorities. Kennedy also authorized the assassination of Fidel Castro and actively participated in the Cuban missile crisis decisions. As attorney general, Kennedy publicly investigated organized crime and as senator from New York was a member of "The War on Poverty" program initiated by President Johnson.[51]

Sirhan Sirhan, the assassin of Robert F. Kennedy, had immigrated from Jerusalem to New York and later to California. Raised by a family of religious zealots, he hated all Jews and therefore killed Kennedy, whom he regarded as Jewish. Sirhan believed that Kennedy's policies would favor the survival of Israel if elected president. Sirhan has repeatedly sought parole but was denied thirteen times.[52]

The Assassinations of George Moscone (1929-1978) and Harvey Milk (1930-1978)

On November 27, 1978, Dan White, a member of the board of supervisors of San Francisco, California, entered the office of the mayor, George Richard Moscone, and shot and killed him. White then went after supervisor Harvey Milk and shot and killed him as well.

Arrested and tried for these deliberate homicides, White was convicted of both murders. Nevertheless, the jury recommended and the judge agreed to give White a five year sentence on the grounds he had eaten too much "junk" food. In 1985 White committed suicide.

The murders of Moscone and Milk arose from a citywide dispute in San Francisco related to the increasing political power of homosexuals in that city. In 1977 Milk was elected to the board of supervisors of San Francisco and thereby became the first openly homosexual politician to achieve election. At that time his election was a national sensation because homosexuality was rejected by public opinion and was also illegal in every state of the union. Moscone supported Milk and actively participated in the elections of women and minorities to San Francisco offices. In view of these political conditions and the fact that the pay of supervisors was poor, Dan White resigned his position as supervisor, only to change his mind and ask Moscone to reappoint him. Moscone refused and White then killed him and Milk, whom he despised as a homosexual.[53]

Moscone was the product of Catholic private schools. He earned a law degree, served in the navy, and entered politics in 1960. He became a member of the state senate and majority leader for the Democrats. In 1975, Moscone was elected mayor of San Francisco by campaigning for "gay" rights. He appointed a large number of women and homosexuals to city positions, including the leader of a deviant sect, Jim Jones of "the People's Temple," who became housing commissioner.[54]

Harvey Milk drifted from New York to Florida, to California and back to New York several times. He had earned a degree in mathematics and held a number of jobs related to his background, but found such work boring. After moving to San Francisco to become part of the homosexual community, he ran a camera shop until his election to the city board.

After his murder Milk became a folk hero among the homosexual community. A movie about his life was shown in 2009 and a book about his life was published in 2008. In 2009 Milk was honored with the Medal of Freedom posthumously.[55]

Daniel James White (1946-1985) was 39 years old when he killed himself. He was the second of ten children in his Roman Catholic family. In his junior year he was dismissed from his high school for violence but became valedictorian at another high school. He served in the army for seven years, including an assignment in Viet Nam. On being discharged in 1972 he became a police officer. He quit the police department and joined the firefighters. He was cited by the San Francisco Chronicle for bravery. He then ran for office and was elected to the San Francisco board of supervisors on gaining the support of the police and firefighters' unions. As a board member he saw himself as the defender of home and family against homosexuals, drug users and religious apostates.[56]

One of the consequences of the murder of Mayor Moscone was the rise to political prominence of Diane Feinstein. She was the president of the San Francisco board of supervisors and therefore inherited the mayor's job. She was mayor for ten years, 1978-1988. She was elected to the U.S. Senate from California in 1992 and re-elected in 1998 and in 2004.

The Assassination of Leo Ryan (1925-1978)

Ryan was a member of the House of Representatives when he was assassinated at Port Kaituma in Guyana on November 19, 1978. Congressman Ryan was seated in a small plane at the Kaituma airstrip when Larry Layton and others fired a number of shots at the plane, killing Leo Ryan, three journalists and a member of the People's Temple who sought to escape Guyana. Nine other people were also wounded. All of this violence was the consequence of Ryan's attempt to rescue citizens who had lived in the 11th congressional district in California, which he represented. These Californians had moved to Jonestown, an enclave in the Guyana jungle organized by Jim Jones, a cult leader, who brought a number of California citizens to that remote area.[57]

Jim Jones had founded the People's Temple in Indiana. In 1975 he moved the Temple to San Francisco after his views on racial equality led to considerable harassment in Indiana. In San Francisco, Jones and his Temple members participated in the 1975 mayoral election of George Mascone. This led to the appointment of Jones as Chairman of the San Francisco Housing Authority. Because of his political connections, Jones was publicly praised by vice presidential candidate Walter Mondale. He was also a speaker at the opening of the Democratic Party Headquarters in San Francisco in 1976, leading later that year to a testimonial dinner for Jones attended by numerous California politicians. Nevertheless, Jones moved his Temple to Guyana after a number of media published "exposés" concerning sexual, physical and emotional abuse within the Temple community.[58]

When Jones recognized that numerous members of his church wanted to defect with Congressman Ryan, he evidently directed the shooting of those about to escape. Then, on that same day, Jones induced 909 inhabitants of Jonestown to drink cyanide poisoned Flavor Aid which killed all of them, including children. Jones shot himself to death sometime later.[59]

Larry Layton is the only person convicted of the murder of Leo Ryan. He was sentenced to life in prison on March 3, 1987 and released in April of 2002.[60]

The Assassination of Allard K. Lowenstein (1929-1980)

On March 14, 1980 Dennis Sweeney murdered Allard K. Lowenstein in his Manhattan office. Sweeney entered Lowenstein's office and shot him several times. Lowenstein had been a member of the House of Representatives for one term from 1968 to 1970, when he was defeated in an effort to gain a second term. Thereafter, Lowenstein became the head of Americans for Democratic Action and thereafter ran once more for Congress in 1972 but was defeated again. He continued his effort to gain elected office when he ran for the U.S. Senate in 1974 and again in 1976 and in 1978, only to lose each time.[61]

Lowenstein, a graduate of the Yale University Law School, practiced so-called "liberal" politics. This included an effort to reopen the investigation of the assassination of Robert Kennedy on the grounds that, in Lowenstein's opinion, Sirhan Sirhan was not the killer of Kennedy. Lowenstein was appointed as head of the United States delegation to the United Nations Commission on Human Rights.[62]

Lowenstein had briefly worked at Stanford University, where he met Dennis Sweeney. Sweeney labeled himself an anti Viet Nam war activist and promoter of black civil rights. He had worked in the voter registration drives in Mississippi in the 1960's. Sweeney was convicted of the murder of Lowenstein and served eight years in a psychiatric hospital. He was released in 2000.[63]

The Assassination of John Lennon (1940-1980)

On December 8, 1980, at around 10:50 p.m., Mark David Chapman shot John Lennon in the back four times at the entrance of a New York City apartment building. Although lacking musical talent, Lennon had the ability to project his personality onto the screen and to write popular songs which are regarded as major contributions to rock and roll history. There can be little doubt that popular music is limited to a foot pounding rhythm accompanied by a great deal of noise and a political message. This is of course not comparable to the music of Verdi, Beethoven, Mozart, or Gershwin. Instead, such music must be understood as a means of stimulating the emotions aroused by the kind of circular interaction which large crowds develop in a manner similar to the crowd reactions produced by political demagogues.[64]

Lennon was born in England and became popular in that country and in the United States because he associated with three other musicians who sang his songs as a group and called themselves "The Beatles." Lennon became associated with George Harrison and Paul McCartney and a drummer, Ringo Starr. Lennon wrote such songs as "Hello, Little Girl," "P.S. I LoveYou," "I Want to Hold Your Hand," and numerous other tunes easily written, simply sung, and soon forgotten amidst innumerable other such bands, singing groups and noisemakers whose popularity earned the writers and performers vast amounts of money. Lennon also wrote an essay entitled "Woman Is the Nigger of the World." A drug user, married twice, Lennon protested against a number of issues then important. He had two sons, one from each of his wives.[65]

Lennon appeared in a number of television shows. He also wrote poetry such as, "Tomorrow will be Muggy, followed by Tuggy, Wuggy and Thuggy." His popularity around the world earned him such exaggerated titles as "greatest musician," "immortal," and other gross labels which, in the course of time, have evaporated as media driven hyperbole.[66]

Mark David Chapman was born in 1955 in Fort Worth, Texas. He was twenty-five years old when he shot John Lennon in the back four times outside the Dakota apartments in New York City. Lennon's wife was present when Lennon was killed, as were several associates. In view of the horror of seeing the murder of her husband, Lennon's wife Yoko Ono and others screamed in horror. Yet Chapman calmly sat down in the lobby of the building and read *The Catcher in the Rye*, a book he carried with him at all times. Chapman had a history of violence. He was told by God to plead guilty to the killing of Lennon. Furthermore he did not know why he was tried in a court for the murder nor did he deny the killing. No motive for the assassination has been discovered. There can be little doubt that Chapman is not a normal person in the psychological sense, although he was not found "insane," which is a legal term.

The murder of Lennon leads to the conclusion that the price of prominence is that it attracts people who are angry, aggressive, and possibly violent. Therefore no absolute security for so-called "celebrities" is possible.

The Assassination of Meir Kahane (1932-1990)

On November 5, 1990, El Sayyid a Nosair killed Meir Kahane in a second floor conference room of the New York Marriott Hotel East Side in Manhatten. Nosair was motivated by religious hate. Taught to seek the death of any who believe in Judaism, Nosair shot Kahane who was an orthodox rabbi and citizen of Israel where he served in the parliament.

In the late 1960's Kahane had founded the Jewish Defense League while he was still living in the United States. Born in Brooklyn, Kahane moved to Jerusalem, Israel in 1971. The Jewish Defense League sought to protect New York Jews from racist attacks in the streets of New York and other American cities. The JDL also worked diligently to rescue Jews living in the erstwhile Soviet Union by promoting their emigration to the United States and Israel.[67]

In 1971 Meir Kahane moved to Israel where his father had been born. There he founded the "Kach" party. That party was dedicated to expelling Arabs from Israeli territory. The party also viewed divine law as expressed in the Bible as superior to Israeli civil law. In 1984 Kahane was elected a member of the Israeli parliament, the Knesset, and served as a representative for four years when he was expelled because of his views. These views included the opinion that non-Jews, i.e. Arabs should be paid to leave Israel lest they become a majority and once more persecute the Jews in their own land. He proposed that Arabs who would not leave even if paid $40,000 be forcibly deported.[68]

The killer of Meir Kahane was adjudicated "not guilty" of murder by a jury composed of anti-Jewish activists. He was nevertheless found guilty of gun possession, assault and coercion and sentenced to 7.5 years in prison. [69] In 2002 it was revealed that Nosair was paid by Osama bin Laden to kill Kahane and that he was also involved in the attack on the World Trade Center. [70]

The Assassination of Dr. George R. Tiller (1941-2009)

On May 31, 2009, Dr. George R. Tiller was shot to death in the lobby of the Reformation Lutheran Church in Wichita, Kansas. Dr. Tiller was an usher that Sunday morning. Tiller performed numerous late term abortions. This angered the anti-abortionists in his state and elsewhere. For thirty years they made every effort to shut down his clinic but were not successful until Scott Roeder murdered him.[71]

Tiller had been the target of anti-abortion activists for thirty years. The anti-abortionists blockaded his clinic, had him prosecuted, boycotted his suppliers, demonstrated with signs reading "Tiller the baby killer," filed lawsuits against him, made death threats and bombed his clinic. In 1993, an anti-abortionist tried to kill him by shooting him five times. Tiller's wounds did not kill him and so Roeder tried again. Tiller was a Republican, a churchgoer, a former Navy officer, and a member of the oldest country club in Wichita. He viewed himself as a "Freedom Fighter" and denounced radical conduct.[72]

Scott Roeder of Merriam, Kansas was arrested in Gardiner, Kansas on the day of the killing. Charged with first degree murder and aggravated assault, Roeder had vandalized a women's clinic shortly before he killed Dr. Tiller. According to his former wife, Roeder was and is mentally ill. His instability may in part be revealed as Roeder worked for four different employers in only six months before his arrest. Roeder was also involved in a number of anti-government activities. Police discovered a large number of weapons in Roeder's car. He was convicted on a weapons charge, which the Kansas Court of Appeals overturned because the police had no authority to search his car.[73]

The murder of Dr. Tiller led to the usual denunciation of violence by the anti-abortion believers. So-called "liberals" accused so-called "conservatives" of stirring up hatred of abortionists and therefore held them responsible of the killing of Dr. Tiller. Tiller is of course not the only doctor murdered for conducting abortions. Including Tiller, eight abortionists have been murdered in the United States.

NOTES

1. Edgar McInnis, *Canada; A Political and Social History,* (New York: Holt, Rinehart and Winston, 1962), 299-306.

2. T.P. Slattery, *The Assassination of D'Arcy McGee,* (Toronto: Doubleday Canada, 1968).

3. Richard L. Bushman, *Joseph Smith: Rough Stone Rolling,* (New York: Alfred A. Knopf, 2005), 538.

4. Ibid, 50.

5. Roger W. Lotchin, "Mormons and Gentiles: A History of Salt Lake City," *American Historical Review,* vol. 91, no. 3, (1986), 754.

6. Michael Kauffman, *American Brutus: Jiohn Wilkes Booth and the Lincoln Conspiracies,* (New York: Random House, 2004), 130-134.

7. James A. Christenson and Ronald C. Wimberly, "Who is Civil Religious?" *Sociological Analysis,* vol. 39, no. 1, (1978), 77.

8. Charles W. Ramsdell, "Lincoln and Fort Sumter," *Journal of Soutern History,* vol. III (1937), 285.

9. Lyon G. Tyler, "The South and Secession," *Tyler's Quarterly Historical and Genealogical Magazine,* vol. XIII, (1931-1932), 212-213.

10. Michael Davis, *The Image of Lincoln in the South,* (Knoxville: University of Tennessee Press, 1971), 62-104.

11. Joel H. Silbey, *A Respectable Minority,* (New York: W.W. Norton &Co, 1977), 74-77.

12. David Donald, *Cahrles sumner and the Rise of Man,* (New York: Alfred A. Knopf, 1069), 162-169.

13. Robert Bloom, "As the British Press saw Lincoln," *A Journal of the Liberal Arts,* vol.V, (Spring 1965), 48.

14. No author, "Holds Political Ruin Confronted Lincoln, *New York Times,* (February 9, 1932), 14.

15. *Tylers Quarterly,* vol. 5, :230; vol. 6, :152; vol. 7:7-8, vol.8; 72 vol.14, 230-233.

16. See: Russell Hoover Quinn, *The Constitutions of Abraham Lincoln and Jefferson Davis,* (New York: Exposition Press, 1959), 152, 164, 181. Ludwell H. Johsnosn, "Civil War Military History" , *Civil War History,* v 17, (1971), 130; M.E. Bradford, "The Lincoln Legacy," *Modern Age, vol.*24, 1979-80), 355-363.

17. Gordon Berg, "President Garfield's Proving Ground," *Civil War Times,* vol. 46, no.9, (2007), 42-47.

18. Burton T. Doyle and Homer H. Swaney, *Lives of James A. Garfield and Chester A. Arthur,* (Washington, D.C. Darby Publishers, 1881), 61.

19. Stanley Hirshson, "The Garfield Orbit," *The Journal of American History,* vol. 65, no. 4, (March 1979), 1134.

20. Stewart Mitchell, "The Man Who Murdered Garfield," *Proceedings of the Massachusetts Historical Society,* vol. 67, (October 1941-May 1944), 452-489.

21. No author, "Shot Down at His Door," *The New York Times,* (October 17, 1890), 1.

22. Joseph E. Persico, "Vendetta in New Orleans, " *American Heritage Magazine,* (June 1973), 1.

23. Selig Adler, "The Operation on President McKinley," *Scientific American,* vol. 208, no.3, (March, 1963), 118-130.

24. Arnaldo Testi, "The Gender of Reform Politics: Theodore Roosevelt and the Culture of Masculinity," *Journal of American History,* vol. 81, no. 4 (1995), 1509-1533.

25. Jeffrey Seibert, *I Done My Duty: The Complete Story of the Assassination of President Mc Kinley,* (Bowie, Maryland, Heritage Books, 2002), 430.

26. Gustavo Tosti, "Anarchistic Crimes," *Political Science Quarterly,* vol. 14, (September 1809), 412-417.

27. Edward E. Slosson, "An Experiment in Anarchy," *Independent,* vol.15, (April 2, 1993), 779-785.

28. *Congressional Record,* 57, Cong. I sess.1-12.

29. Sidney Fine, "Anarchism and the Assassination of McKinley," *The American Historical Review,* vol.60, no.4, (July 1955), 798.

30. Andrew Gumbel, *Steal This Vote,* (New York: Nation Books, 2005), 157.

31. Nathan D. Shappee, "Zangara's Attempted Assassination of Franklin D. Roosevelt," *The Florida Historical Quarterly,* vol. 37, no. 2, (October 1958), 101-110.

32. No author, "Scientist Says Report Casts Doubt on Story of Huey Long Death," *The New York Times,* (February 22, 1992), Sec.1, 6.

33. Arthur M. Schlesinger, Jr. *The Politics of Upheaval,* (Boston: Houghton Mifflin Co., 1960), 46-68.

34. No author. *Report of the President's Commission on the Assassination of President John F. Kennedy.* (Washington, DC: The United States Government Printing Office, 1964), Chapter 1, 22.

35. U.S. House of Representatives, Select Committee on Assassinations, (Washington, DC: U.S. Government Printing Office, December 29, 1978) Sec. C., 95.

36. No author, "Dallas Policeman's Wife Also Weeps for her Husband,:" *The New York Times,* (November 29, 1963), 9.

37. Report of the Presidential Commission etc., Appendix XVI 779.

38. Michael Scott Moore, "Did Castro Kill Kennedy?" *Der Spiegel,* (January 14, 2006), 1.

39. William Manchester , *Portrait of a President,* (Boston: Little, Brown, 1967).

40. Earl Caldwell, "Martin Luther King is Slain in Memphis," *The New York Times,* (April 5, 1968), A1.

41. Charles A. Radin, "Panel confirms Plagiarism by King and BU," *The Boston Globe,* (October 11, 1991), 1.

42. Clayborne Carson, Peter Holloran, Ralph E. Luker, Penny Russell, "Martin Luther King as Scholar: A Re-examination of his Theological Writings," *The Journal of American History,* vol. 78, no. 1, (June 1991), 81-85.

43. Thomas F. Jackson, *From Civil Rights to Human Rights: Martin Luther King, Jr. and the Struggle for Economic Justice,* (Philadelphia: The University of Pennsylvania Press, 2007), 85.

44. Ibid., 222-223.

45. Mary S. Robbins, *Against the Viet Nam War: Writings by Activists,* (Lanham, MD: Rowland and Littlefield, 2007), 106.

46. Robert C. Smith, *Contemporary Controversies and the American Racial Divide,* (Lanham, MD. Rowman and Littlefield, 2000), 97.

47. No author, "The Trial That Wasn't," *The New York Times,* (February 23, 1997), 4, 2.

48. Emily Yellin, "Third Inquiry Confirms Others: Ray Alone Was King's Killer," *The New York Times,* (March 28, 1998), A6.

49. No author, "Assassination: The night Bobby Kennedy was shot," *The Independent,* (January 21, 2—7), 1.

50. William Newman, "Rename Triborough for RFK." *The New York Times,* (November 6, 2008), City 1.

51. Arthur M. Schlesinger, *Robert Kennedy and his times,* Boston: Houghton Mifflin, (1978).

52. Carol Oppenheim, "RFK would OK parole, Sirhan says," *Chicago Tribune,* (May 11, 1982), 9.

53. John Cloud, "People told him no openly gay man could win political office," *Time,* (June 14, 1999), 1.

54. Wallace Turner, "San Francisco Mayor is Slain: City Supervisor Also Killed: Ex-offcial Gives Up to Police," *The New York Times,* (November 28, 1978), A1.

55. Chrisitine Bellantoni, "Medal of Freedom for Harvey Milk," *The Washington Times,* (July 31, 2009), 1.

56. Carol Pogash, "Myth of the Twinkie Defense," *San Francisco Chronicle,* (November 23, 2003), D1.

57. Mark Simon, "A Trip into the Heart of Darkness," *San Francisco Chronicle,* (December 10, 1978), A17.

58. Tim Reiterman and John Jacobs, *Raven: The Untold Story of Rev. Jim Jones and His People,* (New York: E.P. Dutton, 1982), 314.

59. Ibid., 390-391.

60. *United States of America vs. Lawrence John Layton,* 666 F.Supp, 1369, no. CR-80-416 REP. U.S. (June 3, 1987).

61. William Henry Chafe, *Never Stop Running:Allard Lowenstein and the Struggle to Save American Liberalism.* (New York: Basic Books, 1993).

62. Richard Cummiongs, *The Pied Piper: Allard K. Lownstein and the Libral Dream,* (New York: Grove Press, 1985).

63. Blaine Harden and Nina Bernstein, "Voices in His Head Muted, A Killer Rejoins the World," *The New York Times,* (July 31, 2000), A1.

64. Les Ledbetter, "John Lennon of Beatles Is Killed," *The New York Times,* (December 9, 1980), A1.

65. Geoff Emerick, "Here. There and Everywhere: My Life Recording the Music of the Beatles," (New York: Gotham Books), 279-280.

66. Ray Connolly, "The Lost Lennon Interviews," *The Sunday Times Magazine,* (September 6, 2009), 15.

67. John T. McQuiston, "Kahane Is Killed After Giving Talk in New York Hotel," *The New York Times,* (November 6, 1990), A1.

68. Ibid, A1.

69. Ronald Sullivan, "Judge Gives Maximum Term in Kahane Case," *The New York Times,* (January 30, 1992), A1.

70. Ralph Blumenthal, "Bombs Used in Trade Center Blast," *The New York Times,* (October 28, 1993), A1.

71. David Barstow, "An Abortion Battle Fought to the Death," *The New York Times,* (July 25, 2009), 1.

72. Ibid, 1.

73. Laura Fitzpatrick, "Scott Roeder: The Tiller Murder Suspect," *Time,* (June 2, 2009), 4.

Chapter Three
Asian Assassinations

AFGHANISTAN

Continuing Assassinations

On February 20, 1919, the son of the Emir of Afghanistan, Aminullah Khan, together with others, killed his father, Habibullah Khan. Aminullah thereby became Khan (Khan is a title given a ruler in a number of Asian countries).

In addition to some personal grievances, the assassins had demanded that the Khan declare war on Great Britain and push the British out of Afghanistan while they were engaged in a major war against Germany and its allies. The British had occupied Afghanistan since 1838 and showed no sign of leaving.[1]

On November 8, 1933, Nadir Shah, the king of Afghanistan was assassinated while distributing awards to high school graduates. He was shot to death by a high school student who sought to revenge himself for the brutality shown his family by Nadir Shah. The student, Abdul Hazara, was hanged, as was his family and more distant relatives.[2]

On April 28, 1978, the first President of Afghanistan, Mohammad Daoud Khan, was assassinated. Daoud Khan had overthrown the king of Afghanistan, King Zahir. Zahir was his cousin and brother-in-law and had served the king as prime minister. Yet, he too became the victim of murder after communist rebels won a short civil war and then shot Daoud and his family in the presidential palace.[3]

On September 14, 1979, Nur Mohammed Taraki, former president of Afghanistan, was killed by his successor, Hafzullah Amin. Taraki had become president of Afghanistan on May 1, 1978, when he succeeded the assassinated Mohammed Daoud Khan. As president, the Harvard educated Taraki allowed women to vote and attempted other liberal reforms. Nevertheless, Taraki was deemed a communist, particularly after he attended a conference in Havana, Cuba. Taraki also associated with the Russian government in that he negotiated

armed support for his government from the Soviet Union in the form of helicopter gunships with Russian pilots and 500 military advisers.

On September 17, 1979, it was reported that Taraki had resigned his presidency in favor of the prime minister, Hafizullah Amin. Yet, this "resignation"
was apparently a false report, succeeded by the report that Taraki had been murdered on the command of Amin.[4]

At least one of the reasons for the assassination of Taraki was his dismissal
of several cabinet ministers. His successor, Amin, was a far more radical communist and friend of the Soviet Union. Amin was far more willing to use the
secret police and other measures to suppress dissent.[5]

Amin was president only until December 1979, when the Soviet army invaded Afghanistan, assaulted the presidential palace in Kabul, and killed Amin.
Supported by the Soviet Army, Babrak Karmal became the next president. He
was living in exile in Moscow at the time of his "election." Amin had been
president for only 104 days.

Amin was mainly known for his brutality. He was accused by the Soviets of
killing 500 political opponents, if not more. He was hated by the relatives of his
victims and others who feared for their lives at the hands of his dictatorship.[6]

On September 28, 1996, the president of Ahghanistan, Mohammad Najibullah, was brutally murdered by the Taliban, a fanatic gang of Islamists whose
purpose was and remains the destruction of the United States and the imposition
of Islamic law on anyone who can be coerced to live with it. Najibullah, a physician, had entered politics in 1977 as a communist. As a member of that party,
he served briefly as ambassador to Iran and then went into exile in Europe. After
the Soviets invaded his country in 1979, he returned and was appointed head of
the secret police. In 1986 he became head of the communist party with the support of the Soviet army. In 1986, he became president followed by the withdrawal of the Soviet troops. This resulted in the capture of the capital, Kabul, by
the Taliban, who then processed to murder all their opponents, including Najibullah, who had sought asylum in the UN compound in that city.[7]

BANGLADESH

The Assassination of Mujibur Rahman (1920-1975)

Mujibur Rahman was murdered on August 15, 1975 by an anonymous group of
army officers in the presidential residence. His entire family was also killed,
except for one daughter who was in Germany at the time. Mujibur Rahman was
the first president of Bangladesh and is considered the "father of his country."
The cause of his assassination may be considered a "victim precipitated" homi-
cide in that Mujibur promoted much enmity against him. This does not mean
that failure as a political leader must of necessity lead to murder. In Bangladesh,

however, this is not surprising, since that country has seen innumerable assassinations during the thirty-nine years of its existence. "There was not a single day," writes Muhammed Tayyeb, "when murder, arson, robbery, and smuggling was not reported in the local or national press."[8]

Bangladesh became an independent country on December 16, 1971. On that day Bangladesh declared its independence from Pakistan under the leadership of Mujibur Rahman.[9]

Mujibur Rahman, although "the father" of his country, was a corrupt and incompetent administrator. He shared power with inept relatives and other "cronies." His policies led to a huge increase in prices and the destruction of democracy as Mujibur Rahman closed down all independent newspapers and began a reign of terror. Political opponents were arrested, imprisoned without trial, and often murdered.

Finally, in 1975 a successful coup ended Mujibur's rule. Since then the country has continued to be one of the poorest on earth. With a population density of 1,300, it can hardly survive.[10]

The Assassination of Ziaur Rahman (1936-1981)

Ziaur was president of Bangladesh from 1975 until he was killed in 1981. As cruel and vindictive as his predecessors, he believed that his harsh rule would end the poverty and overpopulation in his country. Ziaur had declared the independence of Bangladesh in 1971, when he was regimental commander in a port city.[11]

In 1975 Zia seized power after the assassination of Sheik Mujib and promptly made some unpopular statements, including "population control must be our nation's No. 1 priority," and "Bangladesh must feed itself and stop depending on the world for help." His policies led to an increase in food production and a decrease in inflation. He then ran for a five year term as president and was elected overwhelmingly.[12]

FAR EASTERN ASIAN ASSASSINATIONS

CHINA

In view of China's size and age it is remarkable that no Chinese head of state has been assassinated since the grand Khan Sidibala was killed in 1323. Over the years both foreign and domestic politicians have been assassinated in China. Yet they were so few that China's record concerning assassinations cannot be compared to the magnitude of assassinations in other Asian countries such as

India, which has a population of 1.17 billion, not far from that of China, whose population is 1.3 billion.[13]

JAPAN

Japan has a long tradition of assassinations of prominent politicians dating to the 6th century. Killing members of the Japanese nobility continued into the nineteenth century. In the twentieth century, ten politicians were assassinated and in the first decade of the twenty-first century two more politicians were murdered.

The Assassination of Hitoshi Igarashi (1947-1991)

Hitoshi Igarashi was murdered on July 11, 1991 by an unknown killer at his office in Tsukuba University, where he was a professor of Middle Eastern and Islamic studies. Hitoshi Igarashi translated a book, *The Satanic Verses*, by Salman Rushdie, from English into Japanese. Therefore he was murdered on the orders of Ruhollah Khomeini, an Iranianx "Ayatollah" or high priest. Khomeini had issued a fatwa, or decree, ordering any Muslim who could do so to kill the author Rushdie as well as anyone else associated with the dissemination of Rushdie's book on the grounds that Satanic Verses insults the prophet Mohammed. On July 3, 1991, the Italian translator of Rushdie's book, Ettore Capriolo, was stabbed in his apartment in Milan. He survived.[14]

The Assassination of Okubo Toshimichi (1830-1878)

On May 14, 1878, Shimado Ichiro and five others assassinated Okubo as he traveled to a Council of State meeting at the Akaska palace in Tokyo. Those who killed Okubo, then Home Minister and the most powerful man in the Japanese government, claimed that Okubo had wasted the national treasures and disregarded the impoverished population. They also resented Okubo's efforts to modernize Japan on the basis of his earlier travels to England and Germany.[15]

Okubo had traveled widely in Europe and America and recognized the need of Japan to modernize and gain advances from German and English investors. Okubo also traveled to the United States and became determined to westernize his country. All this threatened the power of entrenched local nobility who did not want a centralized government.[16] According to those who knew him, Okubo was remote and cold in his dealing with others. He had no real friends and was at all times interested in business but never showed any interest in other people except as to their usefulness at the moment. Some called his demeanor "composed" and others "firm as a rock." In sum, Okubo became an absolute dictator, which no doubt contributed more to his assassination than any other factor.[17]

The Assassination of Prince Hirobumi Ito (1841-1909)

Ito was assassinated by a Korean patriot on October 26, 1909. Ito had been the governor of Korea and therefore had many Korean enemies, who viewed the century's occupation of Korea by Japan as oppression. An unnamed Korean patriot killed Ito while Ito was on a trip to Manchuria. Ito's rule of Korea was considered particularly harsh. He "put down" a rebellion by Korean patriots and otherwise acted in the most cruel fashion towards "the natives." Korea was occupied by Japan from 1910-1945. It had also been seized by Japan in the 16th century.

The unidentified killer ran towards Ito at the Harbin railroad station in Manchuria and shot him seven times with an automatic pistol. He made no attempt to escape.[18]

The Assassination of Takashi Hara (1856-1921)

On the evening of November 4, 1921, a railroad switchman, Konichi Nakaoka, killed the prime minister of Japan, Hara, at the Tokyo railway station. Hara was on his way to Kioto to attend a political meeting when he was assassinated. Prior to the murder, Hara and other members of the Japanese government had received letters threatening to kill them. It was for that reason that a Japanese delegation, on its way to Washington D.C. was accompanied by a number of secret service men on leaving Seattle by train.[19]

Hara was a supporter of an ever expanding bureaucracy, which finally led to Japanese fascism after his murder. Japanese fascism was accepted by the public and promoted by bureaucrats without any revolution or violence. Japan's pseudo democracy ended within a decade of Hara's assassination and laid the groundwork for the military dictatorship ending in the bombing of Hiroshima and Nagasaki.[20] Takahashi was born the son of a court painter. He was adopted by nobility and raised in a castle. He studied English and American culture and thereafter served in several capacities in various Japanese governments. He worked for the Bank of Japan and was there recognized as exceptionally talented. He became vice chairman of the bank. He was credited with bringing about the recovery of Japan from the great depression of 1929.[21]

The Assassination of Inaukai Tsuyoshi (1855-1932)

On May 15, 1932, a naval officer entered the home of the 29th prime minister of Japan, Inaukai, and shot him to death. At the same time, a number of public buildings were attacked by terrorists who threw bombs at banks and other establishments. The motive for these attacks and the assassination of the prime minister was the belief among the Japanese public that it is legitimate to risk one's life for the sake of the country. Public opinion supported the view that assassinations in the name of a patriotic cause are commendable.[22] A number of assassinations or attempted killings were conducted in the 1930's by numerous Japanese secret societies which made lists of people to be killed because of their official policies. These societies called themselves "blood brotherhoods." They were extreme in their nationalism. These societies collected signatures defending the assassins. Over a million such signatures were collected in favor of the assassins of the prime minister, many signed in blood.[23]

The Assassination of Takahashi Korekiyo (1854-1936)

On February 26, 1936, an attempt was made by a number of Japanese army officers to use force and violence so as to overthrow the government and establish a military dictatorship in its place. On that date, about 1,500 troops seized control of government buildings and killed numerous government officials including Takahashi who was then finance minister. He had previously been prime minister but resigned from that office in 1922. The revolt only lasted three days and was suppressed by the emperor Hirohito. Nineteen men were executed after the revolt and seventy officers were sent to prison. The principal outcome of this short lived revolt was the strengthening of Japanese militarism and the alliance between Hitler's Germany and Japan, which eventually led to the attack on Pearl Harbor.

KOREA

The Assassination of Queen Min (1851-1895)

In the early morning of October 8, 1895, a gang of assassins, bearing swords, entered the queen's residence in the Seoul palace and killed three women. One of them was the queen. The killers did not know the queen but succeeded by these indiscriminate murders. They then burned all three corpses in a nearby pine forest and dispersed the ashes.[24]

The murder of the queen was engineered by the Japanese government, as the Japanese Minister (ambassador) to Korea, Miura, instigated the murder. The Japanese government then recalled Miura and even arrested and tried the killers. Neither Miura nor any of the killers were convicted. The Korean king, the successor of Queen Min, fled to the Russian embassy.[25]

In 1910, Korea was annexed by Japan and remained a Japanese colony until Japan was defeated by the United States in 1945. As a result, the South Korean people view Japan as a greater threat to them than the communist government in North Korea or China.[26]

The Assassination of Park Chung Hee (1917-1979)

On October 25, 1979, Kim Jae Kyu, head of the Korean Central Intelligence Agency, shot and killed the then president of Korea, Park Chung Hee, as he sat at dinner in the CIA restaurant. Five of his bodyguards were also killed. The motive for this assassination was an effort to rid South Korea of the Park dictatorship. Park had abolished all human rights in South Korea, except freedom of religion. The country was being ruled by presidential decree as the legislature was largely appointed by Park. The president was then elected by the "rubber stamp" legislature and popular voting was abolished. Opposition parties were raided by the police and shut down and all criticism of Park was prohibited. Then, opposition members of the National Assembly were forcibly ousted from that body.[27]

PHILIPPINES

No president of the Philippines has been assassinated, although assassination is by no means unknown there. In the 20th century eleven elected or appointed officials have been assassinated in the Phillipines.

VIET NAM

The Assassination of Ngo Dinh Diem (1901-1963)

On November 2, 1963, Nguyen Van Nhung, a captain in the South Vietnamese army, shot and killed the first president of South Viet Nam, Ngo Dinh Diem.

Diem was elected by a large majority of South Viet Nam citizens in 1955 and again in 1959 when the United States had already taken actions to prevent the North Vietnamese communists from unifying the country under their control. The Kennedy administration nevertheless consented to the violent overthrow of the Diem government by General Duong Van Minh. This occurred on November 1, 1963, followed by the subsequent murder of Diem by Minh's agents. Prior to his assassination Diem sought to meet with the U.S. ambassador to Viet Nam, Henry Cabot Lodge, who refused to meet with Diem on orders of President Kennedy.[28]

On hearing of that assassination, the North Vietnamese communist boss reputedly said: "I can scarcely believe the Americans would be so stupid. The consequences of the 1 November coup d'etat will be contrary to the calculations of the U.S. imperialists."[29]

After the Diem assassination South Vietnam was never able to establish a permanent government. Numerous overthrows of the current governments led to the final collapse of South Vietnam in 1975 when North Vietnam overran the entire country, the United States withdrew and a communist system was established there.

The main reason for the assassination of Diem was his religious intolerance. Diem sought to force the Roman Catholic religion on the majority, who were Buddhists. He insulted high ranking officers with respect to their religion and labeled anyone who disagreed with him a communist, although the dissenters were Buddhists. Diem denied promotion to Buddhist officers in the army and exempted land owned by the Catholic church from taxes but would not do so for Buddhist religious establishments. He lost the confidence and support of 85% of the population who were Buddhists and was therefore "dropped" by the United States, with disastrous results.[30]

SOUTHERN ASIA

INDIA

The Assassination of Mohandas Gandhi (October 2, 1869-January 30, 1948)

Mohandas Kramachand Gandhi was assassinated on January 30, 1948 by Nathuram Godse. Gandhi was also known in India as Mahatma, a Sanskrit term meaning "great soul." Gandhi was the leader of the Indian independence movement and is therefore viewed as "the father of the nation." His birthday, October 2, is a national holiday in India.

An astute politician, Gandhi succeeded in his effort to rid India of British rule by adopting tactics that were supported by Indian mores. Before undertaking the role of liberator, Gandhi gathered experience in the civil rights movement then in progress in South Africa, which was also ruled by Britain.

In 1915, Gandhi became the leader of the Indian National Congress, which sought to end poverty, insure women's rights, bring about Indian economic self reliance, and, above all, achieve independence.[31]

Gandhi was educated in Indian schools and at the University of London, where he studied law. The practice of law led him to move temporarily to South Africa, as he accepted a job with an Indian legal firm to work in Natal, South Africa, which at that time had a good sized Indian population. During the civil rights movement in South Africa, Gandhi first adopted the nonviolent protest movement that eventually succeeded in driving the British out of India. This movement may best be called "nonviolent resistance" but also included contempt for blacks, whom Gandhi called Zulus and whom he viewed as racially inferior.[32]

During the First World War, Gandhi actively recruited Indian soldiers for the British cause, a stance that dumbfounded his friends in the nonviolence movement he had advocated for so many years. Nevertheless, Gandhi employed non-cooperation, nonviolence and peaceful resistance during the 1920's and into the 1930's. The British responded to these efforts by the Indian National Congress by arresting and jailing Gandhi in 1922 for "sedition," which meant that he led a campaign of mass civil disobedience. He was released after two years.[33]

Throughout the 1920's and 1930's, Gandhi negotiated with the British government again and again with a view of gaining Indian independence from Britain. In 1934, three attempts were made to assassinate him.

During the Second World War, Gandhi refused to support the British effort against Nazi Germany, leading to mass arrests and violence all over India, as the British viewed Gandhi and his followers as supporters of the enemy. Gandhi was imprisoned in 1942 in the Aga Khan palace. Then, at the end of the war, the British agreed to quit India, leading to the partition of India into Hindustan and Pakistan, which was and is almost entirely Muslim. Gandhi opposed partition and earned a great deal of enmity from both religious groups for his stance.[34]

The dispute between the Muslims and Hindus in India became more and more violent as partition became effective in 1948. Hindus demanded that all Muslims be deported to Pakistan and Pakistan threatened violence against India. Gandhi demanded that India make payments to Pakistan for the destruction of Muslim homes in India and that violence on both sides cease. The outcome of his efforts was his assassination. Thereafter Pakistan and India went to war, which settled nothing but left both atomic powers fearing each other.[35]

Nathuram Godse (1910-1949) used a semi-automatic Beretta pistol to shoot Mohandas Gandhi and kill him in January of 1948. Godse and his friends believed that Gandhi was sacrificing Hindu interests to Muslim aggression. He blamed Gandhi for the partition of India and was particularly opposed to the payment of 520 million rupees by India to Pakistan. Godse also believed that the partition of India into India and Pakistan was caused by Muslim fanaticism. He resented that Gandhi eventually agreed to that partition.[36]

The Assassination of Indira Gandhi (1917-1984)

On October 31, 1984 two of Indira Gandhi's bodyguards, Satwant Singh and Beant Singh, killed Indira Gandhi with their service weapons in the garden of the prime minister's residence in New Delhi. Thirty-one bullets had penetrated her and she died on the way to a hospital.

Indira Gandhi was the daughter of the first prime minister of India, Jawaharlal Nehru. She was married to Feroze Gandhi, not related to Mohandas. She became prime minister of India in January of 1980 and remained in office until her assassination in 1984. Indira Gandhi held a number of political offices before becoming prime minister. This was the product of her family connections. She was educated in India and in England. On her return to India she married Feroze, leading to the production of two sons. After the death of her husband in 1960 and her father in 1964, she devoted herself entirely to politics. She became minister of information and broadcasting. In 1966 she was elected prime minister. She continued in that role during the India-Pakistan war of 1971 and was elected to a second term that year.[37]

During her second term, Gandhi was accused of widespread corruption. She was ordered by the Supreme Court to relinquish her seat in parliament. She refused to do so and imposed a state of emergency, which allowed her to rule directly without consent of parliament. This led to violence in the streets, as supporters and opponents of Gandhi fought each other. Thereupon all elections were canceled, citizens were detained indefinitely and all publications subjected to censorship. Finally Indira Gandhi ruled by decree until her murder.[38]

The Assassination of Rajiv Gandhi (1944-1901)

Rajiv Gandhi was assassinated by Thenmozhi Rajaratnam on May 21, 1991. Rajaratnam was also known as Dhanu. She approached Gandhi at a public meeting and detonated a belt laden with explosives. This killed her as well as Gandhi and a number of others. The motive for the killing was the dispute between India and Sri Lanka, or Ceylon, arising from the entrance of the Indian Peace Keeping Force into Ceylon and its reputed use of atrocities against the Tamil militant organization which seeks to separate part of Ceylon from the state of Sri Lanka and form another nation in the disputed area.

SRI LANKA (CEYLON)

The Assassination of S.W. R. D. Bandaranaike (1899-1959)

On September 26, 1959, the prime minister of Sri Lanka, Bandaranaike was shot by Talduwe Somarama, a Buddhist monk. He died shortly thereafter. Somarama visited Bandaranaike and shot him as they were about to shake hands on meeting. When the prime minister fell to the floor, his killer shot him a second time. One consequence of that assassination was that Mrs. Bandaranaike became the first woman to become prime minister anywhere.[39]

Bandaranaike was influenced by socialist, if not communist ideology, a view which was most strongly resisted by the Buddhist clergy. There are those who claim that the assassination was organized or at least encouraged by the United States Central Intelligence Agency.[40]

NEAR EASTERN ASSASSINATIONS

IRAN OR PERSIA

The Assassination of Xerxes I (519 BCE-465 BCE) and Xerxes II (d. 424 BCE) of Persia

In 465 BCE, Xerxes was murdered by the commander of the royal body guard, Artabanus. Xerxes was the emperor of Persia, a huge ancient empire mentioned several times in the Jewish Bible. It has been speculated that Xerxes the Great, as some historians have called him, was the Ahasverus mentioned in the *Book of Esther*. His eventual successor was Xerxes II, who ruled only 45 days when he was assassinated by Pharnacyas and Menostanes on the order of Sogdianus, a brother of Xerxes II. Sogdianus was killed a few months later in 423 BCE by Darius, who then ruled Persia until 404 BCE[41]

The Assassination of Nader Shah (1698-1747)

In more recent times, several Iranian heads of state have been assassinated. On June 19, 1747, the king or shah of Iran, Nader Shah, was assassinated by his own bodyguard, Salah Bey, and two other accomplices, whom he killed before he died himself. Nader was probably killed at the instigation of his nephew Adil Shah, who then succeeded him. Within a year, the same fate befell Adil Shah, who was eventually succeeded by Karim Khan in 1760, the year Afghanistan separated from Iran.[42]

Nader Shah has been called the Napoleon of Persia, because he invaded and ruled all of present- day Iran, Afghanistan, parts of India, and parts of central Asia. These campaigns ruined the economy of Iran and forced the population to pay immense taxes. Nader suffered a number of ailments, leaving him in a state of anger and belligerence at all times. His cruelty increased as his illness became worse. He went so far as to blind his own son. Fearing for their own lives, his bodyguards assassinated him in 1747. His nephew, Adil Shah, succeeded him but remained on the throne only a year.[43]

The Assassination of Nasser-al-Din-Shah (1831-1896)

Nasser al Din was assassinated by Mirza Reza Kermani on May 1, 1896. He was the first Persian king to visit Europe and was honored by Queen Victoria on his visit in 1873. During his visit, Nasser al Din met with British Jews and suggested that the Jews buy land and establish a Jewish state in the Near East. Nasser also introduced a number of English inventions, including a postal service, a railroad, banking, and newspapers. He was also the first Iranian to use photography, and painted and wrote poetry.[44]

Mirza Reza Kermani, who assassinated Nasser al Din, resented the treatment of Afghans by the Iranians and therefore killed Nasser at Din.[45]

The Assassination of Haj Ali Razmara (1901-1951)

Haj Ali Razmara was assassinated by Khalil Tahmassebi on March 7, 1951. Razmara had been prime minister of Iran since 1950, after a military career which began with hisgraduation from the French military academy at St.Cyr. Razmara sought to conclude an agreement with the Anglo-Iranian Oil Co. on terms far less favorable to Iran than expected by the National Front, headed by Dr. Mohammed Mossadegh, who became prime minister within two months of Razmara's assassination.[46]

Razmara eliminated numerous government appointments and trimmed the government payroll. His money saving measures made him extremely unpopular among landowners who had received large subsidies from the state. After his murder, the National Front demanded that the oil industry be nationalized, a demand Razmara had rejected. This led to his denunciation by the Ayatolla Kasani, who justified the assassination on the grounds that Razmara would not nationalize the country's oil resources. The nationalists thereupon killed the education minister, Dr. Abdul Hamid Znaganeh, and plotted to kill the Shah of Iran. In the end, the Iranian parliament voted to nationalize the oil industry. The Anglo Iranian Oil Co. was dissolved and expelled. Mossadegh remained in power until the U.S. and Britain succeeded in returning the exiled Shah of Iran, Pahlevi, to Iran, and forced the resignation of Mossadegh. That in turn led to the establishment of the Iranian Republic under Ayatollah Khomeini and the final exile of the Shah in 1979.[47]

The Assassination of Hassan Ali Mansur (1923-1965)

Mansur was assassinated on January 22, 1965, when Mohammad Bokharaii fired three shots at him as he was leaving his car. That murder was ordered by Ayatollah Rafsanjani, who later became president after the Shah had been overthrown and the Iranian revolution had seized power. Mansur had been appointed prime minister by Shah Reza Pahlavi. Mansur was in favor of American friendship and support. Mansur appointed mostly American or European educated officials. During his tenure, the Iranian parliament passed the Geneva Convention American Force Protection Act. This led to loud denunciation by the Ayatollah Khomeini from his exile in Turkey. When the Shah was overthrown and the Iranian revolution proclaimed by Rafsanjani and others, they bragged about the murder of Mansur.[48]

The Assassinations of Mohammad Ali Rajai (1933-1981) and Mohammad Javad Bahonar (1933-1981)

On August 30, 1981 Massoud Kashmiri delivered a bomb into the office of the president of Iran, Mohammad Ali Rajai, and killed him together with the Prime Minister, Mohammad Javad Bahonar. Three other men were also killed in the blast. The killer belonged to the People's Mujahedin. He worked as a security guard for the president and was therefore in a position to kill him. Rajai had been president only 27 days and Bahnar was in office only three days when both were killed. The killings were connected to fighting for power between a number of political parties within Iran.[49]

IRAQ

The Assassination of Feisal II (1935-1958)

Numerous Iraqi politicians and religious leaders have been assassinated during the half century since the murder of Faisal II, king of Iraq. Abdul Sattar Sabaa Al-Ibousi and a gang of killers, who rounded up the king and his entire family, including his wife, mother, and aunt, and several servants, killed Faisal on July 14, 1958. All were shot to death in the courtyard of the royal palace. The next day the prime minister of Iraq, Nuri al-Said, was also brutally murdered. These murders led to the abolition of the monarchy and the establishment of a military dictatorship. After a number of years of constant fighting between various factions within the military, Saddam Hussein succeeded in becoming the absolute ruler of Iraq until his downfall during the second Iraq war. The immediate cause of this revolt by army officers against the king was the alliance Faisal had formed with the British. Many Iraqis resented this alliance, which they viewed as an assault on their sovereignty. Dissatisfaction with the Iraqi monarchy developed during the Second World War, when a military overthrow of the government led to the alliance between Iraq and the German government. This alliance did not last long, since the British and their allies restored the king within a few weeks. Faisal had been educated in England.[50] The list of assassinated politicians and religious leaders is impressive. It must be understood that there has never been a separation between the state and religion, so that those killed decimated the ranks of both institutions. The list of assassinated Iraqis includes four Ayatollahs and innumerable politicians in and out of office at the times of their murders.[51]

ISRAEL

The Assassination of Rudolf Kastner (1906-1957)

Rudolf Kastner was assassinated by Zeev Eckstein on March 3, 1957. Kastner was in no manner a government official or leader of anything. His assassination nevertheless was the culmination of years of accusations and counter-accusations claiming that Kastner was a Jewish Nazi collaborator or that he was the heroic savior of Hungarian Jews.

Kastner was a Hungarian lawyer and journalist who had joined the Aid and Rescue Committee in German occupied Hungary in 1944. At once, Hungary's Jews were deported to the gas chambers at Auschwitz in Poland at the rate of 12,000 a day. Kastner thereupon negotiated with the Nazi killer Adolf Eichmann, senior officer of the SS killing commandos, to permit 1,685 Jews to leave Hungary for Switzerland in exchange for money, gold and diamonds. This led Israeli historian Yechiam Weitz to write that Kastner saved more Jews than any other Jew before or since.[52]

Despite Weitz's opinion, an Israeli citizen, Malchiel Greenwald, published a pamphlet in Israel in 1953 accusing Kastner of having been a Nazi collaborator. Kastner was accused of giving positive character references to three SS officers who therefore escaped prosecution for war crimes. The accusations led to a two year long libel trial in Israel ending in the verdict that Kastner "had sold his soul to the devil" on the grounds that Kastner saved his relatives and friends when he could have warned all the other Hungarian Jews that "resettlement," as the Nazis called it, was in fact mass murder in gas ovens.[53]

Kastner was killed on March 3, 1957. A year later, in 1958, the Israeli Supreme Court overturned the verdict of the lower court, holding that Kastner's sole motive was the saving of Jewish lives and that the allegation he was a Nazi collaborator was libelous. In 2008, a feature film, *Killing Kastner*, was released in Israel and the United States. The film supports Kastner's heroism. Nevertheless, the controversy concerning Kastner has not ended. It cannot ever end because some will view his success in saving the lives of 1,685 Jews as heroic. Others argue that Kastner saved only his own relatives and friends as well as "prominent" rabbis at the expense of 800,000 Hungarian Jews who were murdered.[54]

The dispute concerning Kastner should not allow us to overlook that the German killers were responsible for the dilemma confronting Kastner and that no one can today know how any of us would have reacted in the situation Kastner faced.

The Assassination of Yitzhak Rabin (1922-1995)

Yitzhak Rabin was assassinated by Yigal Amir on November 4, 1995, when Amir shot Rabin in Tel Aviv during a public rally for peace. The motive for the killing of Rabin was an effort to prevent Rabin from giving Israel's Arab enemies large segments of Israeli territory in order to appease them. Many Israelis view such surrender of Israel's territory as akin to the Munich accords of 1938, in which Britain and France agreed to give Germany the Sudetenland, which belonged to Czechslovakia. This did not satisfy the Germans, who promptly invaded the remainder of the Czech Republic. The record has shown that no matter what concessions Israel makes to the Arabs, no concession is ever enough.[55]

Rabin subscribed to the so-called Oslo Accords, which were designed to relinquish a large part of Israel to the terrorist organization, Fatah, whose purpose is the destruction of Israel and the mass murder of Jews, wherever they may live. Fearing such an outcome of negotiations between Rabin and the terrorist leader Yassir Arafat, Yigal Amir killed Rabin in the irrational hope of preventing the destruction of Israel by murder. The consequence was that Shimon Peres became temporary prime minister, followed by Ariel Sharon.

Instead of bringing about a peaceful resolution to the Israeli-Arab conflict, the Oslo Accords led to the killing of 854 Jews and the wounding of 5,051 additional Israeli citizens. The accords were based on the Israeli belief that the Palestinians had given up the ambition of destroying Israel. The Israelis made innumerable concessions to the Palestinians, who viewed each concession as a sign of weakness and therefore attacked Israel more and more.[56]

A number of Israelis have been assassinated since 1933, when Haim Arosoloff, a Zionist leader, was gunned down in Jerusalem. None were major politicians.

JORDAN

Jordan, originally known as Trans-Jordan, is a segment of Israel. It was severed from that country during the British occupation of Israel after the First World War. The British gave the territory east of the Jordan River to the Bedouins, who established an Arab state there. Its first king was Abdullah I.[57]

The Assassination of Abdullah I (1882-1951)

On July 1, 1951, Abdullah visited the Al Aqsa Mosque in Jerusalem, where he was shot dead by Mustafa Ashu, who was reputedly an agent of the former "Grand Mufti" of Jerusalem, Amin al-Husayni. The motivation for the assassination was the fear by Husayni and his supporters that Abdullah sought to make peace with Israel. Husayni was then living in Lebanon.[58]

Husayni had spent the years of the Second World War in Berlin as an associate of Adolf Hitler, the German dictator. Husayni believed that the Germans would win the war and that he would then be established as the Nazi dictator of the Middle East, with a view of killing the Jewish population of Israel. Husayni was promised the leadership of an independent Arab state if the Nazi empire were to win the war. Meanwhile, he was living in a Berlin villa where he spent his monthly stipend in an effort to recruit an Arab military unit to fight with the Germans on the eastern front. In this he succeeded, as an Arab-Muslim SS unit was recruited which killed most of the Jews in Salonika, Greece, and in other parts of that country.

After Germany had lost the war, Husayni sought to destroy Israel by inciting the Arab nations surrounding that country to invade and destroy the Jewish community there. This failed in 1948 (and all subsequent efforts) and led king Abdullah to the conclusion that Jordan needed to conclude a peace treaty with Israel and end the efforts at invasion and destruction. Fearing that Jordan would no longer assist in the plans to kill the Jews and that other countries might follow Jordan's example, Abdullah was assassinated before he could carry out his plans. Nevertheless, his grandson, Hussein, became king of Jordan after him and did indeed conclude a peace treaty with Israel.[59]

In 1971, Wasfi al-Tal, then prime minister of Jordan, was shot to death on a visit to Egypt.

LEBANON

It is justified to call Lebanon the assassination capital of the world. Since 1970, at least 29 prominent politicians have been murdered there. Not all were prime ministers. Some held that office, while others were leaders of parties or newspaper publishers, legislators, generals or police investigators. Here are a few examples.

The Assassination of President-elect Bashir Gamayel (1947-1982)

On September 15, 1982 a powerful bomb destroyed the headquarters of the Lebanese Christian Phalangist party, killing eight men, including the president-elect of Lebanon, Bashir Gemayel. More than fifty people were wounded. The killer of Gemayel was Habib Tanious Shartouni on behalf of the Syrian intelligence service, who accused Gemayel of seeking to make peace with Israel. Furthermore, Gemayel was a Christian and therefore despised by the Muslim majority. The killer of Gemayel, Shartouni, spent eight years in prison but escaped to Sytia in 1990 when Lebanon was occupied by Syria.[60]

The Assassination of Rashid Karami (1921-1987)

On June 1, 1987, Rashid Karami was murdered by Samir Geagea, who had planted a bomb on the helicopter Karami was using to fly from Tripoli to Beirut. Karami was the only one killed, while three of his aides were wounded. Geagea was sentenced to death for this assassination. However, the death sentence was commuted to life imprisonment and finally to amnesty in 2005.[61]

Karami was born into a prominent Lebanese family. His father and brother were members of the Lebanese government, his brother having been prime minister three times. Karami entered politics soon after graduating from law school and held the office of prime minister eight times between 1955 and his murder in 1987. His principal political effort was directed at giving Muslims equal rights with Christians. He was responsible for the Lebanese civil war and supported extremists seeking to destroy Israel.[62]

The Assassination of Rafik Hariri (1944-2005)

On February 14, 2005, the Syrian government murdered Prime Minister Hariri by detonating a large bomb as he was driving in a Beirut street. The United Nations investigation revealed the Syrian plot to kill Hariri.[63] Subsequently the United Nations created a military tribunal to investigate the assassination of Hariri, particularly since the Lebanese minister of industry, Pierre Gamayel, became the fifth anti-Syria Lebanese politician to be murdered since Hariri was killed in February 2005.[64]

This tribunal had been hampered by numerous obstructions coming from Syria but also from a number of factions within the Lebanese political establishment. One outcome of the assassination was the withdrawal of Syrian forces from Lebanon. Further, the United Nations Security Council demanded that the Lebanese government arrest the killers of Hariri. This could hardly be done as the terrorist gang Hizbullah is powerful enough to resist the government. This means that the Lebanese government does not have the power to guarantee the safety of witnesses. It is therefore highly unlikely that the tribunal will ever succeed in convicting the killers of Hariri or satisfy International Law regarding the numerous murders of politicians in Lebanon.[65]

SAUDI ARABIA

The Assassination of Faisal ibn Saud (1904-1975)

On March 25, 1975, Faisal ibn Musad Abdel Aziz, nephew of the king, Faisal, shot and killed the king during a reception. The killer was deemed to be mentally ill. The killer had been institutionalized after saying repeatedly that he meant to kill the king. Although the murder of the king was viewed with alarm in Saudi Arabia, it made little difference in either the internal or external condition of the kingdom.[66]

Faisal was one of the many sons of Ibn Saud, founder of the kingdom. He was appointed to a number of offices, including minister of foreign affairs and commander of the army during the 1934 war with Yemen. Using a number of methods and intrigues, Faisal succeeded in ousting his brother, also named Saud, from the position of king, which he assumed in 1964. He was known for his efforts at reform, in that he allowed women to gain an education, improved the financial condition of the country, and introduced television, which was resented by the most fundamentalist followers of Islam. It is widely believed that the motive for killing him was his support for these reforms.[67]

An ally of the United States, he opposed communism during the "cold war" and as a true believer in Islam sought the destruction of Judaism and the Jewish community.[68]

YEMEN

The Assassination of Imam Yaya (1869-1948)

On February 19, 1948, the king of Yemen, Yaya Hamid el Din, was assassinated together with three of his sons and a chief advisor. Suspicion centered on another son of the 85-year-old monarch to the effect that the son may have been the assassin or at least participated in the conspiracy against the ruler. That son became head of the new government. He was one of several sons of the king who had been imprisoned for "political plotting." In any case, the assassination was evidently caused by infighting within the ruling family and therefore had no major significance for the country or its foreign relations. The assassination merely means that one absolute dictator took the place of a previous one, so that the lives of the citizens remained the same.[69]

TURKEY

Nineteen Turkish politicians, journalists, businessmen, writers and academics have been assassinated in that country since Mahmud Sevket Pasha was murdered in 1913. He was prime minister of Turkey. The other victims of assassinations were not in politics or were never heads of the Turkish state.

NOTES

1. J. W. McLaughlin, "Escaped Briton Tells Full Story of Afghan Plot," *The New York Times,* (May 29, 1919), 1.

2. Louis Dupree, *Afghanistan,* Princeton, N.J. *The Princeton University Press,* (1973), 474.

3. Martin Ewans, *Afghanistan: A short history of its people and politics.* (New York: Harper Collins, 2002), 88.

4. David B. Edwards, *Before Taliban :Generations of the Afghan Jihad* (University of California Press, 2002), 87.

5. No author, "Taraki Yields Afghan Presidency and Party Posts to Prime Minister" *The New York Times,* (September 17, 1979), A1.

6. Thomas T. Hammond, *Red Flag over Afghanistan,* (Boulder., Colorado, Westview Press, 1984).

7. Milton Viorst, *In the Shadow of the Prophet: The Struggle for the Soul of Islam,* (Boulder, Colorado, Westview Press, 2001), 25.

8. Muhammed A. Tayyeb, "Bangladesh: The Dilemmas of Independence," *Asian Affairs,* vol.5, no.3, (January-February, 1978), 171.

9. No author, "Birth of a Nation," *The New York Times,* (December 25, 1971), 16.

10. Ibid, 169-170.

11. Les Ledbetter, "Bangladesh Reports Death Of President Ziaur Rahman," *The New York Times,* (May 30, 1981), 20.

12. Ibid, 20.

13. Steven R. Weisman, "Japanese Translator of Rushdie Book Found Slain," *The New York Times,* (July 13, 1991), 11.

14. Ibid, 11.

15. Tsuchiya Takao, "Transition and Development of Economic Policy," in: Keizo Shibusawa, *Japanese Society in the Meiji Era,* (Tokyo, Obunsha Publishing, 1958), 118-119.

16. W.G. Beasley, "Councillors of Samurai Origin in the Early Meijii Government, 186809) *Bulletin of the School of Oriental and African Studies,* XX (1957), 98-99.

17. Shibusawa, 1-6.

18. No author, "Prince Ito Assassinated," *The New York Times,* (October 26, 1909), 1.

19. No author, "Japanese Premier Stabbed to Death by Korean Fanatic," *The New York Times,* (November 5, 1921), A1.

20. Richard J. Samuels, "When Leadership Failed," *The American Sociologist,* (Spring/Summer, 2003), 39-40.

21. Myung Soo Cha, "Did Takahashi Korekiyo Rescue Japan from the Great Depression?" *The Journal of Economic History,* vol. 63, no. 1, (March 2003), 127-144.

22. Hugh Byas, "Army to Stop Agitation," *The New York Times,* (May 16, 1932), 1.

23. No Author, "Political Killings Frequent in Japan," *The New York Times,* (August 18, 1935), B5.

24. Stephen Bonsal, "The Obliteration of the Kingdom of Korea," *The New York Times,* (July 28, 1907), SM1.

25. Lawrence Battistini, "The Korean Problem in the Nineteenth Century," *Monumenta Nipponica, vol.*8, no.1, (1952), 64-66.

26. Bradford Trbach, "Korea-Japan Tension Is Centuries Old," *The New York Times,* (November 14, 1994),A16.

27. Sam Jameson, "Even in Death, Park's Authoritarian Shadow Looms Over Korea," *Los Angeles Times,* (November 4, 1979),,E1.

28. No author, *The Pentagon Papers,* (Boston: The Beacon Press, 1971), 76.

29. Mark Moyar, *Triumph Forsaken: The Vietnam War, 1954-1965,* (Cambridge, England: Cambridge University Press, 2006), 286.

30. Seth Jacobs, *Cold War Mandarin: Ngo Dinh Diem and the Origins of Amerca's War in Vietnam, 1950-1963,* (Lanham, MD.: Rowan and Littlefield), 91.

31. Sabyasachi Bhattacharya, *The Mahatma and the Poet:* (New Delhi: National Book Trust, 1997), 1.

32. Surendra Bhana, *The Making of a Political Reformer: Ghandi in South Africa 1893-1914),* 149.

33. Rajmohan Gandhi, *Patel: A Life,* (Ahmedabad, India: Navajivan Publition House, 1990), 131.

34. Louis Fischer, *The Essential Gandhi: An Anthology of his Writings on his Life, Work and Ideas* (New York: Vintage Books, 2002), 308-309.

35. Vinay Lai, "Hey Ram: The Politics of Gandhi's Last Words," *Humanscape,* vol. 8 no. 1, (January 2001), 34-38.

36. No author, "The Killing of Mr. Gandhi," *The Times of London,* (November 16, 1949), 3.

37. Katherine Frank, *Indira: The Life of Indira Nehru, Gandhi,* (New York: Houghton Mifflin Co.), 278-284.

38. Paul R. Brass, *The Politics of India Since Independence,* (Cambridge, England, Cambridge University Press, 1995), 40.

39. No author, "Ceylon's Premier is Killed; Assassin, a Monk, Seized," *The New York Times,* (September 26, 1959), 1.

40. K.M. DeSilva, "The Bandernaikes in the Islands Politicis," *Round Table,*no..350, (1999), L241-280.

41. Albert T. Olmstead, *History of the Persian Empire,* (Chicago: University of Chicago Press, 1970), 289-90.

42. Michael Axworthy, *The Sword of Persia: Nader Shah, From Tribal Warrior to Conquering Tyrant,*(New York: Palgrave Macmillan, 2006), 243-286.

43. Ibid, 243-286.

44. Catrine Clay, *King, Kaiser, Tzar,* (London: John Murray, 2006), 67

45. Hamid Dabashi, *Iran: A People Interrupted,* (New York: The New Press, 2006), 67.

46. Stephen Kinzer, *All the Shah's Men,* (Hoboken, NJ: John Wiley & Sons, Inc, 2003), 66.

47. Ibid. 72.

48. No author, "Premier of Iran Shot by Student," *The New York Times,* (January 22, 1965), 6.

49. No author, "Blast Kills Iran Leaders," *The Los Angeles Times,* (August 31, 1981), 1.

50. John F. Burns, "The Vote, and Democracy Itself, Leave Anxious Iraqis Divided," *The New York Times,* (January 30, 2005), 1.

51. Felix Belair, "President Bids U.N. Act Today on Mideast After Pro-Nasser Coup Ousts Iraq King," *The New York Times,* (July 15, 1958), 1.

52. Leora Bilsky, "Judging Evil in the Trial of Kastner," *Law and History Review,* vol. 19, no. 1, (Spring 2001), 19.

53. Anna Porter, *Kasztner's Train,* (Vancouver: Douglas & McIntyre, 2007), 10.

54. David Kranzler, *The Man Who Stopped the Trains to Auschwitz,* (Syracuse, NY: Syracuse University Press, 2000), 103-104.

55. Clyde Haberman, "Assassination in Israel," *The New York Times,* (November 5, 1995), *11* 6b.

56. Daniel Pipes, "Why Oslo's Hopes Turned to Dust," *The New York Post,* (September 9, 2003).

57. Isaiah Friedman, "How Trans-Jordan was severed from the territory of the Jewish National Home," *Journal of Israeli History,* vol. 27, no. 1, (March 1, 2008), 65.

58. Tom Segev, "Courting Hitler," *The New York Times,* (September 26, 2008), Sunday Book Review, 1.

59. Eugene L. Rogan and Avi Shlaim, *The War for Palestine,* (New York: Cambridge University Press, 2007), 104-124.

60. No author, "Phalangists identify bomber of Gemayel as Lebanese Leftist," *The New York Times,* (October 3, 1982), World 1.

61. Antoine J. Abraham, *The Lebanon War,* (Westport, Connecticut: Greenwood Publishing Group, 1996), 195.

62. Peter B. Flint, "Rashid Karami, Cool Persuader in a Land of Strife," *The New York Times,* (June 2, 1987), A6.

63. Sam F. Ghattas, "Hariri Tribunal Under Way," *The Washington Times,* (March 4, 2009), 1.

64. Julia Preston, "World Briefing: United Nations: Syria balks at Hariri Tribunal," *New York Times,* (November 25 , 2006).

65. Middle East Policy Council, "The Hariri Tribunal: Politics and International Law" *Middle East Policy,* vol. 15, no. 3, (Fall 2008), 80.

66. Juan de Onis, "Motive Unknown," *The New York Times,* (March 26, 1975), 1.

67. Mohammad Hassanein Heykal, "The Saudi Era," *Journal of Palestine Studies,* vol. 6, no.4, (Summer 1977), 160.

68. Eleanor Abdella Doumato, "Manning the Barricades: Islam According to Saudi Arabia's School Texts," *Middle East Journal,* vol.57, no.2, (Spirng 2003), 230-247.

69. Homer Bigart, "Strange War in Strange Arabia," *The New York Times,* (March 10, 1957), SM8.

Chapter Four
Latin American Assassinations

BERMUDA

Bermuda is is neither part of North America nor South America. Located more than 900 miles east of Savannah, Georgia, in the Atlantic Ocean, the island and the archipelago surrounding it has been a British colony since the early 17th century. It is governed by a British appointed governor and a legislature. Sixty percent of the inhabitants are black.

On March 10, 1973, the then governor, Sir Richard Sharples, was shot to death by Erskine Durrant "Buck" Burrows, who also killed Hugh Sayers, the aide to Sir Richard. Even Sharples' dog was killed with him. Burrows had also killed the police commissioner George Duckett and the owner of a supermarket and its bookkeeper, Victor Rego and Mark Doe.[1]

Burrows said that he wanted to prove that the white, British, upper class rulers of Bermuda were no better than the black majority living there and that these bosses died just like anyone else.

It is significant that Burrows and another defendant in another murder conviction were the last persons suffering the "death penalty" in any British territory. The death penalty was abolished in stages beginning in 1965 when it was abolished in England and ending in 1999 when it was also abolished in the British military.[2]

COLOMBIA

Five presidential candidates have been assassinated in Colombia since 1987. In that year Jaime Pardo Leal, leader of the Patriotic Union party, was murdered. In 1989, Luis Carlos Galan, the leader of the Liberal Party, was assassinated. In 1990, the same fate reached Bernado Jaramillo Ossa, leader of the Patriotic Union Party. Then, also in 1990, Carlos Pizarro Leongomez, leader of the M-19 party, was gunned down, followed in 1995 by the assassination of Alvaro Gomez Hurtako, a former presidential candidate.

DOMINICAN REPUBLIC

The Assassination of Rafael Trujillo (1891-1961)

On May 30, 1961, the dictator Rafael Trujillo was shot to death on the street in Santo Domingo. He was ambushed by eleven conspirators and killed with the support of the United States government. This means that the Central Intelligence Agency encouraged, funded, and promoted this assassination.[3]

Trujillo was a tyrant who exploited the people of Santo Domingo in the most brutal and personal manner. He forced the people to acknowledge a personality cult including monuments to him placed all over the country. That country, the Dominican Republic, has a population of 10 million living on two thirds of Hispaniola, an island shared by Haiti.

Married and divorced numerous times, Trujillo became dictator in 1930 by use of massive election fraud. Opponents of Trujillo were killed and elections abolished as a cult of personality dominated all institutions in the country.

Trujillo also enforced that all government employees had to contribute 10 percent of their salary to his political party and also instituted an identity card, so that anyone not carrying such a card could be arrested as a vagrant.[4]

Despite his murderous regime, Trujillo had an "open door" policy, so that the Dominican Republic was the only Latin American country willing to accept Jewish refugees from Hitler's Germany as a consequence of the Evian conference of 1938. Trujillo was motivated to do so because he wanted to increase the white population of the island, which is a predominantly mixed race nation. He therefore donated 26,000 acres of land to accommodate 800 Jewish settlers from Germany.[5]

Trujillo left a considerable amount of money to his family. After his assassination, the country underwent constant "palace revolutions" in that successive military officers overthrew the current government only to be kicked out by the next revolutionary. The United States invaded the Dominican Republic to restore order and insure adherence to American interests.

MEXICO

The assassinations of Francisco I. Madero (1873-1913) and Emiliano Zapata (1880-1919)

On February 22, 1913, Francisco I. Madero was shot and killed on the order of the then President of Mexico, Victoriano Huerta. Madero had become president in 1911 by assembling various political factions in Mexico who were opposed to the dictatorship of Porfirio Diaz.

Madero came from a wealthy family who allowed him to travel to Europe and to study there. He also enrolled at the University of California at Berkeley to improve his English. A follower of spiritualism, Madero believed that he was in contact with the spirit of Benito Juarez, who had been president of Mexico from 1858-1872.

Madero also founded and edited a newspaper devoted to his political ambitions. His book *The Presidential Succession of 1910* became a bestseller in Mexico and boosted his chances of election. The dictator Diaz had Madero arrested but he succeeded in fleeing into the United States.[6]

Madero's "crime" was that he campaigned all over Mexico to prevent the re-election of Porfirio Diaz. Diaz was, however, reelected by means of massive fraud. Subsequently, Madero entered Mexico City in 1911 with armed men and succeeded in spreading the revolution against the dictator Diaz throughout Mexico by April of that year. Diaz then resigned and moved to Europe. On June 7, 1911, Madero became president of Mexico. Several military commanders then organized rebellions against Madero. These were defeated until Victoriano Huerta, the commander of the Mexican armed forces, succeeded in capturing Madero in 1913 with the help of the American ambassador Henry Lane Wilson. Wilson wanted to overthrow Madero and therefore supported Huerta. Huerta, having gained power, assassinated Madero when he was 39 years old. [7]

Emiliano Zapata was murdered on April 10, 1919, by Jesu Guajardo, a colonel in the Mexican army. Zapata had followed an invitation by Guajardo to meet him for a discussion conerning Guajardo's interest in switching his support from the Mexican government to those rebelling against it. Gudjardo shot and killed Zapata on his arrival for the meeting.

Over the years, Zapata has become a national icon. Streets and towns and housing developments are named after him. Signs with inscriptions that "Zapata lives" are common in Mexico and there are those who believe that Zapata did not die but fled to some obscure rural place. At the Stanford University in California there is a Casa Zapata dormitory.[8]

The Assassination of Alvaro Obregon (1880-1928)

On July 17, 1928, the president of Mexico, Alvaro Obregon, was murdered by Jose Leon Toral. Obregon was shot in a restaurant by Leon Toral, a priest who believed that he could change the Mexican government's view of religious matters. Obregon was an ally of Mexican president Plutarco Elias Calles, who persecuted the Catholic clergy of Mexico in the 1920's.[9]

Obregon was regarded as the military victor of the Mexican revolution. In view of his popularity, Obregon decided to run for president in 1920 and won the election. He served one term and was followed by Plutarco Calles, his hand-picked successor. Thereafter, the Mexican Congress abolished the one term limit for the presidency. This allowed Obregon to run once more. He was elected but was killed before he could take office.

Jose de Leon Toral was a member of the League for the Defense of Religious Freedom, a Catholic organization which opposed the presidency of Obregon and Calles because both presidents closed churches and arrested priests suspected of supporting the dictator Victoriano Huerta. When two of Toral's friends were wrongly convicted and executed for plotting to kill Obregon, Toral decided to kill him. Toral believed that killing Obegon would bring about "the kingdom of Christ." He was executed in February 1929.[10]

The Assassination of Leon Trotsky (1879-1940)

On August 20, 1940, Jaime Ramon Mercader del Rio Hernandez fatally wounded Leon Trotsky in his home in Mexico, leading to Trotsky's death two days later. Trotsky had been struck with a pickax by a man he believed to be his friend.[11]

Leon Trotsky was murdered on the orders of the Soviet dictator Joseph Stalin, a.k.a. Josep Jughashvili. Stalin was the winner of a political struggle for the leadership in the Soviet Union after the death of Vladimir Lenin a.k.a. Ulyanov, in 1924. Lenin was the first Soviet dictator. Stalin succeeded in forcing Trotsky into exile outside of Russia, particularly because Trotsky had been the first "People's Commissar for Foreign Affairs" and the founder and first commander of the Red Army as well as the "People's Commissar of War."[12]

Trotsky was born Lev Davidovich Bronstein in 1879. Although of Jewish ethnicity, he had no religion. He joined the Russian worker's party and other revolutionary groups seeking to rid the country of the Czar. This led to his exile from Russia on two occasions when he lived in London and later in New York City. Upon the success of the 1917 Russian revolution, Trotsky returned to Russia and became one of the leaders of the Soviet state. He was deported from Russia in 1929 and then moved to Turkey, France, Norway, and finally Mexico. During these years, Trotsky wrote several books and numerous journal and newspaper articles. These criticized Stalin and the direction taken by the Communist party in Russia. Trotsky's writings were distributed to communists everywhere, leading Stalin to fear that Trotsky could persuade communist elites to oppose him. Therefore Stalin had Trotsky killed. In fact, Stalin organized "show trials" against Russian communists who were suspected of supporting Trotsky.[13]

The killer Mercader was a native of Spain. During the 1936 civil war in Spain, Mercader was recruited by the Soviet Union as a spy. Ordered to kill Trotsky, Mercader used a fake passport to enter Mexico. There he rented an apartment near the home of Trotsky, whom he met by being introduced by a mutual friend. That gained him entrance to Trotsky's home. Imprisoned for twenty years, Mercader was released in 1960 and then feted in the Soviet Union and in Cuba as a "hero" for having killed Trotsky with a pickax.

EL SALVADOR

El Salvador is a small country located at the Pacific Ocean next to Nicaragua in Central America. It has only 21,000 square kilometers, or 8,108 square miles, with a population slightly more than five million. Nevertheless twenty political assassinations have occurred there between 1913 and 1989. Of these, eighteen assassinations occurred after 1974.

The Assassination of President Manuel Enrique Araujo (1865-1913)

On February 4, 1913, Manuel Araujo was seriously wounded when Virgil Mulatillo and Fermin Fabian Perez attacked him with machetes. Araujo died five days later. No effort was made to investigate the reason for this assassination. The killers were shot by the military.

Araujo was president of El Salvador from 1911-1913. The descendant of a Portuguese family, he studied medicine. After graduating from the University of El Salvador, he studied surgery in Europe.

Elected in November 1910, he served less than two years. During those two years, Araujo founded the National Guard. He also appointed "justices of the peace" in all Salvadorean municipalities and established a Ministry of Agriculture.

El Salvador was an exceptionally violent county in the 1980s. Governed by military opportunists, the nation became a common staging ground for assassinations as various factions and the government fought for power. In the course of the fighting, three American nuns of the Maryknoll Order, Ita Johnson, Maura Clarke, and Dorothy Kazel, were murdered in El Salavador along with a volunteer, Jean Donovan.[14]

These killings were by no means the only murders of prominent clergy in El Salvador in the 1980's. In fact, the archbishop of that country, Oscar Romero, was assassinated in the spring of 1980. Romero was regarded as a prominent defender of human rights, a view despised by that country's military dictatorship. Locked in a civil war, government forces as well as rebels slaughtered over 8,000 civilians in 1980 alone.[15]

Violence was so pronounced in El Salvador that a bomb was thrown into the crowd at Romero's funeral, leading to the trampling to death of mourners. In addition, snipers shot into the crowd of mourners. Attacks against Roman Catholic clerics continued in the years succeeding 1980 until 1992 which marked the end of the 12 year civil war. That war was fought in the main because both landowners and civil rights guerrillas were dissatisfied with the government. The war ended with the United Nations sponsored peace accord of 1992. In 2011 the country was still extremely poor and subject to a great number of violent deaths.[16]

BOLIVIA

The Assassination of Ernesto Guevara (1928-1967)

On October 9, 1967, Mario Teran shot and killed Ernesto Guevara in a Bolivian prison. Teran shot nine times before Guevera died. Teran was a soldier in the Bolivian army.

Guevara has been elevated to heroic proportions not only in Latin America but also among millions of disaffected people around the world as a hero of the Cuban revolution and of all who feel that they are the victims of injustice and oppression. Popularly known as "Che," an abbreviation of the name "Jose," Guevera participated actively in the Cuban revolution which overthrew dictator Fulgencio Batista in 1959. Guevara had met Fidel Castro and his brother in Mexico. There he joined the Castro brothers in their successful effort to establish a communist dictatorship in Cuba. That succeeded after a two- year civil war. During the fighting, Guevara distinguished himself and was appointed second in command by the dictator Fidel Castro. Once the revolution had substituted one dictator for another, Guevara occupied a number of important positions in the new government. He participated in killing opponents by delivering them to firing squads, brought about "agrarian reform," held the position of national bank president, and traveled to numerous countries to represent state socialism.[17]

Guevara was also instrumental in bringing Soviet nuclear ballistic missiles to Cuba, thereby threatening the United States and precipitating the Cuban missile crisis in 1962. Guevara wrote a great deal, including a manual on the conduct of guerilla warfare as well as a diary of his numerous motorcycle travels throughout South America.[18]

Guevera was born in Argentina. Widely read and interested in both social and physical sciences, he became a physician at the University of Buenos Aires. His travels throughout South American convinced him to leave medicine and enter politics so as to alleviate the misery of the poor throughout the continent. He became a Marxist enemy of the United States, first in Guatemala, then in Cuba, and later in the Congo in Africa. From there he traveled to Bolivia, where he joined a guerilla force seeking to overthrow the Bolivian government. This resulted in his capture and assassination.

A truly large number of books, journal articles, movies, plays and his own diary have been published about Guevara. In Argentina, several high schools bear his name and there are numerous Che museums. The Cuban Peso exhibits his picture and there are even some Latins who pray to him for assistance. Despite all of this posthumous adoration, there are an equal number of publications denouncing Guevara as a killer and destroyer and participant in violence, killing innocent people for causes they did not support and ideologies they despised.[19]

A considerable mythology has developed around Guevera's life. Because Guevera was an advocate of mindless action for the sake of action, numerous bombers of innocent civilians around the world have claimed to be followers of "Che." Ignorant of his real life, people who know nothing about him invoke his name, as did an Arab guerilla who believed Che to be an Arab from Jaffa.

Guevera's picture is widely disseminated among all kinds of adolescent rebels who have no idea who he was. As time goes on, the myth and the reality diverge more and more, just as has been true of Abraham Lincoln and others who made history by their unusual lives and forceful actions. Guevara was a cold blooded killer of his political enemies and chief executioner of the Castro regime. Yet, in Hollywood he is feted as a rock star and sex symbol. This is the product of Cuban propaganda, which depicts him as a supporter of the poor. Yet, those who now adore him would undoubtedly have ended in one of his prisons or firing squads.[20]

NICARAGUA

The Assassination of Anastasio Samoza Garcia (1896-1956)

On September 21, 1956, Rigoberto Lopez Perez, a twenty-seven year old poet, walked into a country club where the president of Nicaragua, Anastasio Somoza Garcia was celebrating his nomination for another term as president and shot him in the chest. Somoza died two days later.

Somoza Garcia was "elected" for twenty years, from 1936 until his assassination, because he was a major landowner, because the military supported him, and because he was supported by the United States government. He ruled as a dictator, as did his son who followed him.

Somoza Garcia was supported by the United States and therefore supported the Allies during the Second World War. The United States lent Nicaragua large sums of money and also increased its military capabilities. This made the country almost entirely dependent on the United States, which absorbed ninety percent of its exports. Somoza Garcia enriched himself and his family. He held numerous enterprises and was estimated to possess $60 million. The Somoza dynasty came to an end with the violent overthrow of Somoza Garcia's son, Somoza Debayle, in 1979.[21]

ARGENTINA

The Assassination of Juan Jose Torres (1920-1976)

Torres was murdered in Argentina in 1976. At the time of his assassination he was a refugee from his own country, Bolivia. He had fled to Argentina because he feared for his life after he was deprived of the presidency by the violent overthrow of the earlier government.

Torres' body was found on a rural road in Argentina by a ranch hand. Torres had been blindfolded and was murdered and his body left 65 miles from Buenos Aires. More than 320 people were killed in Argentina in 1976, beginning with the violent overthrow of Isabel Martinez de Peron, president of Argentina. Torres had been president of Bolivia only ten months, from October 1970 to August 1971. He viewed himself leader of "a revolution of the people," a common claim by numerous South American militarists. He was labeled as "leftist" by his "rightist" enemies (These labels are derived from the era of the French revolution of 1789. The French Assembly of 1791 included those who sought radical measures to end the French monarchy. They were sitting left of the speaker's chair in the general assembly while those seeking some compromise were seated on his right).

In 1976, when Torres was a general in the Bolivian army, he was responsible for the assassination of Ernesto "Che" Guevara. Yet, five years later he was himself as far "left" as Guevara had ever been. This led his enemies to believe that he would lead Bolivia into the Soviet sphere of influence and into imitating Cuban communism. He was overthrown and fled to Peru and from there to Argentina.

During his military career, Torres was involved in several violent changes in the Bolivian government and consequently accumulated numerous enemies. His assassins were never identified.[22]

The reason for this failure to find the killers is best understood in the light of "Operation Condor." That label was attached to a series of assassinations plotted by the intelligence services of five South American countries and the United States in 1974. Included were Argentina, Bolivia, Chile, Paraguay, Uruguay, and the U.S.A. The purpose of this plot was to eliminate from South America all those deemed to be communists or communist sympathizers. A good number of the targets of these assassinations had, like Torres, fled to Argentina. There the mass killings organized by the government were called The Dirty War and consisted of the disappearance of thousands of citizens. Numerous prominent politicians were killed, wounded or placed on a "hit list" as possible collaborators with "leftists." Included on such a "hit list" was former congressman and mayor of New York Ed Koch and former Secretary of State Henry Kissinger.

To date (2011) there are still many Argentine mothers who protest publicly that their children disappeared in the 1970's.[23]

PERU

The Assassination of Francisco Pizarro (1476-1541)

On June 26, 1541, a cadre of Pizarro's enemies forced their way into his palace in Lima, Peru and stabbed to death the conqueror of the Inca Empire. Those who murdered Pizarro and some of his followers were friends of Diego Almagro, whom Pizarro had killed because Almagro sought to kill Pizarro.[24]

Pizarro is known to history as the destroyer of the Inca Empire, which had existed at least since the 13th century. The Spanish explorers who destroyed Inca civilization were very few. In fact, Pizarro's army was a good deal smaller than that of the Incas. He nevertheless succeeded in literally "wiping out" the Incas because the Incas were not immune to the diseases brought to South America by the Spanish, in particular, smallpox. Moreover, the Spanish sought to enrich themselves by seizing gold and silver mined in the Peruvian mountains.[25]

Pizarro, a former swineherd, had never gone to school. He was therefore illiterate and cruel. He had captured the Inca emperor and demanded a roomful of gold in exchange for the emperor's life. When the gold was delivered, Pizarro had him killed despite the agreement.[26]

Historians have placed a great deal of emphasis on the acquisition of land by the Spanish conquerors. In addition, the conversion of the native Americans to Christianity has been emphasized. It is however evident that the main motive for the conquests was the acquisition of gold and other metals. The Pizarro family became wealthy as the result of the conquest of Peru, Ecuador, and Panama by looting temples, cemeteries and private homes of the South American people. Likewise, the Spanish treasury was filled with gold stolen from the South American nations, particularly the Incas.[27]

After the assassination of Francisco Pizarro, his brothers were temporarily able to profit from his wealth but were accused of having participated in the murder of Diego Almagro and therefore jailed, so that on their release after 18 years they had lost their investments. It was not gold or money which ensures Pizarro's reputation but his brutality in destroying whole civilizations in the New World.

NOTES

1. No author, "Bermuda Governor and Aide Are Killed By Shots in Capital," *The New York Tines,* (March 11, 1973), 1.
    2. Ibid, 1.

3. Robert D. Crasweller, *Trujillo: The Life and Times of a Caribbean Dictator,* (New York: MacMillan, 1966), 182.

4. Maxine Block, *Current Biography: Who's News and Why,* (New York: H.W. Wilson Co., 1941), 976.

5. Crasweller, *Trujillo,* 199.

6. Enrique Krauze, *Mexico: Biography of Power. A History of Modern Mexico, 1810-1996.* (New York: Harper Collins, 1997), 246-247, 264.

7. Ronald M. Schneider, *Latin American Political History,* (New York: Westview Press, 2006), 168.

8. Samuel Brunk, "The Sad Situation of Civilians and Soldiers: The Banditry of Zapatismo in the Mexican," *The American Historical Review,* Vol.101, no.2, (April 1996), 331-353.

9. Emrique Krauze, *Mexico: Biography of Power,- A History of Modern Mexico,* (New York: Harper Collins, 1997), 403.

10. Ibid, 403.

11. Arnaldo Cortes, "Trotsky Dies of His Wounds," *The New York Times,* (August 22, 1940), 1.

12. Robert Conquest, *"The Great Terror: A Reassessment,* (New York: Oxford University Press, 1991), 418.

13. John Dewey, "Not Guilty," (New York: Harper & Brothers, 1938), xv, 422.

14. Juan de Onis, "U.S. Suspends New Air to Salvador Till American Deaths Are Clarified," *The New York Times,* (December 6, 1980), 1.

15. No author, *The New York Times,* (November 29, 1980), 22.

16. Michael Ring, "El Slavador Today: The Hope and the Challenge," *Enemies of War,* www.pbs.org. itvs. Enemies of war/perspectives3. html.

17. Paco Ignacio Taibo, *Guevara, also known as Che,* (New York: St. Martin's Press, 1999), 691.

18. John Lee Anderson, *Che Guevara: A Revolutionary Life,* (New York: Grove Press, 1997),.22-23.

19. Andrew Sinclair, *Viva Che! The Strange Death and Life of Che Guevara,* New York: Sutton Publishing, (1968), 80-127.

20. Helena Zhu and Joan Delaney, "Che Guevera: Hypocritical Darling of Pop Culture," *The Epoch Times,* (February 23, 2009), 1.

21. Tim Merrill, *Nicaragua: A Country Study,* (Washington, D.C., United States Government Printing Office, 1993).

22. No author, "Torres, Ex-President of Bolivia, Found Murdered in Argentina," *The New York Times,* (June 4, 1976), 10.

23. Claudia Lagos and Patrick J. McDonne, "Pinochet-era General is Caught," *Los Angeles Times,* (August 3, 2007), 1.

24. William Prescott, *History of the Conquest of Peru,* (New York: Modern Library, 2005; originally 1847), 547.

25. Kim McQuarrie, *The Last Days of the Incas,* (New York: Simon and Schuster, 2007), 89.

26. Ibid. p.89.

27. Rafael Varon Gabai and Auke Pieter Jacobs, "Peruvian Wealth and Spanish Investment," *The Hispanic American Historical Review,* vol. 67, no. 4, (November 1987), 660.

Chapter Five
African Assassinations

MUSLIM NORTH AFRICA

ALGERIA

The Assassination of Mohammed Boudiaf (12919-1992)

On June 29, 1992 the president of Algeria, Mohammed Boudiaf, was shot and killed by Lembarek Boumaarafi, a lieutenant in the Algerian army. The assassin was shot to death at once by a bodyguard after a gunfight broke out in which 41 people were wounded. The murder had been organized by The Islamic Salvation Front, a large Algerian fundamentalist party.

Boudiaf was popular because he had been one of the leaders in the fight for Algerian independence from France. However, he was an outspoken opponent of the fundamentalists and corruption by government officials.[1]

EGYPT

The Assassination of Ahmed Maher (1888-1945)

On February 25, 1945, the prime minister of Egypt, Ahmed Maher, was shot and killed inside Parliament as he was about to read a declaration of war on the "Axis" powers, i.e. Germany and Italy. He was about to walk to the speaker's platform when a lawyer, Mahmud Issawi, stood up and fired directly into Maher. Arrested, he said that he favored a Nazi victory and had for some time been a pro-Nazi activist in Egypt.[2]

The Assassination of Anwar Sadat (1918-1981)

On October 6, 1981, the Egyptians celebrated the "victory" of the Egyptian army of October 1973 in which Israel not only defeated the Egyptians but also had invaded Egypt past the Sinai Peninsula on their way to Cairo. Only American intervention prevented the Israelis from planting their flag there. Nevertheless, the Egyptian government labeled that defeat a great victory and sponsored a parade by the armed forces. During that parade, Khalid Islambouli, a lieutenant in the army, strode forward and shot and killed Sadat, the president of Egypt, as he was seated in the front row of the reviewing stands.[3]

Islambouli was not the only one to shoot. Several other conspirators shot and killed the Cuban ambassador, a general, and the Coptic bishop. In addition, 28 were wounded. An insurrection had also been organized but failed.[4]

Islambouli was executed in 1982. The motives for the killing of Sadat were related to the wish to "liberate" Jerusalem from Jewish control and from the conviction of the conspirators supporting Islambouli that an Islamic state should be established in Egypt. Neither of these objectives was achieved by the assassins who, like so many others, achieved no change in policies by their own government.[5]

Egyptian "jihadists" and other militants had resented that President Sadat visited Jerusalem in 1977 and spoke to the Israeli parliament. That effort by Sadat to bring about peace with Israel led to much anger on the part of army officers and other "patriots" who were ready to assault Israel once again.[6]

AFRICAN STATES SOUTH OF THE SAHARA

BURUNDI

Burundi is a country in East Africa. It is "landlocked" between Rwanda and Tanzania. At one time a French colony, French is still in use alongside Kirundi. The population is somewhat less than nine million in more than ten thousand square miles.

Between 1961 and 1994, five Burundi heads of state were assassinated. First was Louis Rwagasore, son of a king of Burundi before it became a republic. He was a prime minister who was killed only two weeks after taking office. The motive for the killing may have been religious hate. Likewise, Pierre Ngendandumwe, also prime minister, was assassinated eight days after beginning a second term. The motive for the murder was linked to ethnic hatred between Tutsi and Hutu tribes.

Joseph Bamina was prime minister from January 26 to September 30, 1965 when he was assassinated. Then, in 1993, Melchior Ndadaye was assassinated after only three months in the office of prime minister, once more becoming the victim of Tutsi and Hutu rivalry. In February of 1994 Cyprien Ntaryaminra became president of Burundi. In April of that year his plane was shot down and he died together with the president of Rwanda. Once more ethnic fighting erupted, as a literal genocide ensued.[7]

CONGO

The Assassination of Marien Ngouabi (1938-1977)

On March 19, 1977 Barthelemy Kikadidi, an army officer, shot and killed the president of the Congo, Marien Ngouabi. Congo had a population of only 1.4 million in 1977. Ngouabi was a communist who associated his country with Cuba, the former Soviet Union and China.[8]

The killing of president Ngouabi was the outcome of a feud between him and the former president, Alphone Massamga-Debat. Debat was convicted of the murder of Ngouabi and executed on March 25, 1977. Debat did not actually shoot Ngouabi but was known to have employed the killer Kikadidi. Debat was a former president of the Congo but was ousted in a "coup" in 1968, a coup organized by Ngouabi. [9]

The Assassination of Patrice Lumumba (1925-1961)

There can be little doubt that Lumumba, prime minister of the Congo, was assassinated by a Belgian police commissioner, Frans Verscheure, and a Belgian Captain, Julien Gat. Belgium had been the colonial ruler of the so-called Belgian Congo from 1908 until 1960, when the Congo attained its independence. The Congo occupies over 905 thousand square miles in the western part of Africa (Alaska has 656 thousand square miles). Because of its size and its resources, the United States and the then Soviet Union became bitter rivals concerning the influence each country had over the government of the Congo after it gained its independence in 1960. This rivalry was enhanced by the wish of both countries to control the copper and rubber resources found there. In addition, diamonds and gold have been found there. Therefore both the United States and the Soviet Union wanted to dominate that country even after the formal severing of ties between Belgium and the Democratic Republic of the Congo. Independence was gained by peaceful means at a conference held in Brussels. Patrice Lumumba was appointed prime minister under the presidency of Joseph Kasa Vubu.[10]

Shortly after independence was achieved, a civil war broke out in the Democratic Republic of the Congo involving a declaration of independence by the province of Katanga. The United Nations sent troops to suppress this rebellion. Unable to do so, the UN withdrew and was succeeded by Soviet troops, who also failed to suppress the civil war. In the course of these events, Lumumba was regarded by the United States government as an ally of the Soviet Union and a communist. Therefore, President Eisenhower instructed the Central Intelligence Agency to poison Lumumba or get rid of him by some other means. Aided by the CIA station chief in the Congo, Lumumba was arrested and executed by a Belgian firing squad.[11]

LIBERIA

The Assassination of William R. Tolbert (1913-1980)

On April 12, 1980, seventeen noncommissioned officers of the Liberian army led by master sergeant Samuel Doe entered the presidential palace and killed the president, William R. Tolbert. Tolbert's body, together with twenty-seven other victims of the assault, was dumped into a mass grave.

Doe was appointed president of Liberia by the Army Redemption Council, which had seized control of the country on the grounds that it was being governed by corrupt officials. Doe appointed a number of younger officers to government positions and released those imprisoned by Tolbert.[12]

The Assassination of Samuel Doe (1951-1990)

On September 9, 1990, Prince Y. Johnson tortured and killed Samuel Doe in Monrovia. Johnson videotaped the torture of Doe. The video was shown on news reports around the world and depicted Johnson drinking beer while Doe's ear was being cut off. Other horrors were also recorded. Johnson was an ally of Charles Taylor, who organized the fight against Doe and succeeded in killing him and making himself president of Liberia. Doe had used a number of "rigged" elections to keep himself in power by shutting down newspapers and controlling all communications.

MADAGASCAR

The Assassination of Richard Ratsimandrava (1931-1975)

Ratsimandrava became president of Madgascar, an island off the southeast coast of Africa, six days before he was assassinated while driving from the presidential palace to his home. He was president from February 6 to February 12. He was killed by the "Republican Security Forces," an armed gang dissolved by his predecessor, Gabriel Ramanantsoa. This assassination led to a civil war between the supporters of a former president and the military government. Ratsimandrava was succeeded by "the National Committee of Military Leadership."[13]

NIGERIA

The Assassination of Abubakar Balewa (1912-1966)

On January 15, 1966, Chukwuma Nzeogwu killed the prime minister of Nigeria, Balewa. This assassination was a part of a military takeover of the country, leading to a civil war between those loyal to the president and those who had organized his murder and overthrow. A number of other Nigerian officials were also killed and their houses burned down. The killings included the wives of the victims, as Major General Johnson Aguiyi-Ironsi took over a new military government.

Subsequently Agiuiyi-Ironsi was also assassinated on July 29, 1966 only a little more than six months after he seized power from his assassinated predecessor. The same fate befell Murtala Ramat Mohammed (1938-1976), who was assassinated by Lieutenant Colonel Buka Suka Dimka. Mohammed was succeeded by Shehu Shagari in October of 1979.[14]

The assassinations were motivated by a lust for power by military men who had the means to kill and who invited their own demise ipso facto.

RWANDA

The Assassination of Juvenal Habyarimana and the Rwandan Genocide

On April 6, 1994, an airplane carrying the president of Rwanda, Juvenal Habyarima, and the president of Burundi, Cyprien Ntaryamira, was shot down. Both presidents died in the ensuing crash. This double killing became the catalyst for the ensuing civil war between the Hutu and Tutsi ethnic groups in Rwanda. Members of the Rwandan armed forces have been accused by the Rwandan government of firing a missile which brought down the 'plane carrying the two presidents.[15]

The ensuing civil war left 800,000 Tutsi dead. In addition numerous Hutus were also killed. Some historians have claimed that the then Hutu dominated government plotted to kill President Habyarimana, thereby setting off ethnic violence. The current Rwandan government has accused France of participating in the assassination plot.[16]

The Rwandan genocide began with the publication of a journal called Kanguka, which published constant incitement for violence against the Tutsis. The consequent fighting between the two ethnic groups led to the establishment of an

UN peacekeeping force, which was utterly ineffective and incapable to achieving its mission.[17]

An International Criminal Tribunal for the Genocide in Rwanda meets in Arusha, Tanzania. That court has heard testimony to the effect that the genocide was planned by the Rwandan government and was carried out by mayors and members of the police. The victims were identified by their skin color so that the lighter colored Tutsi became the easily identified Tutsi.[18]

SOMALIA[19]

The Assassination of Abdirashid Ali Shermarke

On October 15, 1969, Shermarke was shot dead by one of his own bodyguards. This killing was organized by the army, who then seized power. The only visible motive for this assassination was the ambition of the commander of the army to rule the county.

Somalia became an independent country in 1960 after it had been a United Nations trust territory under Italian administration. Together with British Somaliland, it became a republic surrounded by the Gulf of Aden and the Indian Ocean.[20]

Somalia has not had a stable government since independence, so that there are instead numerous local governments. It is in the light of this anarchy that the murder of President Shermarke illustrates the chaos ruling there.

SOUTH AFRICA

The Assassination of Henrik Verwoerd

On September 6, 1966, Henrik Verwoerd, then prime minister, was shot to death inside the Assembly building. This was preceded by an attempt to kill Verwoerd. On April 9, 1960, David Pratt, a South African farmer, shot Verwoerd, who survived and returned to work two months after the shooting. Pratt was declared insane and sent to a mental hospital, where he hanged himself.

Verwoerd defended the "apartheid" policies of his government, policies that were viewed as "racist." He was called "the architect of apartheid." Nevertheless, there is no evidence that his policies led to his assassination.[21]

NOTES

1. Youssef M. Ibrahim, "Algerian President Fatally Shot at Rally," *The New York Times,* (June 30, 1992), 1.

2. No author, "EGYPT;'War and Death," *Time,* (March 5, 1945), 1.

3. No author, "The Sadat Assassination," *The New York Times,* (October 7, 1981, D1), 3.

4. Mark Sageman, *Understanding Terror Networks,* (Philadelphia: University of Pennsylvania Press), 31-34.

5. Hamied N. Ansari, "The Islamic Militants in Egyptian Politics," *International Journal of Middle East Studies,* vol.16, no.1, (March 1984), 128-144.

6. Henry Kamm, "Sadat in Jerusalem: Day of Challenge," *The New York Times,* (November 21, 1977), 77.

7. Robert Krueger, *From Bloodshed to Hope in Burundi: Our Embassy Years During Genocide,"* (Austin: University of Texas Press, 2007).

8. Reuters, "Ngouabi Dies of his Wounds," *The New York Times,* (March 20, 1977), 1.

9. No author, "Former President Executed in Congo," *The New York Times,* (March 26, 1977), 7.

10. Godfrey Mwakikagile, *Nyerere and Africa: End of an Era,* (New York: New Africa Press, 2006), 147-205.

11. Ludo de Witt, *The Assassination of Lumumba,* (New York: Verso Publishing, 2001).

12. No author, "Tolbert of Liberia is Killed in a Coup by Sergeant," *The New York Times,* (April 13, 1980), 1.

13. No author, "Malagasy Head of State Killed Six Days After Taking Office," *The New York Times,* (February 12, 1965), 11.

14. Lloyd Garrison, "Nigerian Regime Rocked by Coup; Control in Doubt," *The New York Times,* (January 16, 1966), 1.

15. Joseph Kron, "Extremist Hutu Officials Blamed in '94 Rwandan Assassiantion," *The New York Times,* (January 11, 2010), A6.

16. Ibid. A6.

17. Linda Malvern, *Conspiracy to Murder: The Rwandan Genocide,* (New York: Verso), 49.

18. Melvern, *Conspiracy,* 25-28.

19. Ken Menkhaus, "Governance Without Government in Somalia," *International Security,* vol. 31, no.3, (2007), 74.

20. No author, "Policeman Slays Somali President," *The New York Times,* (October 16, 1969), 1.

21. C.J. Beyers, "Hendrik Verwoerd," *Dictionary of South African Biography,* vol.4, (Durban, South Africa, Butterworth, 1981), 730740.

Chapter Six
Anarchy and Terrorism

I.

Between 1894 and 1910, a period of sixteen years, six heads of state were assassinated in Europe and the United States. In 1894, the president of France, Marie Francois Sardi Carnot, was killed by an anarchist, Sante Caserio. In 1897, the prime minister of Spain, Antonio Canovas del Castillo (1828-1897), was assassinated by the anarchist Michele Angiolillio. In 1898, the Empress Elizabeth of Austria (1837-1898) was assassinated by Luigi Luccheni. In 1900, the king of Italy, Umberto (1844-1900), was assassinated by Angelo Bresci. In 1901, the president of the United States, William McKinley, was assassinated by Leon Czolgosz, and in 1912, the prime minister of Spain, Jose Canalejas (1854-1912), was assassinated by Manuel Pardinas.

Earlier, in 1881, the Czar of Russia, Alexander II, was assassinated by Nikolai Rysakov. These and numerous other assassinations and attempted killings of government officials were carried out in the name of anarchy, a philosophical movement which gained adherents in Europe and in part in America with a view of eliminating all government.

The term anarchy derives from the Greek anarchos, meaning "without rulers." The belief in a society without government may have originated in the writings of some oriental philosophers, although that is not certain. In Europe, a number of prominent writers promoted anarchy with the result that some of their followers killed heads of state, calling these murders "propaganda of the deed."[1]

The most cited author promoting anarchy in the nineteenth century was Pierre Joseph Proudhon (1809-1865). A religious bigot who advocated the mass murder of European Jews,[2] Proudhon published his first essay, "On the Utility of Sunday Observance," in 1839. The next year, in 1840, Proudhon published his most sensational work, entitled "What Is Property?" Here he critiques private property and government and answered his own question: "private property is theft."[3]

In addition, Proudhon announced that he was an anarchist and that all government is oppressive. He objected to the earning of income from the labor of others, such as rent and interest. Like Karl Marx, he objected to the profit earned by the capitalist because the workers would starve if they did not allow their own exploitation. He therefore advocated an exchange economy in which value would be calculated by the cost of production and the labor invested in it.[4]

At first Proudhon sought to replace government with "scientific socialism" in which the Academy of Sciences would make all decisions based on statistics. Later he adopted the voluntary contract as the chief means of coordinating economics and politics. He believed that individual contracts between people of equal bargaining power could replace all government. He wanted government to institute these changes and then disappear voluntarily.[5]

In the late 1840's Proudhon proposed that workers' associations be formed which would provide sickness and pension benefits to its members, provide a technical education for the members, and abolish the division of labor by rotating all jobs.[6]

Proudhon believed, as did Karl Marx, that workers' associations, not the government, would insure "the principle of equivalent exchange" without violence. He talked about the workers conquering the world by the force of principle.[7]

In 1848, Proudhon published a two volume work called System of Economic Contradiction or The Philosophy of Poverty. He argued that the existing economic system must bring about exploitation and misery. Following Hegel, he claimed that the economic system could not be reformed but needed to be replaced by a synthesis he called mutualism.[8]

Seeking to abolish all government, Proudhon proposed that a spontaneous order would arise through free interaction in which every citizen would "do what he wishes and only what he wishes."[9]

Proudhon published a considerable literature designed to influence the French to abolish government, private property, banking and other institutions in favor of his numerous suggestions, none of which were realized because the public rejected them. In sum, Proudhon rejected all government in these words: "...to be governed is to be at every operation, at every transaction, noted, registered, enrolled, taxed, stamped, measured, numbered, assessed, licensed, authorized, admonished, forbidden, reformed, corrected, punished." He continued his definition of government: "It is under the pretext of public utility, and in the name of the general interest, to be placed under contribution, trained, ransomed, exploited, monopolized, extorted, squeezed, mystified, robbed; then at the slightest resistance, the first word of complaint, to be repressed, fined, despised, harassed, tracked, abused, clubbed, disarmed, choked, imprisoned, judged, condemned, shot, deported, sacrificed, sold, betrayed, and, to crown all, mocked, ridiculed, outraged, dishonored. That is government, that is its justice; that its morality."[10]

Although Proudhon sought to kill the Jewish population of Europe, he did not otherwise advocate violence. He believed that a violent revolution would not be necessary because the "abstract idea of the right" would persuade all people to adopt a stateless society through reason. None of this made much sense in the real, political world. The anarchists, including Proudhon, rejected political parties because they viewed parties as a variety of absolutism. Yet, without a political party, they could not advance their ideas and make them reality. It was therefore a Russian anarchist, Michael Bakunin, who added violence to the teachings of Proudhon and thereby made anarchy more effective.[11]

Michael Bakunin died in 1876, five years before Alexander II, the Czar of Russia, was assassinated in 1881. Alexander was killed by a bomb thrown at him by one of three conspirators. The first effort to kill Alexander failed as the bomb thrown at him only wounded but did not kill him. Then the second bomb was thrown and Alexander died shortly thereafter of the wounds he had received. For months prior to this assassination numerous members of a Russian anarchist society made efforts to kill the Czar but failed each time.

There can be little doubt that those determined to assassinate Alexander were inspired by Bakunin, who had devoted his life to the destruction of the Russian state and the establishment of anarchy, meaning the abolition of all government. Bakunin participated in the revolutions of 1848 in Paris, in Vienna, and in Berlin and other German states, and was therefore imprisoned for eight years.[12]

Bakunin believed in "revolution of the deed" as well as "propaganda of the deed," which sought to emphasize that men shape their own destinies. He rejected books and writings of all kinds as useless in advancing the cause of anarchy despite his prodigious writings, which he never finished. He started numerous books but did not leave a single finished work at his death.[13]

Bakunin influenced a number of later revolutionaries and anarchists. Bakunin was infected by a psychotic hatred of Jews, a common European cultural phenomenon that led to the successful slaughter of six million European Jews in the gas ovens of the Second World War. No doubt, anarchism contributed its share to this greatest of all crimes. Eldridge Cleaver, an American anarchist and Jew baiter, expressed his indebtedness to Bakunin in his book *Soul on Ice*.[14]

Unlike Karl Marx, who expected revolutions to occur in Germany and other industrialized countries, Bakunin foresaw the revolutions in the agrarian societies in Russia and China where there were no organized factory workers who, in Bakunin's view, were tainted by the aspirations of the middle class. Bakunin hoped for a revolution based on revenge by the peasants and the lower working class in urban societies which Marx had called a "Lumpenproletariat" and which consisted of the unemployed, the outlaws and all social "failures." Bakunin predicted the Russian revolution of 1917, which he believed would result in the liberation of mankind. Instead it led to the Stalinist dictatorship, which is continued in somewhat milder form in the post Soviet era of the 21st century.[15]

Bakunin believed in immediate revolution. Here too he differed from Marx, who thought that revolutionary forces would emerge over time. He wanted a violent destruction of all social institutions, including the end of parliamentary democracy, which he viewed as a "shameless fiction." He opposed constitutions and laws and hoped that war would bring about revolutions, including unrestrained uprising and anarchistic destruction. He wanted to convert war into a national rebellion, as occurred in Russia in 1917 when the Russian armed forces were defeated by Germany and then turned against their own government. Like Lenin after him, Bakunin wanted no dealings with liberal socialists. He demanded the abolition of representative government, the end to the army and the police, and the leveling of income as proposed by the President of the United States, Barack Obama, in 2010.[16]

Bakunin promoted such unrealistic ideas as the establishment of a clandestine organization which would prevent a dictatorship after the revolution had succeeded. Such a group would of course become a burdensome dictatorship, a contradiction of Bakunin's so called liberal principles. According to Bakunin, the end justified the means in that a "temporary" dictatorship was envisaged. In fact, no such "temporary" dictatorship was and is possible. Dictatorships are self perpetuating, as the bosses never want to give away their power. [17]

II.

One of the persistent features of the anarchist movement has been the denunciation of Jews. This religious bigotry was also supported by some former Jews, such as Karl Marx, who wrote an entire anti-Jewish tract later used as propaganda by the German Nazi government. This should not be surprising, since it has always been an aspect of European culture to persecute and murder Jews. This hatred was originally an aspect of Christian as well as Muslim theology, as the founders of both religions resented that the Jews of their day would not convert to their beliefs. Among Christians, this resulted in the Christ killer accusations which finally resulted in the holocaust and the mass murder of six million European Jews. Among Muslims, the wish to eradicate all Jews is seen in killings of all kinds directed at the people of Israel as well as the few Jews sometimes found in Muslim lands.[18]

In the nineteenth century, scientific advances weakened the religious basis for anti-Jewish action. Therefore, anti-Judaism was translated into racial anti-Semitism, which pretends that Jews are a race to be exterminated like vermin. The label "anti-Semitism" was coined in 1873 by Wilhelm Marr, a German journalist who founded The League of Anti-Semites, deriving the word "Semite" from the linguistic classification of Hebrew as a "semitic" language (according to the Bible, Sem was one of the sons of Noah).[19]

Because all of western and Muslim literature, philosophy, entertainment, religion, myth and popular culture has preached the hatred of Jews for 1,900 years, the numerous political and philosophical movements in western and Muslim civilization continue these hatreds in various forms to the present day. After the holocaust, the phrase "anti-semitism" fell into disrepute. It was therefore revived in the form of rejecting the national liberation movement of the Jewish people, called Zionism, and hatred of Israel.

In the nineteenth century, the anarchists were infected by this psychotic hate, which even included anarchists of Jewish descent. Many ethnic Jews supported the anarchist movement because they believed that the "Jewish problem" would go away once anarchy had been achieved. One of these Jews was Moses Hess, who wrote a book called *The Holy History of Mankind* in 1837, to the effect that the Jewish future in Europe would have to be assimilation into the universal socialist revolutionary movement. This foolish notion was at once undermined by the Russian revolutionary group "Narodnaia Volia," who considered the persecution of Jews a positive step on the way of achieving the social revolution. In addition, the so-called "Dreyfus Affair" demonstrated to the Jews of Europe that their mass murder was imminent, although few were willing to recognize the degree of the danger. Most Jews pretended to themselves that the false accusations against Captain Alfred Dreyfus were merely a temporary setback in their effort to become accommodated to the cosmopolitan society promised by the anarchists.[20]

Proudhon and Bakunin believed that anarchists should renounce all national loyalties and strive for a nationless universe. This was not the view of Peter Kropotkin, one of the leading Russian anarchist writers of the late nineteenth century. Together with Hillel Solotaroff and Bernard Lazare, he believed that nationalism could accommodate anarchy. For that reason, Kropotkin, Soloratoff and Lazare were willing to support Zionism as a temporary means of dealing with the Jewish Problem until the state withered away in favor of anarchy. Kropotkin also rejected Zionism on the grounds that Jews were incapable of colonizing "Palestine" and that Zionism was only a religious movement. Proudhon called Jews the sworn enemy of mankind, who should be sent to Asia or destroyed. Proudhon also called Jews a nation of parasites not fit for socialism. It is no doubt astonishing to those not acquainted with Jewish history that any would follow anarchy in view of such evaluations of the Jewish people.[21]

A prominent German Jewish anarchist was Gustav Landauer, who published a newspaper called Der Sozialist. Like other Jews, he too became disillusioned with the limited progress made by Jews in Europe after the 1913 Beilis blood libel, in which the Russian government accused Menachem Beilis of using Christian blood for ritual purposes.[22]

More influential than Landauer was Rudolf Rocker, who published an anarchist periodical called *Arbeiter Front* in England. Rocker claimed that nationalism or any national feeling was not natural, but imposed on people by those in power and the political machinations of heads of state. Like Landauer, Rocker believed that the special problems of the Jews would be solved once "the revolution" became successful.[23]

Hillel Solotaroff, a Russian born American Jew, studied medicine and then engaged in journalism favoring anarchy and the eventual unity of mankind by the abolition of government and the sharing of wealth. Yet, Solotaroff, like the other Jewish anarchists, was awakened to reality when in 1903 a pogrom occurred in Kishinev. The word "pogrom" may be translated as "outrage," and usually meant an attack on the Jewish minority in Eastern Europe, who were assaulted and murdered at intervals, particularly in the vicinity of the Easter festival. When a Christian boy, Mikhail Ribalenko, was murdered by a relative, the government of Russia chose to pretend that "the Jews" had killed the boy so as to use his blood in the Passover ritual. This claim resulted in an attack on the Jews of Kishinev, leading to the death of 49 Jews, the wounding of 92 Jews, and the destruction of 700 houses.[24]

This and numerous other anti-Jewish events taught Solotaroff that anarchism would not save them and that assimilation would not satisfy their enemies. Solotaroff foresaw that the European Jews would eventually be slaughtered, an event proved true between 1933 and 1945. Solotaroff recognized that Jews who believed that they would become integrated into European society were instrumental in promoting their own physical destruction.[25]

The eleven million Jews in Europe in 1939 were finally slaughtered because they would not and could not believe that the Christian community meant what they said. There was never a time in all of European history, since the Roman Emperor Constantine made Christianity the official religion of the empire in 311 by the Edict of Milan, that Jews were not subject to the utmost cruelty and brutality available in each age, finally leading to the holocaust.[26]

III.

Peter Kropotkin (1842-1921) was a Russian anarchist writer who descended from Russian nobility. He was called Prince by some of the media but rejected that title vehemently.

Kropotkin was a theoretical anarchist whose writings were most influential in the nineteenth and early twentieth centuries. Although few of those who threw bombs and assassinated heads of state were capable of reading the extensive intellectual literature produced by Kropotkin and others, their ideas became the contents of anarchist newspapers and journals and were introduced to the assassins by those vehicles of communication. These ideas also entered into the speeches of anarchist orators so that a direct link between assassinations and anarchist literature can easily be established.

Kropotkin began by demanding that the private means of production be transferred to common ownership. He further wanted to abolish all political systems in favor of "integrated communities."[27]

Kropotkin wrote that a future society would be without government and a free communist society. He did not endorse communism in the sense that Karl Marx had proposed, since Marx meant to have a government consisting of the dictatorship of the proletariat. By free communism Kropotkin meant a society with both economic freedom and political freedom. He believed that a society of equals could be established, governed by associations and federations, all organized by individual initiative for the benefit of everyone and without coercion of any kind.[28]

Kropotkin believed that his new society would come about after revolution destroyed the old society, which exploits urban workers and farmers. He rejected the vision of Marx concerning the proletariat, but thought that people would voluntarily share the wealth, set up communal stores, and have farmers supply food for production workers in a mutual arrangement of cooperation and friendship. No enforcement of any of these arrangements was envisaged, as Kropotkin wanted no government.[29]

Kropotkin wrote that material wealth belongs to the society at large and not to any one individual. He therefore proposed the confiscation of property, beginning with the expropriation of buildings such as palaces and villas, which should be put at the disposal of the homeless. Since there would be no government in the society of the future, Kropotkin did not explain how such confiscation could be brought about. Kropotkin argued that justice demands that every person has a right to life and welfare and that his scheme would insure that this is met.

According to Kropotkin, agriculture would eventually become collective and integrated into industrial production located in rural areas. This would lead to thousands of farmers living together on communal lands, happily farming and making farm labor enjoyable.[30]

Kropotkin also promoted the liberation of women from their traditional household chores and advocated their equality with men. He foresaw the invention of various labor saving devices such as the dishwasher, the washing machine, electric stoves, and the sewing machine. Yet he placed most of his trust in the absence of any government so as to insure freedom. He thought the state would be replaced by arrangements between the producer and consumer, depending only on the people becoming aware of his program and their will to create the utopian world he had promised. Kropotkin was by no means the pacifist he claimed to be. In 1879, at an anarchist congress in Switzerland, Kropotkin advocated "propaganda of the deed" and urged "propaganda by speech, written word, by dagger, gun and dynamite." He influenced others to assassinate and kill, although he never did so.[31]

Much criticized, Kropotkin has nevertheless been quite influential, in that his views gave rise to a number of social movements in Europe, including the Rote Armee Fraktion in Germany, which terrorized that country in the 1970's.[32]

IV.

"Propaganda by the Deed," a phrase coined by Errico Malatesta (1853-1932), consisted of assassinations or attempts at killing "heads of states" in Europe and America.

Malatesta began his anarchist career at an early age. When only fourteen, he wrote a letter to King Emmanuel II of Italy, complaining about some local injustice. For this he was arrested. He attended a medical school but was soon expelled for joining an anti-government demonstration. He thereupon joined the Italian section of the communist party, leading a year later to a meeting with Bakunin in Switzerland.

Five years later, having read much of the anarchist literature of his day, Malatesta, Andrea Costa, and Carlo Cafiero, together with a band of other anarchists, invaded two villages in the Campania region of Italy, where they burned the tax registers and declared an end to the reign of king Victor Emanuel. Although the townspeople welcomed them, they would not join the insurrection. Instead troops arrived and broke up the band of anarchists.[33]

After traveling to a number of European cities and Egypt, Malatesta stayed in London for two years and then returned to Italy in 1883. There he wrote a pamphlet, Between Peasants, advocating anarchy. In 1884 he was imprisoned for this writing but escaped to Buenos Aires, where he spread his anarchist ideas. Again in London in 1889, he wrote another pamphlet, Anarchy. Two years later he returned to Italy and edited a paper called Agitation. In 1898 he was imprisoned on the island of Lampedus but once more escaped to London and later the United States. Once more in London in 1900, he traveled to Amsterdam in 1907 and was then arrested in London in 1909 but not imprisoned. In 1913, Malatesta returned to Italy and participated in a demonstration in Ancona. He then moved back and forth from Italy to London and back to Italy where he urged workers to strike with some success. Yet, the turmoil caused by these incitements did not lead to anarchy but the ascent of Benito Mussolini to become dictator in Italy and the suppression of all dissent. Malatesta died in 1932.[34]

Johann Most (1846-1906), a native of Bavaria, Germany, came to the United States in 1882 after having been jailed in numerous countries in Europe for agitating in favor of anarchy. In this country, too, he was jailed for writing a violent editorial supporting the murder of European kings in his German language publication Freiheit or Liberty.

Born into a Roman Catholic family, Most refused to attend mass as an adolescent and was jailed for this refusal. He later boasted that he never entered a church again. Beginning in 1871, he became a socialist agitator in Vienna, where he was tried and found guilty of "high treason." Having been released from prison by reason of a general amnesty, he moved to Chemnitz, in Saxony, now a state within Germany but then an independent country. He was expelled from Saxony and moved to Mainz, where he entered politics. He was elected to the German parliament and moved to Berlin. In the "Reichstag" or parliament he gave a violent speech in favor of the Paris uprising and was jailed for incitement to riot. He served two years in prison. He continued to agitate against all government but moved to England to promote his views. There he published Freiheit and publicized the views of Bakunin. His doctrines were so violent that even some anarchists abandoned him and his ideas. On the assassination of Czar Alexander II in 1881, Most issued a special edition of his paper and commended the assassins and advocated pillage and massacre. This led to his arrest and 18 months in prison for advocating murder. His paper was closed. On his release in 1882, Most moved to New York City, where he published Freheit once more. In the United States he was received with great enthusiasm by his anarchist followers. He spoke in numerous American cities, making extreme comments and cursing government and "the establishment." On the assassination of President McKinley, Most congratulated the killer, Czolgosz. He was again arrested and served one year in prison for "disorderly conduct." Before going to jail, he gave a speech in New York which was so emotional and arousing that it led to riots and demonstrations. In his later years he was somewhat less flamboyant, but shortly before his death he wrote his autobiography, which once more cursed all authority.[35]

The violent speeches and writings of Most and others were not wasted. They influenced a number of assassins, who not only killed prominent politicians and heads of state but also killed some victims who had no political positions.

On February 12, 1894, Émile Henry tossed a bomb into a crowded restaurant in Paris, wounding numerous guests and killing three. Pursued by a waiter and a police officer, Henry shot and killed both, so that he was guilty of five murders, for which he was executed in May of that year. Henry had associated with the most violent anarchists of his time and defended the "propaganda of the deed." He had repeatedly moved to London and back to Paris, studying anarchist literature in English and French. When Augusta Valliant threw a bomb into the French Chamber of Deputies, Henry proclaimed that deed "heroism" and defended Henry in a long article in a French publication.[36]

Jean Adam (Koenig stein) Navaho (1859-1892) became a folk hero among anarchists at the end of the 19th century. He had bombed a restaurant, killing and wounding numerous people. He also placed bombs into the homes of French officials, who were held responsible for the brutal beatings of anarchists and who had allowed the police to shoot and kill nine demonstrators during a workers' confrontation with the police. Navaho had also murdered a 93-year-old man in the course of robbing him and had engaged in grave robbery of wealthy deceased. He was executed for these crimes and was then glorified as a martyr to the anarchist cause. A song was composed in his honor and the word ravacholizer came to mean "to revenge" an injustice.[37]

The killing of anarchists for murder led to more murder and more attacks. To revenge the killing of Ravachol, Auguste Vaillant threw a bomb into the French Chamber of Deputies from the visitors' balcony. No one was killed but a number of deputies were injured. Vaillant was convicted and also guillotined.[38]

This led to an explosion in the restaurant Foryot where Vaillant had been arrested. No one was convicted of that bombing. However, in 1948 the historian Alexandre Zevacs claimed that the bomb in that restaurant had been placed there by Paul Delasalle, a well known anarchist at that time. Delasalle's widow denied this claim. Another suspect in that bombing was Felix Feneon, an art critic and employee of the French war ministry. Feneon was well acquainted with the terrorist Henry and other extremists and expressed similar sentiments. Feneon was arrested together with others but was acquitted by a "hung" jury. He subsequently remarked that "propaganda by the deed" had done more for anarchy than all the writings of Peter Kropotkin.[39]

V.

There can be little doubt that Emma Goldman (1869-1940) was the leading advocate of anarchy in the United States during the last part of the 19th century and the first three decades of the twentieth century. Goldman immigrated to the U.S.A. in 1885.[40]

One year later, in 1886, the "Haymarket Riot" influenced Goldman to become an anarchist. The "Haymarket Riot" began with a demonstration in favor of striking workers. In the course of the demonstration someone threw a bomb at police supervising the demonstration. The police fired into the crowd and killed numerous demonstrators and eight police officers. Subsequently four men were hung on conviction for murder, although there was no evidence that these four had thrown the bomb. This injustice infuriated Goldman and others and led to her belief that all government was oppressive and unjust. Therefore she joined the anarchists.[41]

After a brief, unsuccessful marriage leading to an early divorce, Goldman lived many years with a fellow Russian immigrant, Alexander Berkman. She and Berkman plotted to kill Henry Clay Frick in order to revenge the seven steel workers who were killed when they were attacked by Pinkerton detectives during a strike. Frick had hired the detectives so that they could allow strikebreakers to enter the steel plant of which Frick was the manager during Andrew Carnegie's absence. Berkman entered the office of Frick on July 23, 1892 armed with a revolver. He fired at Frick three times. He wounded Frick but did not kill him. Frick and two associates subdued Berkman and he was imprisoned for 14 years. Goldman and Berkman viewed this attempt to assassinate Frick as "propaganda of the deed."[42]

In 1893 the United States suffered a major depression. Unemployment rose to better than twenty percent, leading to huge demonstrations. These demonstrations permitted Goldman to speak to masses of unemployed people. On August 23, 1893, she spoke to 3,000 people in Union Square in New York, telling the unemployed to take action. She shouted: "take everything by force." This speech led to her arrest on charges of incitement to riot. She was convicted and spent ten months in prison. On her release she was greeted by three thousand followers. Subsequently she traveled in Europe and met the anarchists Errico Malatesta and Peter Kropotkin. In 1899 she participated in organizing the International Anarchist Congress.[43]

When President McKinley was assassinated in Buffalo, New York in 1901, his killer, Leon Czolgosz, claimed that he was inspired to murder the president by the speeches of Emma Goldman. That led the police to arrest Goldman and those living with her. She was incarcerated for two weeks while every effort was made to link her to the crime. This did not succeed, as she had nothing to do with the assassination. However, she refused to condemn Czolgosz, for which she was vilified in the press and labeled "the high priestess of anarchy."[44]

Goldman was an outstanding speaker and activist. She illegally distributed information about birth control and used her journal Mother Earth to incite its readers in favor of anarchy. In 1917, she and Berkman were imprisoned for two years for advising men not to register for the draft during the First World War. On their release, Goldman and Berkman were deported to Russia, where they witnessed the Russian revolution. She left Russia because the Communists imposed a dictatorship on the country and prohibited free speech. She moved to England and from there to France and Canada. [45]

Despite the persecution of the German Jews by Hitler and his followers on his accession to power in 1933, Goldman declared that she would not fight Germany, claiming that the democracies were "only fascists in disguise."[46]

In 1934 Goldman was briefly allowed to lecture in the United States but thereafter lived in Canada. She died in Toronto in 1940.

Another American anarchist born in the nineteenth century was Benjamin Tucker (1854-1939). Like all anarchism writers, Tucker was influenced by the works of Proudhon, whose books he translated into English after spending some time in France. He was also acquainted with the works of Herbert Spencer, Lysander Spooner, William Greene and Josiah Warren. Tucker called his own philosophy Anarchistic Socialism, with the aim of "depriving capital of its resources."[47]

In 1882 Tucker had returned to the United States and began to publish a journal he called Liberty. In it he called capitalists thieves and denounced all government. However, he was a Quaker pacifist and never advocated violence, physical force or armed insurrection. He believed in passive resistance, such as the use of strikes and trade on a voluntary basis in opposition to the profit system. He thought that consent of all the governed is anarchism and opposed majority rule, which he viewed as a form of aggression. He believed that cooperation would become voluntary if only the state were abolished and with it compulsory cooperation. He thought that individuals have the right to resign from the state, so that compulsion would end.[48]

According to Tucker, American workers lived in such poor conditions and were so badly exploited because four monopolies, supported by authority, caused these disabilities of the laboring man. These four monopolies, he argued, were: the money monopoly, the land monopoly, tariffs, and patents. Tucker viewed interest and profit as a form of exploitation made possible by the banking monopoly, which was in turn imposed on workers by coercion. He called interest theft; rent a form of robbery, and profit he called plunder. Nevertheless, he defended the right to do wrong as he saw it.[49]

Tucker believed that land should only be owned by those actually using it and not by investors or others who did not work on the land. He also opposed state control of banking and the practice of needing a charter to be allowed into the banking business. He agreed with Marx that laborers do not receive a fair wage compensating them for their work.[50]

Tucker opposed all forms of organization such as labor unions, and also rejected laws imposing a short workday, insurance or pensions. He believed that strikes would finally give the laborer all that he earned and that "labor, which creates all, shall have all." He thought that each man should live on the fruits of his labor and no man should have an income from capital. This, he thought, would result in anarchist workers living in freedom as prosperous individuals. Tucker also believed that protection should be furnished by voluntary associations who would use force only in the name of justice and never protect those who sought to collect rent.[51]

Tucker was an adamant atheist. He was so insistent on this position that shortly before he died in 1939 he called in his French housekeeper and told her to be a witness that on his death bed he did not believe in God.[52]

VI.

Although French anarchists were essentially defeated by the end of the First World War and the terror attacks had come to an end in that country, anarchy became a major German problem in the 1970's with the founding of the Red Army Faction (Die Rote Armee Fraktion). Those who founded this organization in 1970 were once more influenced by the teachings of Proudhon and Bakunin with emphasis on "propaganda by the deed."

Founded by Andreas Baader, Gudrun Ensslin, Horst Mahler and Ulrike Meinhof, the group was held responsible for 38 deaths and innumerable injuries, arson, and destruction of property in its twenty-eight years of activity. The RAF or the Baader-Meinhof gang came into being as a result of the visit of the former Shah of Iran, Mohammad Reza Pahlavi (1919-1980) to Berlin in 1967. The protests against that visit were followed by violence when in 1968 Andreas Baader and Gudrun Ensslin bombed two Berlin department stores.[53]

In fact, the action of the RAF had ended in 1991 with the assassination of Detlev Rohwedder, a German politician assigned to oversee the privatization process in the former East Germany. The group announced its formal dissolution on Hitler's birthday, April 20, 1998.[54]

After 1991, there were two unplanned violent episodes involving members of the RAF. The first was the suicide of Wolfgang Grams at a train station in Bad Kleinen on June 27, 1993. Grams and Birgit Hogefeld spotted a police unit who they suspected were about to arrest them for the murder of Rohwedder. Before shooting himself, Grams had shot and killed one of the police officers. [55]

Horst Ludwig Meyer and his companion, Andrea Klump, both members of the RAF, were discovered in Vienna, Austria on September 15, 1999. Meyer shot at the Austrian police and was killed in the succeeding shootout. Andrea Klump was arrested at the scene and later convicted of several crimes. She was charged with bombing a bus with several Jewish refugees from Russia. The attack, organized and financed by the Palestine Liberation Organization, took place in Budapest, Hungary in 1991.

In 1988 Klump traveled to Spain in the company of Meyer. There she plotted an attack on a hotel in Rota because it housed a contingent of NATO military personnel. They planted a bomb in the hotel which did not explode. Meyer and Klump fled the scene and were not found. Klump had lived in Lebanon from 1984 to 1988, where the Palestine Liberation Organization taught her how to make bombs to be used against American installations in Europe.[56]

The RAF began to attack public installations with the firebombing of two department stores in 1968. Thereafter, the RAF robbed banks, bombed police stations, army barracks and embassies. They took hostages and killed some of them. These killings were sometimes revenge killings to "get even" with the government for jailing some of their RAF comrades. The majority of the abductions and killings were politically motivated and targeted judges, administrators, and industrialists.

The RAF anarchists assaulted German society in the course of three "generations." From 1970-1975 the "first" generation consisted of the founders of the RAF and some thirty "hangers on." These founders, i.e. Baader, Meinhof, Ensslin, and Mahler, were involved in bank robberies, arson, and murder. In April 1975 the German embassy in Stockholm was seized and two of its employees were murdered. One month later, Baader, Ensslin, Meinhof, and an associate, Jan Carl Raspe, were sentenced to life in prison. In 1976 Meinhof killed herself in prison and in 1977 Baader and Ensslin killed themselves in prison. Their followers claimed that they had been murdered by the prison administration.[57]

Another member of the founding group of the RAF was Horst Mahler, who was released from a fourteen -year prison term for arson and bank robbery in 1981. He then joined the National Democratic Party, which was in effect the Nazi party of postwar Germany. This should not be surprising, since all RAF members were committed to anti-Jewish propaganda. The members of the RAF frequently traveled to Arab countries, where they were welcomed by Muslim terrorists.[58]

The suicides of Meinhof, Baader and Ensslin were viewed as murder by the RAF members, who decided to revenge these killings. They therefore began by killing the chief German prosecutor, Siegfried Buback, and two prominent bankers.

Buback was killed by Brigitte Mohnhaupt and Christian Klar. Mohnhaupt was released from prison after serving 24 years and Klar was released in 2008, both having been convicted of the murder of Buback and Buback's driver, Wolfgang Göbel ,as well as Georg Wurster, the head of the driver service.

Buback was killed as he was driven to work. A motorcycle drove alongside his car as the motorcycle passenger fired 15 bullets into Buback's car, killing him and Göbel. In 2007, these murders once more agitated Germans, as it appeared that the actual gunman in these killings was Stefan Wisniewski who was never prosecuted.[59]

Hans Martin Schleyer was assassinated by the RAF on October 18, 1977. An unrepentant Nazi, Schleyer had been a member of the murderous SS (Sturm Staffel) in Hitler's entourage. He was repeatedly promoted to various positions in the Nazi hierarchy. His wife was the daughter of a Nazi official. After the defeat of Germany in 1945, Schleyer was promoted to a number of industrial jobs, including the presidency of the Geman chamber of commerce, and simultaneously, director of the large automobile producer Daimler Benz, executive director of the German employers association, and the Federation of German Industries.

In short, Schleyer profited from his Nazi connections and loudly proclaimed his Nazi views even after Germany had become a so-called democracy. All this angered the members of the RAF, who kidnapped Schleyer on September 5, 1977, a kidnapping organized by Brigitte Mohnhaupt. This was achieved as Schleyer, driven by his chauffeur and surrounded by other cars serving as bodyguards, was stopped at an intersection as a car backed into the street and a baby buggy was pushed in front of his car. His convoy stopped and three men fired their guns at Schleyer, whose driver and one bodyguard were killed. Schleyer was brought to Brussels, where he was killed when it became known that three RAF members had committed suicide in prison.

On Sunday, July 30, 1977, Susan Albrecht and two male companions visited the Ponto mansion in Dresden. Ponto was the chairman of the powerful Dresden bank and well acquainted with Albrecht, whose family were friends. Albrecht's father was a wealthy lawyer. Although the Ponto mansion had all kinds of protection devices, Susanne Albrecht was admitted to the Ponto living room carrying a bunch of roses. The Pontos were leaving for a South American vacation and believed Albrecht meant to say "farewell." Instead she pulled a gun from behind the flowers and shot Jürgen Ponto to death.[60]

Albrecht had been closely associated with various Arab terrorist organizations and participated in distributing anti-Jewish propaganda. She had traveled to Yemen and other Muslim countries, where she was trained in using violence. She was arrested in Frankfurt, Germany in 1991 and sentenced to twelve years in prison but released after six years.[61]

There is good reason to believe that Stefan Wisniewski was also involved in the murder of Bruback. Wisniewski was convicted of murder, arson and kidnapping in a variety of actions in the 1970's and released in 1999. Since then his involvement in the Buback killing is being investigated by the German court.

These three prominent victims of the RAF were by no means the only ones killed. In addition there were at least 34 more killings attributable to the RAF, together with bank robberies, assaults, and bombings. Of the 99 RAF members convicted or sought for various crimes by the German government, 45 were women. This high percentage of female participation in violence does not seem to fit the "normal" level of women's violence. For example, Irmgard Möller, an early member of the Baader-Meinhof gang, killed three people when she drove a car full of explosives into a U.S. army barracks in Heidelberg in 1972. Likewise, Petra Schelm fired her handgun at police who were chasing her. The police fired back and Schelm was killed. She was wanted for bank robbery and for participating in murder. She had been trained in urban warfare at a PLO camp in Jordan. Angela Luther participated in the bombing of a police station in Augsburg and in the bombing of the U.S. army barracks in Heidelberg. Brigitte Mohnhaupt was involved in the murder of Jürgen Ponto and Sieglinde Hofmann participated in the kidnapping and murder of Hanns Martin Schleyer.[62]

The extraordinary involvement of women in the Rote Armee Fraktion may be explained by the social position of women in Germany in the years prior to the 1960's. The mothers of the RAF participants were living under Nazi rule. This meant that even the minor advantages women had attained in the years after the First World War were erased by Nazi doctrine. Accordingly, women were the subjects of men and of the state and had no independent rights whatever. Of course, men too were subject to the violent dictatorship of the Hitler years. However, men could attain high positions in the Nazi hierarchy, which was not possible for women. Women, in Nazi ideology, were mere breeding grounds for the perpetuation of the "master race."

Anarchy and Terrorism

Therefore, when the Nazi regime had been removed, those girls born shortly thereafter sought to liberate themselves from the views of their elders who had been raised or influenced by the rigid ideology concerning women already existing in Germany before the advent of Nazism. Women now demanded some equality. Women demanded the right to an education. Women demanded the right to vote and be elected and some demanded the right to sexual freedom. Amidst these demands there were those who saw the state as repressive and responsible for the perpetuation of gender inequalities. This view was particularly supported by those whose were disgusted by the widespread empowerment of former Nazi officials like Schleyer. Between 1949, when Germany became independent again, and the 1970's, when the RAF was most in evidence, former Nazi tyrants were readmitted to the judiciary as judges and prosecutors, former race theorists were reinstated to the faculties of universities, and a host of Nazi officials ran the government agencies of the new Federal Republic of Germany. It appeared to some that nothing had changed and that force and violence were their only recourse.

On April 20, 1998 the British news agency Reuters received a letter at their Cologne (Köln) office, mailed from Chemnitz. The letter read in part: "Nearly 28 years ago, on May 14, 1970, the RAF was born in a liberation action. Today we end this project. The urban guerilla battle of the RAF is now history."[63]

Italy also suffered a tremendous epidemic of terrorism between 1969 and the end of the 1980's. Like Germany, Italy had been a fascist dictatorship, although by no means as murderous as the Nazi regime. Nevertheless, during the fifteen years ending in 1984, 351 Italians were assassinated and 768 wounded by terrorists.[64]

Israel has been he target of terrorist attacks for over sixty years and the United States became the victim of Arab terror on September 11, 2001. The 21 Arab countries are all dictatorships; democracy or personal liberty are unknown among them. Like Germany and Italy, these repressive regimes breed anger, hatred and resentment which is projected against outsiders as it is too dangerous to express such sentiments inside the Arab world.

In addition, many in the Arab world concern themselves with ancient and medieval history in a manner totally forgotten by the western world except for professional historians. In Arab society there is resentment stemming from the comparison between western achievements and Arab culture lag. While the Christian world was handed a resounding defeat by the Muslim Arabs in 1187, the Christian world surpassed Muslim civilization thereafter and to the present day.[65]

Resentment in the Arab world is focused on the need of all Arab countries to import every scientific device, from television to automobiles from America and western Europe. This resentment is augmented by the fact that the industrial powers are largely dependent on Arab oil. Believing that they can gain political ends through violence, Arab terrorists have murdered private citizens and assaulted military installations as well.

Although the Arab countries earn vast sums from the sale of oil, the income derived from these sources is distributed only to a few dictators and their friends and families and does not reach the population of these countries. The poverty of the average person in Arab countries leads to frustration and anger directed at those outsiders who seem more successful than the local population, who are oppressed by the Arab bosses and dictators.

Religious fundamentalism adds fuel to the fire. This view of the world considers all non-Muslims enemies and teaches its followers that non-Muslims need to be converted to "the truth". Since the over 2 billion Christians in this world are unlikely to accept such conversion, many Muslims resort to force to impress their intended targets of the truth of their cause. All of these resentments are particularly aimed at the mere 13 million Jews who, because of their small number, seem easily slaughtered by so overwhelming a majority of Arabs and Muslims.

Those who seek to carry out violent attacks against the "unbelievers" are almost always young men between the ages of 22 and 34. This was also true of those who carried out the atrocities in Germany and Italy in the 1970's.[66]

The relationship between violent behavior and age is not restricted to the terrorists from Arab countries. In the United States, 65 percent of violent crime is committed by young men in the age group 15 to 35. [67]

Muslim countries routinely teach their schoolchildren hatred for the United States and western civilization. Since these countries have high birth rates, their population is and will continue to be relatively young so that males in the crime prone ages will be plentiful. In these countries, the growth rate for the population is about 2.82%, as compared to 0.16% in developed countries. It can therefore be expected that terrorism stemming from Muslim sources will not abate soon.[68]

Because the demographics guarantee continued terrorism aimed at the United States, it is in the interest of the U.S.A. to become oil independent and either exploit American resources in Alaska and elsewhere or to promote the use of atomic energy, which has been so successful in France and other industrialized nations.

VII.

Anarchy and terror have been constant companions of human existence for centuries. In the 19th, 20th and 21st centuries, these social movements have become more prominent, even if not more effective than heretofore. While anarchy, the proclaimed wish to end all government, has failed and has mostly disappeared from Europe where it was strongest, terrorism has taken its place. Usually, ter-

rorism is defined as an attack on uninvolved civilians for political gain. It is assumed by the media and the public generally that terrorists have specific political aims and that their terror attacks would cease once their aims are realized.
The evidence is otherwise, in that sociologists have shown that terrorism and
anarchy have quite different roots than the proclaimed political goals of their
votaries.[69]

The history of anarchy and terrorism plainly shows that these destructive
organizations rarely, if ever, attain their goals by killing uninvolved civilians. In
fact, terrorism is a fundamental failure, as the terrorists have really not been able
to translate their violence into real success. Terrorist attacks may kill people, but
they do not achieve political advantages or political power. The fact is that not
one terrorist organization has achieved its political aims by attacking civilians.[70]

Terrorists like to claim that they are using terror tactics as a last resort
against oppressive governments. The fact is that the most oppressive governments do not suffer terrorism. Terrorism and anarchy are found almost entirely
in democracies like Germany and Italy or in "benevolent" dictatorships. In these
countries there are constitutionally protected peaceful means of protest, which
the terrorists refuse to use.[71]

Terrorist organizations usually make extreme demands and an absolute refusal to compromise. They usually derail all negotiations by increasing attacks
just when some solution to the conflict appears to get results. These terrorist
organizations often support the same aims as normal political parties, but use
bombs just the same. They seldom participate in negotiations. An example was
the exceptional amount of terror committed by the so-called Al Aqsa Martyrs at
the very time when the then prime minister of Israel, Ehud Barak, conceded the
entire Gaza and West Bank territories to them.[72]

Terrorist organizations usually change their announced objectives in order
to stay "in business." This is best illustrated by the manner in which "al-Qaida"
changed its objectives again and again. First they fought the occupation of Afghanistan by the Russians. Then they targeted the fighting in Bosnia. Thereafter
they attacked Christians in the Philippines, then in Russia, thereafter in Spain
and in Muslim countries and finally, on September 11, 2001, they attacked the
United States. Evidently, Osama bin Laden needs new enemies all the time in
order to justify mastery of his terrorist movement.[73]

This shift in terrorist targets can be illustrated again and again among terrorist groups in Arab countries, in South America, in France and in Germany.

It is also remarkable that the majority of terrorist attacks have been carried
out by unknown perpetrators. These anonymous attacks come from people who
ask for nothing and who make no demands. The terrorists who attacked the
World Trade Center and the Pentagon and sought also to attack the White House
on September 11, 2001 did not make any prior demands. No effort was made to
coerce anyone or to proclaim some terrorist goal.

Terrorists often attack other terrorists. Instead of fighting for the common cause, terrorists groups seek to destroy each other. This is illustrated by the fighting between various factions of the Arab terrorists in Israel, the infighting between the Marxist groups in Argentina and the fratricide in Chechnya.[74]

Terrorist organizations usually persist long after it has become evident that they cannot win and that they cannot advance their "cause." Other terrorist organizations continue even after they did in fact achieve their announced goals. It is for this reason that terrorist organizations will invent new rationales for terrorism even when the former reasons have been rendered moot. This then indicates that terrorist organizations are much more interested in violence, killing, and bombing than in any particular cause. Succinctly, terrorists want to remain terrorists, with or without a cause, since it is the terror itself that attracts its members, not the announced reasons for the attacks on civilians.[75]

Therefore observers of the terrorist "scene" conclude that those who engage in terrorist acts, be they motivated by so called "anarchy" objectives or other "causes," are much more interested in participating in terrorist organizations for social and personal reasons than for the political causes announced in the media. Strong, affective ties with other terrorist members are the driving force behind these groups. Terrorist organizations furnish their members with the same sense of belonging as religious organizations, who usually speak of a sense of "communion" or solidarity as the terrorists participate in actions which allow them to belong to a reference group that approves of them and their actions.[76]

There is considerable evidence that the greatest number of those who engage in terrorist behavior have been socially isolated and feel rejected, lonely, and without purpose until they join a terrorist organization. Their purpose is to achieve social solidarity rather than to attain any political objective.

SUMMARY

Between 1894 and 1910 six European heads of state were assassinated. These and a number of additional murders were the product of the anarchist movement as proclaimed by the French author Proudhon and the Russian writers Bakunin and Kropotkin. Seeking a stateless society, they encouraged "propaganda by the deed," meaning assassinations of government officials. These writers were also the forerunners of the Jewish genocide of the 1930's and 1940's.

Influenced by the works of Proudhon, Bakunin, and Kropotkin, the Italian Malatesta and the French anarchists Henry, Ravachol and Vaillant threw bombs into restaurants and the Chamber of Deputies in Paris.

In the United States, the leading anarchists, Emma Goldman and Benjamin Tucker, held fiery speeches and issued tabloids intended to rouse the population to anarchy without success.

In Germany the Red Army Faction murdered prominent bankers and industrialists and similar groups did so in Italy. An exceptional number of women were involved in this violence. The German terrorists were closely associated with the Arab terrorists whose membership is mostly drawn from disaffected and isolated young adults seeking companionship and a cause giving them a reason to exist.

NOTES

1. Neville Bolt and Jaz Azari, *Propaganda of the Deed*, (London: The Royal United Services Institute, 2008).

2. Bernard Lewis, *Semites and Anti-semites*, New York: Norton, (1984), 111.

3. K. Steven Vincent, *Pierre Joseph Proudhon and the Rise of Prench Republican Socialism*, (Oxford: Oxford University Press, 1984), 60.

4. Pierre Joseph Proudhon, *What Is Property?* (New York: Dover Publications, 1970), 277.

5. Ibid, 330.

6. Vincent, *Pierre Joseph Proudhoun*, 127-163.

7. Ibid, 148.

8. Pierre Joseph Proudhon, *System of Economic Contradiction*, (Boston: Benjamin R. Tucker, 1888).

9. Henry Cohen, Editor, *Proudhon's Solution to the Social Problem*, (New York: Vanguard Press, 1927), 45.

10. Pierre Joseph Proudhon, *The General Idea of the Revolution in the Nineteenth Century*, (New York: The Pluto Press, 1989), 294.

11. Max Nomad, *Apostles of Revolution*, (Boston: Little Brown, 1939), 15.

12. Evgenii Lampert, *Studies in Rebellion*, London, F. A. Preager, Publishers, 1957), 118.

13. Eugene Pyziur, *The Philosophy of Anarchism of M.A. Bakunin*, Milwaukee, Marquette University Press, 1955), 1.

14. Eldrige Cleaver, *Soul on Ice*, (London: Cape Publishers, 1969).

15. George Woodcock, *Anarchism*, (Cleveland, World Publishing Co, 1962), 155.

16. Paul Avrich, *The Russian Anarchists*, (Princeton: The University of Princeton Press, 1967), 129.

17. G.P. Maximoff, *The Political Philosophy of Bakunin: Scientific Anarchism.* (Glencoe, Ill. Free Press, 1953), 304.

18. Gerhard Falk, *The Jew in Christian Theology*, (Jefferson, NC and London: McFarland & Co, 1992).

19. Rudolf Pfisterer, *Im Schatten des Kreuzes*, (Hamburg: Evangelischer Verlag, 1966), 72.

20. George R. Whyte, *The Dreyfus Affair: A Chronological History*, (Basingstoke, England Basingstoke Books, 2008), 331.

21. George Lichtheim, "Socialism and the Jews," *Dissent*, (July-August, 1968), 322.

22. Maurice Samuel, *Blood Accusation: The Strange History of the Beilis Case*, (New York: Alfred A. Knopf, 1966).

23. Rudolf Rocker, *Nationalism and Culture,* (Los Angeles: Rocker Publication Committee, 1937), 200-201.

24. Geoffrey Wigoder, ed., *The New Standard Jewish Encyclopedia,* (New York: Facts on File, 1992), 561.

25. Hillel Solotaroff, "Moments in the national and territorial revival of the Jewish People," *Das Volk* or *The People,* (December 15, 1907)

26. Peter Brown, *The Rise of Christendom,* (Oxford; Oxford-Blackwell Publishers, 2003), 61.

27. Martin A. Miller, *Selected Writings on Anarchism and Revolution,* (Cambridge: MIT Press, 1970), 46-47.

28. Peter Kropotkin, *Memoirs of a Revolutionary,* (New York: Dover Publications, 1971), 398-399.

29. Miller, *Selected Writings,* 189.

30. Roger N. Baldwin, *Kropotkin's Revolutionary Pamphlets,* (New York: Dover Publications, 1977), 71.

31. Crappuillot, Special number, *Anarchy,* (January 1938), 15.

32. Butz Peters, *Tödlicher Irrtum,* (Berlin, Argon Verlag, 2004).

33. Emma Goldman, *Living My Life,* Vol.1, (London: Ptuto Press, 1987), 87.

34. Max Nettlau, *Errico Malatesta,: The Biography of an Anarchist,* (New York: Jewish Anarchist Federation, 1924), 1-96.

35. No author, "Johann Most Dead After Brief Illness," *The New York Times,* (March 18, 1906), 11.

36. No author, "The Guillotine's Sure Work: Details of the Execution of Vaillant the Anarchist," *The New York Times,* (February 6, 1894), 1

37. Howard G. Lay, *"Beau Geste!* (On the Readability of Terrorism) *Yale French Studies,* no. 101, (2001), 87.

38. No author, "The Guillotine's Sure Work," 5.

39. John Rewald, "Extracts of an Unedited Journal by Paul Signac," *Gazette des Beaux Arts,* vol. 6. no.36, (December 1949), 113.

40. Alice Wexler, *Emma Goldman: an Intimate Life,* (New York: Pantheon Books, 1984), 13.

41. Emma Goldman, *Living My Life,* (New York: Alfred Knopf, Publishers, 1931), 24.

42. No author, "Chairman Frick Shot," *The New York Times,* (July 24, 1892), 1.

43. Wexler, *Emma Goldman,* 84-89.

44. Candace Falk, *Emma Goldman: A Documentary History of the American Years,* (Urbana: The University of Illinois Press, 2008), 461.

45. John C. Chalberg, *Emma Goldman: American Individualist,* (New York: Pearson Longman), 46.

46. Alice Wexler: *Emma Goldman in Exile,* (Boston: Beacon Press, 1989), 236.

47. Benjamin R. Tucker, *Instead of a Book, by a Man Too Busy to Write One; a Fragmentary Exposition.* (New York, Arno Press, 1972), 404.

48. Victor S Yarros, "Philosophical Anarchism: Its Rise, Decline and Eclipse," *The American Journal of Sociology,* vol. 41, no.4, (January 1936), 470-483.

49. Benjamin R. Tucker, "Rights and Individual Rights," *Liberty,* (January 7, 1882), 3.

50. Benjamin R. Tucker, "Solutions to the Labor Problem," *Instead of a Book,* 475.

51. Martin Blatt, *Benjamin R. Tucker and the Champions of Liberty,* (St. Paul and New York, 1986), 299.

52. Paul Avrich, "Oriole Tucker Richè'" *Anarchist Voices,* (Princeton, NJ: Princeton University Press, 1996), 11.

53. Diego Gambetta, "Heroic Impatience," *The Nation,* (March 22, 2010), 25.

54. Karl Ellerbrock, "Detlev Rohwedder," In: *Neue Deutsche Biographie,* (Berlin, Germany, Duncker & Humboldt, 2005), vol. 22, 7.

55. Butz Peters, *Tődlicher Irrtum,* (Frankfurt am Main, Germany, Fisher Publishers, 2007), 694-701.

56. Kirsten Grieshaber, "World Briefing: Europe-Germany: Sentencing in 1991 Attack on Jews," *The New York Times,* (September 29, 2004), A 11.

57. Paige W. Eager, *From Fighters to Terrorists: Women and Political Violence,* (London: Ashgate Publishing (2008), 54-55.

58. J. Smith and Andre Moncourt, *The Red Army Faction: A Documentary History,* (Oakland, CA PM Press, 2009), 616.

59. Der Spiegel Staff, "Germany Revisits RAF Terrorism Verdict," *Der Spiegel,* (April 23, 2007), 1.

60. No author, " The Brutal Murder of an Old Friend Makes Her the Dark Queen of Terrorism, " *People,* vol.8, no.26, (December 26, 1977) :1.

61. No author, "German Terrorist Sentenced for '77 Killing," *The New York Times,* (June 4, 1991),A8.

62. J. Smith and Andre Moncourt, *The Red Army Faction: A Documentary History,* (Oakland, CA: PM Press, 2009), 325-612.

63. Diego Gambetta, "Heroic Impatience," *The Nation,* (March 22, 2010), 25.

64. Richard Drake, "The Red and the Black: Terrorism in Contemporary Italy," *International Political Science Review,* vol.5, no.3, (1984) :279.

65. Norman Housley, *Contesting the Crusades,* (Malden, MA: Blackwell Publishers, 2006), 42.

66. A. Merari, "The Readiness to Kill and Die: Suicide Terrorism in the Middle East," In: William Reich, Editor, *Origins of Terrorism,* New York: Cambridge University Press, (1990), 192-207.

67. No author, "Trends in Violent Victimization by Age," (Washington DC: U.S. Department of Justice, Bureau of Justice Statistics, 2008).

68. Population Reference Bureau, *World Population Data Sheet,* (Washington DC, 2009).

69. Alexander Wendt, "Anarchy is What States Make of It: The Social Construction of Power Politics," *International Organization,* vol. 46, no.2, (Spring 1992), 391-425.

70. Robert Pape, *Dying to Win,* (New York: Random House, 2006)

71. Paul Wilkinson, *Terrorism Versus Democracy: The Liberal State Response,* (London: Frank Cass, Publishers, 2000), 59.

72. Robert Malley, "Israel and the Arafat Question," *New York Review of Books,* vol. 51, no.15, (October 7, 2004), 19-23.

73. Jessica Stern, "The Protean Enemy," *Foreign Affairs,* vol.82, no. 4, (July-August 2003), 1.

74. Peter H. Merkl, "Approaches to the Study of Political Violence," In: Peter H. Merkl, *Political Violence and Terror,* (Berkeley: University of California Press, 1986), 45.

75. Martha Crenshaw, "The Causes of Terrorism," *Comparative Politics,* vol. 13, no.4, (July 1981), 397.

76. Chester I. Barnard, *The Functions of the Executive,* (Cambridge, MA, Harvard University Press, 1938), 145-146.

.

Chapter Seven
American Terrorism

TERROR COMES HOME

Europe and the Middle East are not the only areas of the world subject to domestic and international terrorism. Beginning with the Ludlow Massacre, the United States has also been the target of terrorists motivated by a variety of causes. Included in some of these causes which motivate some Americans to use violence are the Animal Liberation Front, the Army of God, the Black Liberation Army, the Earth Liberation Front, the Ku Klux Klan, the Symbionese Liberation Army, and the Weathermen. All of these groups and many more claim to liberate something or someone by killing, burning, assaulting, or maiming those viewed as an obstacle to the goals the group seeks to achieve. The terrorists are not always private citizens. Government can also sponsor terror against its own citizens, as illustrated by the Ludlow Massacre of April 20, 1914, in which the Colorado militia and private "security" guards killed 19 people.[1]

The Haymarket Riot

The Chicago Haymarket riot and the killing of ten men as well as the wounding of scores of others became one of the most tragic events in American history. Indeed, the deaths of ten citizens seems minuscule to 21st century Americans, who have seen nearly three-thousand murdered on September 11, 2001. In 1886, however, the events of May Day, May 1, of that year seemed enormous. On that day about 50,000 union members working for the McCormick Harvester Company and other employers gathered at the Haymarket at Randolph and Desplaines Streets. The union members protested the killing of strikers by company guards. They also demanded that employers agree to the eight hour work day. Although the gathering was peaceful while a number of speakers harangued the crowd, the Chicago police suddenly attacked. In the course of this melee, a bomb was thrown by an unknown person, leading to the deaths of three union-ists and seven police.[2]

Although the bomb thrower was never identified, the Chicago police rounded up eight anarchist and/or socialist speakers and writers. The eight were charged with murder by the district attorney, not because they had thrown a bomb or murdered anyone directly, but because their speeches and writings were held the root cause of the bombing. In fact, two of the defendants were not at the Haymarket on that day. Nevertheless, all were convicted and seven, August Spies, Michael Schwab, Louis Lingg, Albert Parsons, George Engel, Adolph Fischer, and Samuel Fielden, were hanged for what they said. Indeed, this was a judicial assault on freedom of speech and a direct effort to abolish the first amendment of the U.S. Constitution.[3]

The Ludlow Massacre

The Ludlow Massacre was the outcome of the Colorado coal strike, which be-gan in 1913 and continued into the next year, lasting fourteen months. Although the miners lost the strike at that time, that strike and its aftermath was a major event in the eventual victory of American unions during the Franklin Roosevelt administration twenty years later.[4]

The center of the strike was the "Blood of Christ" mountains in southern Colorado, where bituminous or soft coal was mined for the steel industry for use in producing rails at a time when railroads were expanding into the west. Only three large companies dominated the mining operations. The largest of these was the Colorado Fuel and Iron Co., owned by the Rockefeller family. Because about ten percent of Colorado families depended on this employer, and because almost everyone in two counties was so employed, that company had tremen-dous political power in the state. Therefore coroners' juries almost always ab-solved the mine owners of the numerous deaths their unsafe mines produced every year.[5]

The miners who worked in the canyons near the coal mines also lived in company towns located near the mines. They bought food and equipment at company stores and drank at company owned saloons. Doctors, clergy, teachers, and law enforcers were all employees of the coal companies and the workforce were almost all immigrants from eastern and southern Europe, especially Greece, who knew little English.[6]

In September of 1913, the United Mine Workers announced a strike when the mine owners refused to meet seven demands by the union. These demands were the recognition of the union as collective bargaining agent, an eight hour work day, payment for all work, not just the amount of coal produced, miners to check the scales that weighed the coal they produced because they were being cheated by the mine owners, the right to buy in non-company stores, the right to chose their own doctors, and abolition of the company guard system.[7]

The mine owners met these demands by evicting the ten to twelve thousand strikers and their families from company owned homes, so that the miners and their families were forced to move into tents set up in advance by the union. The operators then brought in a detective agency that had specialized in breaking strikes in West Virginia. The agents of this detective group shone high powered lights on the tent city all night, they fired machine guns at the workers and their families, and beat and murdered a number of members. The purpose was to goad the miners into violent action so the governor would call out the National Guard and make the strike a state government issue so the taxpayers would have to bear the costs. This succeeded, in that the militia declared martial law, suspended all civil rights, jailed thousands of miners including their wives and children, and beat and assaulted the prisoners. Then, on April 20, 1914, the militia sprayed the tent city with gunfire. The people in the tent city fled and the militia burned the tents and looted the possessions left behind. The leader of the tent city, Louis Tikes, was captured and killed. The shooting led to the deaths of 25 people, including twelve children. During the shooting some women and children hid in a pit under one of the tents. They all suffocated when the tent was burned.[8]

After this massacre the miners in Colorado attacked and destroyed mines. The federal government then intervened and the strike ended seven months later. Thereafter, mass arrests were made of the miners. These men were indicted but never tried, as Rockefeller, who owned the mines, wanted the miners to return to their jobs. There are those who claim that conditions in the mines improved as a result of that violence.[9]

On June 5, 2005, the United Mine Workers dedicated a monument at Ludlow to the memory of those who died there.

The Bombing of the Los Angeles Times

On October 10, 1910, the Los Angeles Times building was bombed, killing 21 employees and injuring 100 more. Brothers John and James McNamara were convicted shortly thereafter of setting the explosives. James was sentenced to life in prison after confessing that he had set the bomb. John was sentenced to 15 years for bombing a local iron manufacturing plant.[10]

The bombs were expected to explode at 4:00 a.m., when it was thought that no one would be in the building. Instead the bomb went off at 1:07 a.m., when the building was still occupied. Furthermore, the gas lines under the building were destroyed; causing a fire that killed some of the victims. The next morning several unexploded bombs were found at the homes of the owner of the Los Angeles Times and at the County Hall of Records.[11]

The bombing was called "the crime of the century" by the media, who also denounced unions in general and pictured organized labor as a gang of anarchists and thugs. Indeed, the McNamara brothers, both Irish immigrants, were trade unionists and were both active in the International Association of Bridge and Structural Iron Workers. That association was opposed by the National Erectors' Association, a group of employers whose purpose was to "break" the union by using labor spies, private detective agencies, and strikebreakers. State and local government supported the employers and cooperated in campaigns designed to disband the unions by means of arrests and imprisonments. Violence against union members was also common, leading to a strike in 1906 whose purpose was the retention of their contract. Instead, the employers drove almost all union members out of their plants except for the iron workers at American Bridge, a subsidiary of United States Steel.[12]

The union then turned to violence in retaliation for the violence employed by the plant owners. This consisted of a dynamiting campaign beginning in 1906, with a view of forcing employers to participate in collective bargaining. The violence was not designed to damage factories or kill people. The iron workers blew up parts of 110 iron works without causing major damage.[13]

Employers in the Los Angeles area were determined to prevent unionization among their employees and for that purpose formed the Merchants and Manufacturers Association. Headed by the owner of the Los Angeles Times, Harrison Gray Otis, the association defamed the unions. The Times published endless anti-union material and succeeded in the course of twenty years to rid almost all employers of union members. As a result, wages were lowered, as there was no one to defend the workers. The employers sought to have all employment in California follow an "open shop" arrangement, which undermined the unions ipso facto.[14]

In San Francisco, iron workers struck on June 1, 1910 in an effort to win a $0.50 an hour minimum wage. (Equivalent to $10.50 an hour in 2010). Refusing to pay $0.50 an hour, the Merchants and Manufacturers Association raised $350,000 ($7.5 million as of 2010) to break the strike. A judge issued a number of injunctions prohibiting the strike and "speaking in a loud tone in the public streets." Failing to obey these injunctions led to the arrest of 472 striking iron workers. The strike increased the membership of the iron workers' union temporarily by sixty percent.[15]

Nevertheless, the bombing led to the decimation of the union and the ascendancy of the employers, so that no union was able to gain any membership or political power in California until the 1950's. Nonetheless, the brutal treatment of the iron workers by the employers contributed to the recognition of union demands during the Franklin Roosevelt administration in the 1930's and the passage of the National Labor Relations Act of 1935.

The Wall Street Bomb

Until the Oklahoma City bombing in 1995, the bombing of Wall Street on September 16, 1920 was the worst case of terrorism in the United States history. Although the bombing was never solved in the sense of holding anyone responsible, it is likely that the attack was provoked by the speeches and publications of anarchists such as Goldman and Most. The bomb went off on the street at noon and killed thirty-eight people while maiming hundreds more.[16]

That bombing was unusually cruel. The bomb consisted of dynamite tied to iron weights which acted like shrapnel. As a result people who walked out of nearby buildings were blown apart. Some were beheaded while others lost arms and legs, hands and feet or their scalps. Many pedestrians were engulfed in flames. Other injuries were caused by broken glass and yet others were killed or wounded by the stampede that followed the bombing.[17]

The explosive had been left in a horse drawn wagon across the street from the J.P. Morgan bank. The Morgan bank had frequently been attacked by anarchists and others as an oppressor and warmonger because it lent money to the allies during the First World War. Because the Morgan bank building had thick walls, hardly anyone inside was injured, so that all came back to work the next day. As in most terrorist attacks, the victims were innocent bystanders. The victims were not wealthy bankers, but clerks, bookkeepers, delivery boys, messengers, stenographers, and drivers. These were mostly very young people. Only seven of the 38 dead were over age forty. Five women died alongside four teenagers.[18]

The Morgan bank building stood at the northeast corner of Wall Street and Broadway at the very place where George Washington had been inaugurated and the U.S. Congress met for the first time. The building in which these events occurred had been demolished and a U.S. customs house replaced it, later used as a U.S. Treasury building housing the tax collectors.[19]

This bombing was viewed by the media, at that time only newspapers, as "an act of diabolism unparalleled in the annals of terrorism." The media further speculated that the growing power of "Wall Street" precipitated the attack. The bombing was seen as an attack on capitalism. In addition, this act of terrorism led to the definition of terrorism as a form of political violence designed to induce fear and thus destabilize the social order.[20]

There were also those who believed that the Wall Street bombing was the work of Luigi Galleani (1861-1931), an Italian immigrant who preached anarchy in New York and New Jersey after his arrival in the United States in 1901. He published an anarchist newspaper for fifteen years until the government shut it down in 1918 under the Sedition Act. He also published a bomb-making manual. Followers of Galleani set off bombs, which seldom killed the intended targets such as police chiefs and mayors, but instead killed innocent and uninvolved people who happened to be in the bomb's neighborhood. In June 1919, Galleani was deported to Italy. No evidence that he had committed a crime was available, although he was widely suspected of having bombed a number of sites.[21]

Terrorism became feasible for almost anyone after the invention of dynamite in 1866, because dynamite made it possible to cause mass destruction without being present. At the same time, anarchists and communists began spreading their ideas in speeches and newspapers to the effect that capitalism should be overthrown and a more egalitarian society replace it. It appeared at the beginning of the 20th century that assassination and other violence were the inevitable outcome of class distinctions in America and elsewhere.[22]

No one was ever held responsible for this atrocity, so that there was never an arrest, trial, or conviction concerning this crime. No doubt the bombing was associated with the industrial warfare then so common. As time went by, this dreadful bombing was forgotten, except by some professional historians who know about the brutal exploitation of the workers in the nineteenth century and the early twentieth century. The nineteenth century saw innumerable labor strikes and conflicts between management, supported by government, and opposing the laborers, who were mostly European immigrants. These workers attempted to improve their lot by unionizing, but were met with violent force including shootings, lynchings, clubbings and jailings.[23]

It is of interest that the Wall Street explosion has been forgotten by Americans and that millions believe that the attack on the World Trade Center or the bombing of the Oklahoma office building were unique and unprecedented. The fact is that American history is full of terrorism in various forms and that failure to remember these attacks also leads to failure to guard against such deeds in the future.

Between 1910 and 1978 a number of minor terrorist attacks continued to plague the United States. The entrance of the United States into the First World War ended almost all of the anarchist agitation, which had been responsible for much of the terrorism of the previous forty years. The legitimization of the labor movement during the New Deal administration of Franklin D. Roosevelt and the passage of the National Labor Relations Act in 1935 reduced labor-employer violence to a minimum. The Second World War, and the major gains of organized labor thereafter, eliminated violence caused by labor-employer disputes almost entirely. Nevertheless, terrorism continued in the United States, fueled by other issues.

The Unabomber

Theodore John Kaczynski, born in Chicago in 1942, was a child "prodigy" or exceptionally talented child. He excelled at a very young age and was therefore accepted as a student at Harvard University when only sixteen. He later earned a Ph.D. in mathematics at the University of Michigan and became an assistant professor of mathematics at the University of California at age 25. In 1969, he resigned his position, and two years later he moved into a cabin near Lincoln, Nebraska. There he had no running water and no electricity. He lived a reclusive life, using "survival skills" to maintain himself.[24]

Then, beginning in 1978, Kaczynski sent 16 bombs through the mails to widely scattered targets in the United States, killing three people. He also injured twenty-three others who were either scientists, or someone working for them, or airline employees. He was labeled the "unabomber" on the grounds that his bombs were sent to universities or airlines.

Among Kaczynski's victims were Patrick Fischer, computer scientist at Vanderbilt University, LeRoy Bearnson, electrical engineering professor at Brigham Young University, Percy A. Wood, president of United Airlines, Gil Murray, president of the California Forestry Association, and the New York public relations executive Thomas Mosser.[25]

Kaczynski also sent a bomb to a professor at the University of Chicago who was absent at that time. The package addressed to him was then "returned" to a professor at Northwestern University whose return address was on the package. Suspecting trouble, the "sender" gave the package to the police, who discovered a pipe bomb inside. Other bombs were sent to the University of California at Berkeley where Kaczynski had taught briefly. These packages were not addressed to anyone but nevertheless injured Diogenes Angelakos and John Hauser, both California scientists Angelakos was an electrical engineering professor. He picked up what he thought was a turpentine can left behind by a construction worker, when it exploded, injuring his hand. On May 15, 1985, John Hauser, a graduate engineering student and Air Force pilot, picked up a file box in an engineering laboratory. The "box" exploded and destroyed four fingers of his right hand and injured his arm. He could never pilot a plane again and has permanent damage to his arm.[26]

James V. McConnell, a psychology professor at the University of Michigan, was next to feel Kaczynski's wrath. McConnell was unusually successful in that he wrote a book entitled *Understanding Human Behavior,* which sold more than a million copies and earned the author $250,000 a year. On November 15, 1985, McConnell's assistant Nicklaus Suino opened a package addressed to McConnell when it exploded, injuring both men. Hugh Scrutton was 32 years old, when he died as he picked up a package left outside his computer store in Sacramento. The package exploded, killing him.

Here is a timeline concerning Theodore Kaczynski's life and activities:

•22 May 1942-Ted Kaczynski b•orn, Evergreen Park, near Chicago IL.

•c. 1960-Ted Kaczynski volunteers for psychological experiments of Dr. Henry Murray, former OSS official. This is likely MKULTRA.

•1967-PhD, Mathematics, University of Michigan.

•1969-Resigns from the faculty of the University of California, Berkeley.

•1971-Ted and brother David purchase 1.4 acres near Lincoln, Montana.

•25 May 1978-A package is found in a parking lot at the University of Illinois in Chicago and is taken to Northwestern University in Evanston because of the return address. It explodes when it is opened on May 26, injuring Terry Marker, a security guard.

•9 May 1979-Graduate student John Harris is injured by a bomb at Northwestern University.

•15 Nov 1979-Twelve people suffer smoke inhalation when a bomb explodes in a 727's cargo hold during an American Airlines flight, forcing an emergency landing at Dulles International Airport near Washington

•1980-About this time, the FBI determines that these package-bombing attacks are the work of one person. Their code-name for the case is UNABOM: UN stands for "university," A for "airline," and BOM for the obvious. Once the media starts hearing this code-name, the spelling gets corrupted variously into Unabomer, Unabomber, and Unabomber.

•10 Jun 1980-United Airlines President Percy Wood is injured at his home in the Chicago area.

•8 Oct 1981-A bomb is found in a business classroom at the University of Utah in Salt Lake City. No one is injured.

•5 May 1982-Janet Smith, a secretary, is injured by a bomb at Vanderbilt University in Nashville. The package was addressed to computer science Professor Patrick Fischer.

•2 Jul 1982-Diogenes Angelakos, a professor of electrical engineering and computer science, is injured in a faculty lounge at the University of California at Berkeley.

•15 May 1985-Graduate student John Hauser is injured by a bomb in a computer lab at the University of California at Berkeley.

•13 Jun 1985-A package-bomb mailed to Boeing Co. in Auburn, WA, on 8 May is discovered and disarmed.

•15 Nov 1985-A package-bomb mailed to University of Michigan psychology Professor James McConnell injures his assistant, Nicklaus Suino. McConnell, standing nearby in his Ann Arbor home, isn't hurt.

•11 Dec 1985-Hugh Scrutton, 38, is killed by a bomb near his computer rental store in Sacramento.

•20 Feb 1987-Gary Wright is injured by a bomb left behind a computer store in Salt Lake City, UT.

•22 Jun 1993-Charles Epstein, a geneticist at UC San Francisco is injured by a bomb sent to his home.

•24 Jun 1993-Computer scientist David Gelernter of Yale University in New Haven, CT, is injured in an office.

•30 Dec 1993-The FBI sets up its first web site, devoted to catching the UNABOM assailant. At this point, the FBI has no server of its own, so a NASA computer in Moffett Field, CA, is volunteered for hosting. On 7 May 1995, NASA takes down the UNABOM site, citing safety concerns for NASA employees.

•10 Dec 1994-Advertising executive Thomas Mosser, 50, is killed by a bomb sent to his home in North Caldwell, NJ.

•24 Apr 1995-California Forestry Association President Gilbert Murray, 47, is killed opening a mail bomb in the group's Sacramento headquarters.

•24 Jun 1995-Letters containing the Unabomber's manifesto are mailed to the New York Times, the Washington Post, and Penthouse publisher Bob Guccione.

•24 Jun 1995-An airliner threat is mailed to the San Francisco Chronicle.

•Jul 1995-"There's an intriguing passage that references the Internet. This only confirms my suspicion that the Unabomber not only is knowledgeable about the Net but that he almost certainly traffics on it as well. He is drawn toward the very technology he hates." - Brock M. Meeks, Internet Pundit

•4 Aug 1995-From the Sacramento Bee: "It's clear that the writer has thought about a lot of things and read a lot of things, but I don't see much specifically related to the scholarly discipline of the history of science," said Jack Lesch, an associate professor at UC Berkeley (The Unabomber's Previous Employer as a Faculty Member) who is an expert in the field. "It's conceivable that he took a course or sat in on one, but it's also conceivable that he didn't." Later in the same article: "David Hollinger, a history professor at UC Berkeley, agreed that the bomber's manifesto does not suggest a formal university education."

•19 Sep 1995-The full text of the Unabomber Manifesto, entitled "Industrial Society and its Future," is published in the Washington Post. It clocks in at over 35,000 words, and comes in a special pullout section. The New York Times and the Post split the cost of publishing the manifesto.

•3 Apr 1996-Theodore John Kaczynski, 53, is taken into custody by federal agents.

•5 Apr 1996-Kaczynski is charged with possessing bomb-making materials and held without bail.

•30 Apr 1996-Kaczynski appeals to the Supreme Court to be released due to government leaks.

•18 Jun 1996-Kaczynski indicted in Unabomber attacks.

•7 Jan 1998-Kaczynski attempts to commit suicide by hanging himself with his underwear in the Sacramento County Jail.

•18 Mar 2002-Supreme Court rejects, without comment or dissent, an appeal by Kaczynski for a new trial, based on his being forced to plead guilty to prevent his lawyers from using his mental condition as a defense, and preventing him from representing himself.

The above timeline shows that it took the F.B.I seventeen years to finally apprehend Kaczynski, not because they succeeded in their numerous investigations but because Ted's brother, David, "ratted him out." David Kaczynski collected one million dollars for his identification of his brother as the "Unabomber."

In September 1995, the New York Times and the Washington Post published a Manifesto" by Kaczynski, explaining his actions and denouncing technology and its consequences.

The Bombing of the Oklahoma City Federal Office Building

At 9:02 a.m. on April 19, 1995, a tremendous roar shook the Alfred P. Murrah Federal Office Building in Oklahoma City. Then the building collapsed, killing 168 people, including children in a day care area for pre-school children of Federal employees working there. The bomb had been packed in a vehicle left outside the building. The explosion left a 20 foot wide, 8- foot deep crater in the street. It was later determined that the bomb was made of ammonium nitrate and weighed between 1,000 and 1,200 pounds.[27]

Shortly after the bomb had wrecked the federal building, Timothy McVeigh was arrested in Perry, Oklahoma, by a state trooper for driving without a license plate. His name was run through the National Crime Information Center, a computerized information system supplied by the F.B.I. He was about to be released when the F.B.I. telephoned to ask McVeigh be held on suspicion of having bombed the Murrah building.[28]

This bombing occurred on the second anniversary of the assault by federal agents on the Branch Dravidian compound in Waco, Texas that led to the deaths of over eighty people, including children.

That assault came about because the Bureau of Alcohol, Tobacco and Firearms sought to arrest Vernon Howells, leader of a Christian cult whose members were living in a compound in the vicinity of Waco. Howells called himself David Koresh, the Hebrew name of Cyrus, king of the Persians, and derived from Chronicles 2:33. The government agents used several tanks to punch holes into the buildings housing Howells and his followers. They then forced chemical solutions into the building, followed by the destruction of several sections of the building. The assault led to a conflagration which killed eighty members of the cult and four federal agents.[29]

This assault and its gruesome outcome were observed by Timothy McVeigh, and his friend, Terry Nichols, both former soldiers, recently discharged. Both believed that the U.S. government had declared war on its own citizens and that the Waco debacle and the shootout between Randy Weaver and federal agents at Weaver's Idaho cabin in 1992 proved that federal agents were attacking innocent citizens and that war had been declared against law abiding people in this country.

There is in the United States a segment of the population who feel left out and alienated from their own country and their government. These are people who live in the center of the land, in Kansas or Oklahoma and other states that are seldom mentioned by the media whose only interests are the east coast politicians and the west coast actors. The population of these states is mostly of European origin, white and poor. Many who live there believe that their identity is threatened as the country has become largely black and Hispanic. They believe that the government does not belong to them but has become an enemy seeking to rob them of their ethnicity and identity. Therefore, many of these citizens have armed themselves and attained at least some sense of power and security by owning whole arsenals. The most radical of these people are paranoiac and believe in violence. Moreover, the citizens in states like Oklahoma and Kansas live mainly in rural areas or small towns.[30]

It was this kind of belligerent environment that Timothy McVeigh first encountered when he joined the army and was stationed in Fort Riley, Kansas. McVeigh had graduated from high school in Pendleton, New York, where he was born in 1968. His parents divorced when he was ten. His mother left and he grew up in his father's home together with his two sisters. After high school Tim McVeigh held some dead-end jobs and then became a solider at age 20. He had accumulated a gun collection and considered himself a "survivalist." He stockpiled food and camping equipment. He brought at least twenty guns with him into the army and kept them in a bag in his barracks.[31]

In Fort Benning, Georgia, McVeigh met Terry Nichols, who came from an area in Michigan where distrust of government was a tradition. Nichols was so disgusted with government that he attempted to renounce his citizenship. After both McVeigh and Nichols had been discharged from the army, both men moved to Michigan, where they sold military surplus at gun shows.

In 1995 McVeigh and Nichols decided to "get even" with the government. They viewed themselves at war with a foreign power and sought to fight the perceived injustices they believed had been committed by the government of the United States, both domestically and in foreign countries. Timothy McVeigh was a veteran of the Gulf War of 1991. He had seen slaughter in Iraq and blamed his own government, not the regime of Saddam Hussein, for the death and destruction he had observed.

After his arrest he wrote an essay from his prison cell in which he recalled a Kurdish woman and child killed by chemical weapons. He mentioned the atomic bombing of Hiroshima and Nagasaki and the bombing of the German city of Dresden. He recalled the bombing of Hanoi but not once did he find fault with the Germans, the Japanese, the Vietnamese, or anyone other than the United States. According to McVeigh, the United States was always the culprit, always wrong, and by fiat the aggressors were always exonerated. Timothy McVeigh was killed by prison guards on June 10, 2001.[32]

The second man convicted of the bombing of the Alfred P. Murrah Federal Office building is Terry Nichols. His anti-government views led him to believe that an attack on the Federal Office building was justified on the grounds that the government was perpetually assaulting the rights of American citizens. Nichols had been actively involved in the construction of the bomb that killed 168 victims in April of 1995. In a federal court he was convicted of eight counts of involuntary manslaughter and conspiracy to use a weapon of mass destruction. He was also convicted in an Oklahoma state court of 161 cases of first degree murder, first degree arson and conspiracy. He was then sentenced to 161 life sentences without the possibility of parole.[33]

Michael Fortier was the third person convicted in connection with the Oklahoma City bombing. He was sentenced to 12 years in prison on the grounds that he knew the bombing would take place inasmuch as he had failed to alert "authorities" to the plot, had sold stolen guns and "lied" to federal agents after the bomb shredded the federal building. He was released from prison in January of 2006.[34]

Abortion Clinic Bombings and the Bombing of the Centennial Olympic Park

On July 26, 1996, a pipe bomb exploded in Centennial Olympic Park in Atlanta, Georgia during the summer Olympics. One person was killed and 111 people were injured. The dead woman was Alice Hawthorne, killed at age 44 by a man who did not even know her. Hawthorne was a receptionist at a cable television station. She also owned a small café and ice cream parlor and was a friend to all the other small business owners on Oglethorpe Blvd. in Albany, Georgia. Hawthorne's fourteen-year-old daughter was injured by the same blast that killed her mother.[35]

On January 16, 1997, two bombs exploded at Atlanta North Side Family Planning Services in an Atlanta suburb. Seven people were wounded. The first bomb damaged the building but did not injure or kill anyone. The first bomb led firefighters and investigators as well as reporters to come to the scene of the bombing. Then, an hour later, a second bomb exploded, wounding six people.

There are about 15 bombings or arsons at abortion clinics in the United States each year. In addition, a doctor at a Baton Rouge, Louisiana clinic was stabbed, a Planned Parenthood clinic in Dallas, Texas was robbed at gunpoint, and an abortion clinic in Tulsa, Oklahoma was burned. Paul de Parrie, editor of Life Advocate magazine, praised the bombing and said, "I'm not going to condemn someone that God won't condemn."[36]

On February 21, 1997, a bomb exploded at the Outside Lounge, a bar for lesbians and gays in Atlanta, injuring five people. A second bomb was found and defused. This bombing resembled the bombing at the Atlanta Olympic Park, which also involved a second bomb. Evidently the victims of the bombing were homosexuals, leading a lifestyle of which Eric Rudolph did not approve any more than he approved of abortion.[37]

On January 29, 1998, a bomb exploded at the New Woman All Women Health Care clinic in Birmingham, Alabama, killing a police officer and injuring a nurse. This was the first bombing of an abortion clinic, which led to murder. The bomb killed Robert Sanderson, at age 35 an eight- year police veteran. Subsequently, Dr. David Gunn, an abortionist who practiced in Pensacola, Florida was murdered along with Dr. John Britton, also from Pensacola. In 1994, John Salvi, an abortion protester, murdered Leanne Nichols and Shannon Lowry, who both worked at an abortion clinic in Brookline, Massachusetts. Emily Lyans, a nurse, was badly injured in the blast. She suffered an injury to her eye and severe wounds on both legs.[38]

On October 23, 1998, James Kopp shot Dr. Barnett Slepian. Slepian was standing in his kitchen as a bullet from a high- powered rifle killed him in front of his wife and four children. Slepian was 52 years old and had a large practice in gynecology and obstetrics. He also performed abortions at the Buffalo GYN Womenservices clinic.

Kopp had a history living as a full time anti-abortionist. He moved from town to town and assumed numerous identities and worked odd jobs to support himself. After killing Dr. Slepian, Kopp moved to Ireland and thereafter to France, where he was arrested and deported to the United States. He had been a fugitive since 1998. The French court allowed the deportation on the assumption that Kopp was not to be killed by the U.S. government. France does not have the death penalty. Kopp had been "on the run" for three years.[39]

On October 14, 1998, Eric Rudolph was charged with the three bombings in Atlanta, but not before an innocent man was accused of the Olympic Park bombing. That innocent man was Richard Jewell, the man who discovered one of the pipe bombs placed there by Rudolph, alerted police, and helped evacuate the area before the bomb exploded. No doubt Jewell saved many people from injury and death. At the time, Jewell was a private security guard for Piedmont College. Almost at once after Jewell had risked his life, the F.B.I. and the media targeted Jewell as the bomber. Claiming that Jewell placed the bomb himself so as to become a "hero," the F.B.I. searched his house and publicly accused him of setting the bomb. The media, and in particular the Atlanta Constitution, labeled Jewell a "killer." Reporters rented an apartment across the street from Jewell's home and focused their cameras on his place day and night. He was hounded incessantly as the F.B.I. claimed that Jewell fit their "criminal profile." These false accusations continued for 88 days. Finally the F.B.I. admitted its error but the media kept up their accusations. Finally, in 2006 the governor of Georgia, Sonny Purdue, publicly thanked Richard Jewell on behalf of the citizens of Georgia for saving the lives of those at the Olympic games. Jewell died in 2007.[40]

The Anthrax Attacks

Controversy surrounds the claim by the F.B.I. that Bruce Edward Ivins was responsible for the deaths of five citizens and the illness of seventeen others, all of who were infected by the anthrax virus in 2001. The first victim of the "anthrax attack" was Robert Stevens, a photo editor who worked for a Boca Raton, Florida newspaper called The SunSentinel. The SunSentinel is a supermarket tabloid. Stevens felt unusually tired on Saturday morning, September 28, 2001. The next day he felt feverish and on Monday he was admitted to a hospital because he vomited and became disoriented. Doctors confirmed that Stevens had inhaled the bacillus anthraces of which he died on October 5, 2001. After his death it was revealed that on September 19, 2001, Stevens had received a strange letter containing a white powder. In addition, another employee of the SunSentinel became ill. That employee survived because doctors were alert to the anthrax virus following the Stevens death and treated the latest victim with ciprofloxacin.[41]

In October of 2001 seven members of the media profession contracted anthrax in New York City. One week later an envelope addressed to Senator Thomas Daschle of South Dakota contained the anthrax virus. It was found in the mailroom of the Senate office building in Washington. Twenty-eight employees in the Senate office building were found to have had contact with the anthrax virus as they carried spores in their nasal cavities. All 6,000 people working in the building were treated with ciprofloxacin and the building was closed for three months until it could be decontaminated. The Brentwood, Maryland post office was struck next. Brentwood is only one mile from Washington. The Senate mail was sorted at that post office. Four employees caught anthrax and two died.[42]

One woman in Manhattan and one woman in Connecticut also received contaminated mail and died of anthrax. In Manhattan, a Vietnamese immigrant, Kathy T. Nguyen, died of anthrax, although she worked in a hospital and not in a mailroom. Nguyen lived alone, had no family, and was in no sense a prominent citizen. Yet, she became the random target of the anthrax attacker.[43]

On November 22, 2001, a Connecticut woman, Ottilie W. Lundgren, became the fifth victim to die of inhaling anthrax. Lundren was known to only visit the local library or a nearby beauty parlor but not the post office. Investigators discovered that the anthrax strain that killed her was the same that had been sent to the senate office building and the news media.[44]

The F.B.I. concluded after years of investigating these anthrax attacks, that Bruce E. Ivins was the terrorist who sent the anthrax letters. This suspicion was never verified but led to seven years of harassment of Ivins, who killed himself on July 29, 2008. Dr. Ivins was a leading anthrax researcher who worked for the

U.S. Army Medical Research Institute of Infectious Diseases at Fort Detrick in Frederick, MD.[45]

The anthrax attack has been labeled bioterrorism. That is a method of attacking one's enemies and is older than any knowledge of biology or the existence of microorganisms. An excellent example of the use of bioterrorism was the Tatar attack on the town of Caffa in the Crimea in 1347. The Tatars tossed the corpses of plague victims over the walls of the town. The inhabitants fled and sailed to numerous destinations and thereby spread the "black death" all over Western Europe.[46]

At the end of the Second World War, Russian troops discovered that the Japanese army had developed a military installation used to develop biological warfare. This installation was located near Harbin in Manchuria, a country occupied by the Japanese in 1931. The Japanese had studied anthrax, cholera, and the plague, using Chinese people as "guinea pigs." This led the United States, the United Kingdom, and Canada to research biological warfare after the Second World War.[47]

In 1979, an accident revealed that the Soviet government had for years developed a major network of factories and research centers producing lethal microorganisms, including anthrax. The operation was so vast that the products of this effort could destroy all life on this planet. The accident occurred near the town of Sverdlovsk, when a mistake by a worker led to the distribution of anthrax into the air, leading to the deaths of over one thousand people.[48]

The "anthrax attack" has led to the development of microbial forensics. This new field of investigation traces the origin of a biological agent by using biochemical analysis. Included is the newly available genomic sequencing and carbohydrate fingerprinting. This technique was first used in a criminal case in 1998, when a Louisiana doctor intentionally infected a former girlfriend with HIV.[49]

White Supremacist Murders

On June 10, 2009, security guard Stephen Tyrone Johns was shot by James von Brunn and later died from his injuries at the nation's memorial to the Holocaust. Von Brunn was 88 years old when he was indicted on first-degree murder. This made him eligible for the death penalty. Von Brunn was also shot and died on January 6, 2010. Von Brunn lived in Maryland, where he operated a racist web site that he called Holy Western Empire. He had written a book called *Kill the Best Gentiles* in which he denied the holocaust and claimed that Jews sought world domination.[50]

Von Brunn entered the museum just before 1 p.m. and opened fire without warning. At that time there were hundreds of tourists in the building. Von Brunn carried a long rifle as he entered and shot guard Johns. Other guards returned the fire and wounded von Brunn severely.

James von Brunn had served six years in a federal prison after he entered the headquarters of the Federal Reserve carrying several weapons while threatening to take the members hostage.[51]

Von Brunn was a "white supremacist," as were David Lane, Bruce Pierce, Richard Scutari, and Jean Craig. Pierce and Lane were convicted of murdering Alan Berg, a Denver radio talk show host on June 19, 1984, because Berg was Jewish. Pierce shot Berg 13 times with a Mac-10 submachine gun in the driveway of Berg's townhouse and Lane drove the getaway car. Craig and Scutari were found not guilty by the jury. However, all four were convicted of racketeering and all were imprisoned on those charges since December of 1985. Scutari was sentenced to serve 60 years, David Lane and Jean Craig were sentenced to serve forty years and Bruce Pierce was sentenced to serve 100 years.[52]

There are in the United States a number of organizations devoted to racial, ethnic and religious hate. Those affiliated with these groups use the Internet seeking to attract more members and gain more influence. Some of these groups have been implicated in violent crimes against a number of minorities.

Glaser, Dixit and Green interviewed 38 participants in white racist internet chat rooms to examine to what extent such participants would advocate and/or conduct violence. According to their study, racial intermarriage "evoke(s) the strongest emotional reactions" from avowed racists. Gays and lesbians who are seen as sexual threats are also often the targets of physical assault, while Jews are more likely to be the victims of vandalism on the grounds that "the Jews have all the money."[53]

In-migration of minorities also worried the respondents interviewed in this study, although it did not lead to threats of violence. Such a mild response was also found with respect to job competition from immigrants. It is racial integration which the respondents in this study viewed as a great threat and which led them to threaten violence.[54]

A gruesome example of a racially motivated crime was the murder of James Byrd, Jr. on June 7, 1998 in Jasper, Texas. This horror developed when Byrd, then 49 years old, accepted a ride from Shawn Berry, 24, Lawrence Brewer, 31, and John King, 23. The three white men drove Byrd to a remote rural area where they beat him with numerous objects. They then urinated on his unconscious body, chained him by the ankles to their pick-up truck and dragged him for three miles. In the course of this atrocity, Byrd's head and right arm were severed when his body hit a culvert. Then the three killers dumped the torso in front of a black cemetery. The three men were members of a white supremacy organization.[55]

Two of the killers of Byrd, Lawrence Brewer and John King, were sentenced to death, and Shawn Berry was sentenced to life in prison.[56]

When Vincent McGee, a black man, killed Richard Barrett in Learned, Mississippi on April 22, 2010, one racist killed another racist. The victim of the stabbing was the founder of The Nationalist Movement, an organization devoted to racial intolerance and religious persecution. That organization is opposed to immigration, opposed to civil rights, and opposed to equal opportunities for all races in the U.S. Barret led "white power" demonstrations, defended Ku Klux Klan members in court, and used a picture of Martin Luther King for target practice. He participated in numerous anti-government demonstrations around the county. Then, in 2010 he was killed by McGee, a racist black man.[57]

Austin IRS Attack

On February 8, 2010, Andrew Joseph Stack III flew his airplane into the IRS (Internal Revenue) building in Austin, Texas. He killed himself and one other person, Vernon Hunter, and injured many more. Prior to flying into the IRS building, Stack set fire to his $330,000 home in North Austin and left a lengthy message blaming his problems on the IRS. Stack was sharply critical of the U.S. government, as is his daughter, who commented on her father's suicide-murder to the effect that someone needed to call attention to the injustices imposed on the American people by the IRS.[58]

Stack was known to feel persecuted by the I.R.S., which had taken all of his savings. Stack also blamed his accountants, politicians in general, labor unions, drug manufacturers, and the Catholic Church. No doubt Stack, like many others, was driven to extremes by the conduct of the tax collectors.[59]

Domestic Muslim Terrorism

On November 5, 2009 at 1:30 p.m., Major Nidal Malik Hasan, an army doctor dressed in his uniform, walked out of the soldier's readiness center at Fort Hood, Texas and shouted "Allahu Akbar" or God is Great. With that he pulled two guns from his belt and began shooting at his army comrades for ten minutes. He killed thirteen people and wounded twenty-eight before a lady civilian police officer, Kimberly Munley, shot Hasan and wounded him although she also wounded herself. Hasan became paralyzed below the waist from that shooting.[60]

According to eyewitness Franciso De La Serna, Major Nidal Malik Hasan came out of a building with guns in his hands and calmly shot anyone who happened to be available. Included in the victims was Sgt. Kim Munley, who bled profusely from the wounds she had just received. De La Serna made a tourniquet and wound it around Munley's leg to stop the bleeding. Evidently influenced by Muslim clerics with whom he corresponded, Hasan talked about Muslim suicide bombers as "something glorious."[61]

It appears that since the U.S. invasion of Iraq and Afghanistan, some American Muslims have grown radical in their views and sought to prove their devotion to Islam by killing other Americans. This is documented by an F.B.I. survey which concluded that a number of American Muslims have traveled to Pakistan for training in terrorist camps with a view of killing American soldiers. In addition, there are the actions of Major Hasan, whose conduct differs from that of the other American Muslim terrorists in that he was an officer in the army, had sworn to uphold the constitution, and had also sworn he would defend his country. Born in Virginia and a graduate of Virginia Technical University and the United States Services University of the Health Sciences, he is the son of Palestinian parents.[62]

Prior to shooting and killing his fellow soldiers, Hasan corresponded with Anwar-al-Awlaki, a determined enemy of the United States. Awlaki, a Muslim cleric at a mosque in northern Virginia, was Hasan's prayer leader. Three of Awlaki's followers were participants in the attack on the World Trade Center in 2001, after which Awlaki fled to his home in Yemen. Hasan, although born in the United States and an officer in the U.S. armed forces, listed his nationality as Palestinian on any forms asking for his nationality. Hasan also told fellow soldiers that American Muslims should "rise up against the American aggressors" in Iraq. He claimed that the war against terror was really a war against Islam financed by Jews, a doctrine he preached to patients under his care at Walter Reed Medical Center in Washington, D.C. and at Fort Hood.[63]

While Hasan was on the staff of Walter Reed Medical Center, a number of officers there met to discuss the possibility that Hasan would betray his country and offer intelligence to the enemy if he were deployed in Iraq or Afghanistan. These meetings were the result of Hasan's bizarre statements denouncing the United States and the armed forces of which he himself was a part. Hasan lectured a crowd of fellow doctors at Walter Reed Medical Center that Muslim soldiers should not be asked to fight "fellow Muslims." He also had a business card which had printed under his name "SoA" meaning "Soldier of Allah."[64]

One of the consequences of the Fort Hood massacre has been a review of the shooting by the Department of Defense with a view of discovering why the conduct of Hasan was not included in his evaluation prior to being sent to Fort Hood. The review is to determine whether Hasan's supervisors were negligent in ignoring his threats. It was known to his superior that Hasan constantly discussed religious topics with his patients, that he saw only 38 patients in 30 weeks of outpatient training, that he failed height/weight screening, and that he failed to document the actions of dangerous patients.[65]

On May 1, 2010, a t-shirt vendor alerted police to a smoking car parked with the motor running in Times Square. Inside the Nissan Pathfinder, police found a bomb, crudely assembled, which had not yet exploded. The bomb was packed with gasoline, propane, fertilizer, and fireworks. Since then, F.B.I. agents arrested an American citizen at Kennedy Airport, as he was about to flee to Dubai. Arrested was Faizal Shahzad, a native of Pakistan who lived in Bridgeport, Connecticut. He was charged with attempted use of a weapon of mass destruction after he admitted having placed the bomb into the car and left it there in the hope of killing as many citizens as possible.

In Pakistan, a terrorist, Tauhid Ahmed, said he had been sending emails to Shahzad, and another terrorist, Muhammad Rehan, said in Karachi that he had spent some time with Shahzad when Shahzad visited Pakistan for four months in 2009.[66]

There can be no doubt that the United States is under attack by radical Islamists both from abroad and from domestic terrorists. This attack has continued for a number of years and culminated with the attack on the World Trade Center, the Pentagon and the aborted attack on the White House in 2001. Since then a number of other attacks on the western-Christian world have continued.

SUMMARY

Terrorism has been part of American history since the Haymarket riots of 1886. The Ludlow massacre demonstrated that government is also capable of inflicting terror methods on its own citizens. In addition, groups with all kinds of grievances and causes have used bombings and other forms of violence, as illustrated by the bombing of the Los Angeles Times building, the Wall street explosion, the Unabomber, the bombing of the Federal Office Building in Oklahoma City, the abortion clinic bombings and the killing of abortion doctors, the murders committed by "white supremacists," the IRS building air attack in Austin, Texas, and the domestic violence by American Muslims.

NOTES

1. No author, "Ludlow Massacre Monument Dedicated as US Landmark," *Colorado and Denver News,* (June 28, 2009), 1.

2. No author, "Rioting and Bloodshed in the Streets of Chicago," *The New York Times,* (May 5, 1886), 1.

3. Timothy Messer-Kruse, James O. Eckert, Jr., Pannee Burkel and Jeffrey Dunn, "The Haymarket Bomb: Reassessing the Evidence," *Labor,* vol. 2, no.2, (2005), 39-52.

4. Philip S. Foner, *History of the Labor Movement in the United States :* vol. 5, *The AFL in the Progressive Era, 1910-1915,* (New York: International Publishers, 1980), 85.

5. James Whiteside, *Regulating Danger: The Struggle for Mine Safety in the Rocky Mountains,* (Lincoln, Nebraska, The University of Nebraska Press, 1990), 14-15.

6. Zeece Papanikolas, *Buries Unsung, Louis Tikas and the Ludlow Massacre,* (Salt Lake City: University of Utah Press, 1982), 40.

7. George McGovern and Leonard F. Guttridge, *The Great Coalfield War*, (Boston: Houghton Mifflin Co, 1972), 102.

8. Ibid, 210-231.

9. Ibid, 332.

10. No author, "Fire Kills 19; Unions Accused," *The New York Times*, (October 2 , 1910), 1.

11. Ibid., 1.

12. Alan M. Wakstein, "The Origins of the Open Shop Movement, 1919-1920," *Journal of American History*, v.51, (1964), 460-475.

13. Foner, *History of the Labor Movement*, vol. 5, 7.

14. Michael Kazin, *Barons of Labor*, (Urbana, Illionois, The University of Illinois Press, 1987), 203, 207-208.

15. Foner, *Hisotry of the Labor Movement*, vol.5, 13.

16. Kevin Baker, "Blood on the Street,,"*The New York Times*, (February 22, 2009), 12.

17. No author, "Hospitals Rush Aid to Victoms," *The New York Times*, (September 17, 190), 4.

18. No author, "Col. Charles Neville One Of Bomb Dead," *The New York Times*, (September 17, 1920), 6.

19. Edwin G. Burrows and Mike Wallace, *Gotham: A History of New York City to 1898*, (New York: Oxford University Press, 1999), 296-306.

20. Beverly Gage, *The Day Wall Street Exploded*, (New York: Oxford University Press, 2009), 4.

21. Paul Avrich, *Anarchist Voices: An Oral History of Anarchism in America*, (Princeton, NJ: Princeton Univesity Press, 1996), 135.

22. Ibid.4-5.

23. H.M. Gitelman, "Perspectives on American Industrial Violence," *The Business History Review*, vol. 47, no .1, (Spring 1973), 1-23.

24. Willy Morris, "Kaczynski Ended Career in Math with no Explanation," *The Buffalo News*, (April 6, 1996), 1.

25. George Lardner and Lorraine Adams, "To Unabomb Victims, a Deeper Mystery," *Washington Post*, (April 14, 1996), A01.

26. Ibid.:6

27. David Johnston, "At Least 31 Are Dead, Scores are Missing After Car Bomb Attack in Oklahoma City Wrecks 9 Story Federal Office Building," *The New York Times*, (April 20, 1995) :A1.

28. John Kifner, "Authorities Hold a Man of Extreme Right Wing Views," *The New York Times*, (April 22, 1995) 9.

29. Ross E. Milloy, "An Angry Telephone Call Signals the End of the World for Cult Members," *The New York Times*, (April 20, 1993),A21.

30. Jo Thomas, "The Third Man: A Reporter Investigates the Oklahoma City Bombing," *The Syracuse Law Review*, vol. 59, (2008-2009), 459-469.

31. Dale Russakoff and Serge F. Kovaleski, "An Ordinary Boy's Extraordinary Rage," *The Washington Post*, (July 2, 1995), A01.

32. Irfan Ahmad, "Timothy McVeighs of the Orient," *Economic and Political Weekly*, (April 13, 2002), 1400.

33. Jo Thomas, "Terry Nichols Gets Life Term in Bombing Plot," *The New York Times,* (June 5, 1998), A1.

34. Tim Talley, "After 10 years, McVeigh Associate Leaves Prison,' *The Buffalo News,* (January 21, 2006),A5.

35. Rick Bragg, "A Friend Is Lost and a Street is Full of Bewilderment and Pain," *New York Times,* (July 28, 1996), 1.

36. Rick Bragg, "2 Bomb Blasts Rock Abortion Clinic at Atlanta; 6 Are Injured," *New York Times,* (January 17, 1997), A1.

37. Kevin Sack, "In Latest Atlanta Bombing, 5 Are Inuured at a Gay Bar," *New York Times,* (February 23, 1997), 18.

38. No author, "Chronology of the Bombing Case," *USA Today,* (June 2, 2003), 03a.

39. Corey Kilgannon, "Most-wanted Fugitive is Arrested," *New York Times*, (April 1, 2001), WK2.

40. Luke Cyphers, "Still Seeking Bomb Shelter," *The Daily News,* (October 1, 2000), 94.

41. Leonard A. Cole, *The Anthrax Letters,* (Washington, DC: The Joseph Henry Press, 2003), 46-48.

42. Thomas V. Inglesby et.al. , "Anthrax as a Biological Weapon," *Journal of the American Medical Association, vol.1287, no. 17, (May 2007), 2236-2252.*

43. Alan Feuer, "A Worrisome Medical Puzzle, Wrapped in a Workaday Life," *New York Times,* (October 31, 2001), A1.

44. Paul Zielbauer, "Connecticut Woman, 94, Is Fifth to Die From Inhalation Anthrax," *New York Times,* (November 22, 2001), A1.

45. Amber Dance, "Death Renews Bio-security Debate," *Nature,* vol. 454, (August 2008), 672.

46. Mark Wheelis, "Biological Warfare at the 1346 Siege of Caffa," *Emerging Infectious Diseases,* vol. 18, no. 9, (September 2002), 8.

47. Jeanne Guillemin, "Imperial Japan's Germ Warfare: The Suppression of Evidence at the Tokyo War Crimes Trial," In: Anne L. Clunan, *Terrorism, War or Disease,* Stanford, California, Stanford University Press, (2008), 165.

48. Matthew Meselson, et.al., "The Sverdlovsk Anthrax Outbreak of 1979," *Science,* vol. 266, (1994) :1202-1208.

49. Amber Dance, "Anthrax Case Ignites New Forensic Field," *Nature,* vol. 454, no. 7206, (2008), 813.

50. Sheldon Alberts, "Guard at U.S. Holocaust Museum Slain by Gunman; Washington D.C. Suspect Believed to be White Supremacist." *National Post,* (January 11, 2009), A 17.

51. Ibid, A17.

52. No author, "2 White Racists Convicted in Killing of Radio Host," *The New York Times,* (November 18, 1987), A116.

53. Jack Glaser, Jay Dixit and Donald Greene, "Studying Hate Crime with the Internet: What Makes Racists Advocate Racial Violence?" *Journal of Social Issues,* vol. 58, no.1, (2002), 178.

54. Ibid, 186.

55. No author, "A Trial of Savagery: Reflections on the Death of James Byrd, Jr. in Jasper, Texas," *The Journal of Blacks in Higher Education,* no.20, (Summer, 1998), 110-111.

56. No author, "Third Defendant is Convicted in Dragging Death in Texas," *New York Times,* (November 19, 1999),A33.

57. No author, "More Arrests made in Connection with Barret's Death,"*The Jackson News,* (April 23, 2010), 1.

58. Tony Plohetski, "IRS officials Meet with Employees as Officials Confirm Pilot's Identity, " *American Statesman,* (February 22, 2010), 1.

59. Michael Brick, "Man Crashes Plane Into Texas I.R.S. Office," *The New York Times,* (February 18, 2010), 1.

60. Helen Pidd, "Fort Hood Massacre," *The Guardian,* (November 7, 2009), 4.

61. Bill Hewitt et. al. "Massacre at Fort Hood," *People,* vol. 72, no. 21, (November 23, 2009), 58-62.

62. Joe Wolverton II, "An Officer and a Jihardist," *New American,* vol.26, no.2, (2010), 21.

63. Ibid. :22.

64. Ibid.:23.

65. Arline Kaplan, "The Fort Hood Aftermath - Army accountability and Review and Psychiatrists," *Psychiatric Times,* vol. 27, no. 5, (2010), 42.

66. Mark Mazzetti, Sabrina Tavernise and Jack Healy, "Suspect Charged, Said to Admit Role in Plot," *The New York Times,* (May 4, 2010), A1.

Chapter Eight
The Muslim Assault on Western Civilization

TERROR ATTACKS AGAINST AMERICA

The Iran Hostage Crisis

On November 4, 1979, Muslim students stormed the United States embassy in Teheran, Iran, seized 90 Americans, and demanded that the deposed Shah of Iran, Mohammad Reza Pahlavi, be forced to return to Iran from his refuge in the United States. The Shah had fled his country after the religious leader, the Ayatollah Khomeini, returned from exile in Paris on January 17, 1979. Khomeini established a theocracy based on the Quran and Islamic law and declared his hatred of the United States and all of western civilization.[1]

Early in November, the U.S. government under President Jimmy Carter enlisted the help of a terrorist organization, the P.L.O., to free the American hostages. This was of no avail, as it turned out that the Palestine Liberation Organization sided with Iran against the United States instead of mediating the conflict as promised.[2]

In view of the failure of diplomatic efforts to free the American hostages, President Carter sent a unit of Delta Force, a special forces segment of the United States army, to rescue the hostages by force. On the nights of April 24-25 and April 25-26, 1980, when52 hostages remained in the embassy, eight U.S. helicopters landed 200 miles southeast of Tehran in a salt desert. One helicopter slammed into a fuel transport, both planes ignited, and eight servicemen were killed. The hostages were finally released after 444 days in captivity on the day of President Ronald Reagan's inauguration on January 20, 1981. There can be little doubt that President Carter was not reelected because of this debacle that made the United States appear weak and incompetent in the eyes of the world.[3]

The Attacks on Americans in Lebanon

On October 23, 1983, a suicide bomber detonated a truck full of explosives at a U.S. Marine barracks located at Beirut International Airport. 241 U.S. Marines were killed and more than one hundred wounded. 1800 Marines had been sent to Lebanon as part of an international force assigned to separate warring Lebanese factions. No action was taken by the U.S. government to deal with this attack. Then, in February of 1984, the Marines left Lebanon.

That attack was by no means the first attack against Americans in the region. As early as 1970, the Popular Front for the Liberation of Palestine killed Barbara Ertle of Grandville, Michigan, and that same year fired rockets at the U.S. Embassy in Beirut and then proceeded to rocket the Bank of America, the John F. Kennedy Library, and the American Insurance Co. In 1973, an Arab organization called Fatah killed the American ambassador to the Sudan, Cleo A. Noel, and George C. Moore, another U.S. diplomat.

In January 1978 the Popular Front kidnapped and later killed Frances E. Melroy, U.S. ambassador to Lebanon and Robert O. Waring, U.S. economic counselor. On April 18, 1983, a truck bomb exploded in front of the U.S. embassy in Beirut, killing 63 employees. Innumerable other attacks on American targets continued throughout the 1980's and 1990's, culminating in the attack on the World Trade Center, the Pentagon and the aborted attack on the White House in 2001.[4]

On March 16, 1985, Terry Anderson, chief Middle East correspondent of the Associated Press, was kidnapped in Lebanon by agents of the Iranian backed terror organization Hizb-Ullah. He was not alone. Nine Americans, three Englishmen, one Irishman and one Italian were also abducted in 1985 by a group calling themselves "Islamic Jihad". Before that time, 96 foreign hostages from twenty-one nations were kidnapped in Beirut, of whom 28 were journalists. Anderson and others were finally released in 1991 after six and one half years in captivity.[5]

Iran paid $1 million to $2 million to the terrorists for each hostage released by the kidnappers. Iran did so because they wanted the various terrorist groups to be dependent on Iran and so allow Iran control over Lebanon by using the terrorists as paid agents with power to threaten the Lebanese government. Prior to paying for the hostages' release, Iran had paid the Lebanese terrorists regular monthly amounts to keep the terrorists happy, quiet, and on the side of Iran in the ongoing conflicts within Lebanon.[6]

"The Party of God"

On June 14, 1985, an American airplane, TWA 847, was hijacked on route from Athens to Rome and forced to land in Beirut, Lebanon. The hijackers were members of Hizb-Ullah., "the party of God." They held the passengers for 17 days, demanding that Arab prisoners held in Kuwait and in Israel for terrorism be released. When these demands were not met, the Hizb-Ulla terrorists killed hostage Robert Dean Stetham, a U.S. Navy diver, and threw his body on the airport tarmac.[7]

On October 7, 1985, four members of the Palestine Liberation Front seized the Italian cruise ship Achille Lauro while on its way from Genoa, Italy to Port Said, Egypt. Once in control of the ship, the terrorists, under the leadership of Mohammed Abbas, shot a wheelchair-bound American passenger, Leon Klinghoffer, and threw him and his wheelchair overboard. Klinghoffer was not dead when he was drowned.

After landing in Egypt, Mohammad Abbas and the other terrorists were allowed to fly to their headquarters in Tunisia. Intercepted by American warplanes, they were forced to land in Italy with a view of having them arrested and sent to the United States. Instead, the Italian government allowed Abbas and some of his associates to flee to Yugoslavia and from there to Tunisia, although others were imprisoned. Abbas was tried in absentia and convicted but never spent a day in prison.

Subsequently, Abbas used a speedboat to attack bathers on the beach in Tel Aviv. Thereafter he moved to Iraq, where he was captured by U.S. forces in 2003. He died in prison in Iraq in 2004.[8]

In 1985, five Americans were killed when bombs exploded at airports in Vienna, Austria, and Rome, Italy. Then, in 1986, a bomb exploded on TWA flight 840 en route from Rome to Athens, killing four Americans, and a disco in Berlin was bombed, killing two Americans and injuring hundreds. Libyan members of various anti-American terrorist organizations were responsible for these attacks.[9]

The Lockerbie Horror

Most egregious of all Libyan attacks on Americans was the bombing of Pan Am Flight 103, which exploded over Lockerbie, Scotland, on December 21, 1988. The explosion killed 259 passengers and crew and also killed 11 residents of Lockerbie as the debris from the plane fell on them and their homes.

British and American investigators concluded that the explosion was caused by a device placed on the plane and detonated later by a timing mechanism. The evidence pointed to the involvement of two Libyan nationals, Abdelbaset Ali Mohmed al-Megrahi and Al Amin Khalifa Fhimah. Both were indicted in a Scottish court. The offenses charged were conspiracy to commit murder, murder, and violation of the Aviation Security Act. Because the majority of the victims were Americans, the two suspects were also indicted by an American grand jury. The two men were members of the Libyan Intelligence Service. The British and U.S. governments requested that both men be handed over to British and American authorities. In this they were also joined by France. When Libya refused, the issue was brought to the United Nations Security Council. The Security Council passed a useless resolution attributing guilt to the Libyan government. The Libyans then raised all kinds of legalisms and refused to extradite the killers. In this the numerous Arab members of the United Nations supported Libya.[10]

In view of the international pressure to which Libya became subject, the Libyans agreed to put al-Megrahi and Fhima on trial in Libya. This was not acceptable to the United Kingdom or the United States. Finally, over six years after the 1988 attack, Libya agreed to send both men to the Netherlands for trial. There a Scottish court found Fhima not guilty but convicted al-Megrahi of placing a suitcase on Pan Am Flight 103 in Malta. The suitcase held a Toshiba radio-cassette player rigged with a charge of plastic explosive and a fuse activated by a battery. The plane flew to London and then on toward the United States. Thirty-seven minutes after leaving London, the bomb blew a hole in the jet's side and 259 passengers and crew and eleven on the ground died. One-hundred-ninety of the dead were Americans.

Al-Megrahi was sentenced to life imprisonment as the killer of 270 people. Thirty-five of the murdered passengers were American students enrolled at Syracuse University, where a stone monument to them was erected at the center of the campus.[11]

In August of 2009, the government of Scotland released al-Megrahi on the grounds that medical "experts" expected him do die of prostate cancer within three months. Yet, in July of 2010, al-Megrahi was living in Libya, where he was feted as a hero for having killed 270 people. American senators and others suspect that al-Megrahi was released in an "oil for Megrahi" deal engineered by British Petroleum, one of the largest oil exploration companies in the world.[12]

The 1993 World Trade Center Attack

Six people died and more than one thousand were injured when a bomb exploded in the garage of the New York City World Trade Center on February 26, 1993. This was the first time that terrorists had succeeded in attacking the United States on its soil.

In 1994, four men were convicted of this crime, and two more were convicted in 1997. All were sentenced to 240 years in prison. Among those convicted was Eyad Ismoil, who drove a bomb laden truck into the basement garage of the World Trade Center. Also sentenced was Ramzi Yousef, who built the bomb, and Sheik Omar Abdel Rahman, who planned a war of urban terrorism against New York City.

The attackers flew to Jordan and Pakistan, where they were arrested and returned to the United States. According to Jordanian police, the terrorists regretted that they were unable to topple the 110 story World Trade Center and kill a quarter million people.[13]

A memorial to the six who were murdered had been placed in the World Trade Center complex. It was partially destroyed on September 11, 2001, but has since then been restored. Until the subsequent destruction of the World Trade Center, the attack occurring in 1993 was ignored and forgotten.[14]

Khobar Towers

On Tuesday, June 25, 1996, at approximately 9:50 p.m., a truck bomb exploded outside one building in the Khobar Towers complex in Dhahran, Saudi Arabia. The building was occupied by the majority of the men in the 58th Fighter Squadron of the United States Air Force. The bomb consisted of 20,000 ponds of TNT, killing nineteen American service men and wounding 372 others.[15]

The bomb had been placed in a truck parked against a fence 80 feet away from the high-rise apartment housing the 440th Wing of men who were flying Operation Southern Watch over Iraq to enforce sanctions imposed by the United Nations. When it exploded, the bomb left a crater 85 feet wide and 35 feet deep.

The attack and its gruesome outcome led the Secretary of Defense, William J. Perry, to appoint retired Army general Wayne Downing to head an investigation into the attack and the failure of the officers in charge to prevent it. The Downing report blamed the wing commander, Brigadier General Terry J. Schwalier for not adequately protecting his forces.[16]

The murderous attack was organized by Ahmed Ibrahim Al-Mughassil and was directed and financed by agents of Iran. He bought a tanker truck early in June of 1996 and spent two weeks converting it into a truck bomb. His associate was Ali Saed Bin Ali El-Hoorie, who sat along side of Mughassil, who drove the truck to the Khobar towers. Neither man has so far been found as both left Saudi using fake passports.

Truck Bombs in Africa

On August 7, 1998, at approximately 10:30 a.m., terrorists drove a truck to a parking area near the basement garage of the American embassy in Nairobi, Kenya. They immediately detonated a large bomb killing 213 people, of whom 44 were American embassy employees. Twelve were Americans. Four thousand people in the vicinity of the blast were injured.

There was considerable damage to the embassy as a result of the bombing. Many of the injured happened to drive or walk next to the embassy when the bomb detonated. Others were killed or injured as nearby buildings collapsed.

The terrorists arrived at the embassy gate and demanded entry. The guards refused. Thereupon the terrorists began shooting at the guards and one of them tossed a flash grenade at the guards. The noise led a number of embassy employees to look out the windows to see what was happening and were therefore killed or wounded.[17]

At the same time as terrorists struck the American embassy in Kenya, the American embassy in Dar es Salaam, Tanzania was also bombed. A suicide bomber detonated a bomb on a truck at a distance of 35 feet from the walls of the embassy. The attack killed eleven people and injured 85. One person was missing. No Americans were killed, although several of the injured were Americans. A number of buildings in the vicinity were damaged. In some cases the roof collapsed.[18]

In June of 2001, Mohammed Rashed Daoud al-Owhali was convicted of the bombing of the embassy in Kenya and sentenced to life in prison without the possibility of parole. Owhali was arrested in Kenya when he sought medical help for wounds received in his back as he was running from the bombing. He was arrested in August of 1998 and extradited to the United States.

He was also convicted of a worldwide conspiracy led by Osama bin Laden. Owhali had attended a military camp near the Afghan-Pakistan border, where he was provided with weapons and given training in the use of explosives.[19]

It is significant that the jury members were given numbers in order to hide their names so as to protect them against possible terrorist action. The jury was confronted with a 302- count indictment and with questions concerning willingness to impose the death penalty. Similar precautions involved the jury dealing with the Tanzania bombing. In 2001 Khalfan Khamis Mohammed was convicted of bombing the American embassy in Dar es Salaam, as was Mohamed Odeh and Wadi el Hage. All were sentenced to life in prison. [20]

The Attack on the USS Cole

On October 12, 2000, a small boat carrying detonating explosives was driven into the hull of the guided missile destroyer Cole while the ship was refueling in the port of Aden in Yemen. The blast blew a hole 40 feet in diameter into the Cole, killing seventeen sailors and wounding 33 officers, of whom all but one survived.[21]

The 1983 Beirut bombings, the Khobar Towers attack, and the attack on the Cole were all a part of the worldwide strategy on the part of the al-Qaeda terrorists to conduct a war against the United States and western civilization. These attacks were largely ignored by the U.S. government, as was the 1993 attack on the World Trade Center. Consequently the violence against the United States increased, culminating in the destruction of the World Trade Center on September 11, 2001.

This failure to protect American interests is illustrated by the delivery to the American military of over 100 intelligence reports warning of terrorist car bomb attacks. No action was undertaken to deal with that threat. Indeed, after the bombing of the Khobar Towers, an investigating commission finally declared terrorism "an undeclared war on the United States." [22]

A number of investigations of these attacks led to the conclusion that the U.S. military hardly learned anything from each of these events. Instead the various reports by the several agencies investigating each incident were all seen as isolated from each other until nearly three thousand Americans died when the World Trade Center fell.

September 11, 2001

There are a few events that are remembered for a lifetime by those who experienced them. Some of these events are private, but others are public and so spectacular that people who witnessed them will always remember where they were and what they were doing at the time of the dramatic occurrence. That remains true of the attack on Pearl Harbor of December 7, 1941 as well as the assassination of President Kennedy on November 22, 1963. Because television provided millions with pictures of the horrors inflicted on the people murdered indiscriminately in the offices of the World Trade Center and in the Pentagon building in Washington, the impact of that terrible crime can never be erased from the conscience of mankind. In addition, the world learned of the courageous Americans who prevented the crashing of an airplane into the White House by sacrificing their lives over Pennsylvania.

The events of September 11, 2001 began at 8:44 a.m. when American Airlines flight 11, a Boeing 767 airplane with 93 people aboard, crashed into the upper north tower of the World Trade Center in New York City. The plane had come from Boston and was en route to Los Angeles. During the short flight it was hijacked by Arab terrorists and flown into the office building, with the result that black smoke poured from the gaping hole in the flaming tower. Nineteen minutes later, at 9:03 a.m., United Airlines Flight 175, a Boeing 757 with 65 people aboard, struck the south tower of the World Trade Center. The plane came from Washington en route to Los Angeles. Because the first attack had brought television coverage to the area, the second attack was viewed by millions in horror.

Forty minutes after the second attack on the World Trade Center, American Airlines Flight 77, a Boeing 757 with 64 people aboard, crashed into the south ring of the Pentagon building in Arlington County, Virginia.

Even as the south tower of the World Trade Center collapsed, raining debris and a cloud of dust and rubble all over the area below, United Airlines Flight 93, with 92 people aboard, crashed into the forest in Somerset County, Pennsylvania, killing all passengers and crew members.[23]

The number of people killed by these attacks was close to 3,000. In addition to those on the airplanes, 125 people were killed in the Pentagon attack. Inside the Trade Center another 2,595 died as the towers collapsed, and some jumped to their deaths because of fires in the building. The total death toll therefore was 2,987.

Those who died in these attacks came from seventy-seven countries and every state in the union. Small children were killed, as were the old and the middle aged. More men than women died in this holocaust because more men were doing business inside the trade center.[24]

Nineteen Arab men between the ages of 20 and 28 participated in the hijacking and piloting of the four aircraft selected to carry out the mass murders as planned by Osama Bin Laden and his organization, al-Qaeda (the base). Flight 11 was piloted by Mohamed Atta. The hijackers were Waleed al Shehri, Satam al Sugami, and Abdulaziz al Omari.

United Airlines flight 175 was piloted by Marwan al Shehhi, assisted by the hijackers Fayez Banihammad, Ahmed al Ghamdi, Hamza al Ghamdi and Mohand al Shehri. American Airlines flight 77 was piloted by Hani Hanjour. The hijackers on that plane were Nawaf al Hazmi, Khalid al Mihdhar, Majed Moqed and Salem al Hazmi. United Airlines flight 93 was piloted by Ziad Jarrah. The hijackers were Saeed al Ghamdi, Ahmad al Haznawi and Ahmed al Nami.[25]

Financed with bin Laden's money, some of the hijackers arrived in the United States in April of 2001, although the eventual pilots had come earlier and enrolled in flight training in Florida and in New Jersey. They learned enough to bring on the destruction planned in Afghanistan the year before.

Since September 11, 2001 Americans have responded to these attacks in a dichotomous manner. The response of the United States has been divided into two parts. The first has been the war on Iraq and Afghanistan on the grounds that the erstwhile dictator Saddam Hussein was in part responsible for these attacks and that Osama bin Laden was hiding in Afghanistan. The second response has been to ignore the threat to American democracy coming from Islam and to label the defense of the United States a "war on terror," when in fact Islam seeks to impose its culture on America. Believing that religious freedom must permit Muslims the right to introduce Sharia law into America, the U.S. government has opened the door to the ascendancy of Islamic culture in the country and endangered all the freedoms guaranteed by the U.S. Constitution these 225 years.

At the end of July, 2010, 4,413 Americans have been killed in Iraq since the war began on March 19, 2003. In addition, 1,207 Americans have died in the war in Afghanistan. Over 32,000 have been wounded in both wars.[26]

The attacks of September 11, 2001 demonstrated that the United States had been at war with the Islamists for years without an adequate response from the

American military. That military establishment has been stretched very thin in view of the war on terrorism, the rise in military power in China and Russia, the proliferation of atomic weapons including the threat from Iran, and the ongoing financial crisis, which makes it difficult for the U.S. government to pay for the worldwide commitments engendered by these conditions.[27]

For years the United States has proclaimed to the world that one of our aims in invading Iraq and Afghanistan was not only the defeat of terrorism but also the promotion of human rights, democracy, and the dignity of men and women alike. This objective is almost impossible to achieve because our allies in the Middle East are such as Saudi Arabia, where freedom of expression does not exist, political parties are not allowed, only government media are permitted, and gender discrimination is universal. There is no religious freedom in Saudi Arabia and physical and capital punishment is commonplace. The country is governed by Islamic or Sharia law, which allows the beheading of such "crimes" as sorcery. Amputation of hands and feet and flogging are used in the Saudi criminal justice system, where transvestites and homosexuals are whipped in the most brutal manner. There is no right to legal counsel or judicial review in Saudi nor can suspects call witnesses in their defense. Christianity is prohibited, as is Judaism or any other religion. Only Wahhabi Islam is allowed in Saudi Arabia, while those practicing other forms of Islam are targeted for discrimination. There is a religious police in Saudi which raids religious gatherings by non-Muslims or Muslim minority communities. The religious police also enforce dress codes on women and insure gender segregation at work and in schools. Similar conditions exist in most Muslim countries.[28]

This failure of many of America's allies to maintain any form of democracy makes it exceedingly difficult to claim that the wars fought for human rights, human dignity and democracy have any meaning or any positive outcomes. In fact, the spread of democracy may lead to the use of the ballot box to install the most undemocratic dictatorships in power, as was the case with Hamas in the Palestinian elections of 2006.[29]

Because of the failure of American intelligence services to anticipate attacks on the United States, nearly three thousand Americans died in the 2001 attacks.

Since 2001, when the twin towers of the World Trade Center collapsed, the immigration of Muslims into the United States has continued and increased. It is possible that there are therefore about 3 million Muslims in the country, although some claim that the Muslim population is far larger.

Among these there are "radical" Islamists who seek to impose Sharia law on all Americans. Those who hold these views do not support democracy but wish to enforce Islam by non-violent means Examples of success in this effort are already visible in several states.

In June 2009 a New Jersey judge ruled that a Muslim man was entitled to beat and rape his wife. The judge ruled "This court believes that he (the Muslim man) was operating under his belief that it is, as the husband, his desire to have sex when and whether he wanted to, was something that was consistent with his practices and it was something that was not prohibited."[30]

Tyler Hurd, a 22 year old student at St. Cloud State University in Minnesota, was assigned teacher training at a technical high school. He was accompanied by a service dog which helped him in the event of a seizure which occurred on occasion as a result of a childhood injury.

Muslim students at the high school taunted the dog and threatened to kill the dog on the grounds that, according to Sharia law, dogs are "unclean." The student was forced to leave the teacher training program, as the university administration did nothing to protect him.[31]

In Owatonna, Minnesota, Muslim students assaulted two "white" students who had written papers criticizing the special privileges afforded Muslim students at that school. The papers had been handed out to their friends and came to the attention of the 100 Muslim students in a student body of about 1600. One of the authors of such a paper was assaulted and had to be hospitalized.[32]

In June of 2010, the police department in Dearborn, Michigan, arrested a number of Christians for distributing religious literature on the street during an Arab/Muslim festival. The literature consisted of copies of the Gospel of St. John. The police acted on the grounds that Sharia law prohibits proselytizing. This despite the U.S. Constitution, which guarantees freedom of speech.[33]

In view of these developments, a considerable controversy has occupied New York citizens, and particularly those who lost a loved one in the 2001 attacks. Muslim believers seek to erect a seven story Mosque and Islamic Center at or near "ground zero" or the location of the erstwhile World Trade Center. This is seen as a provocation by those who fear that such a center would be used to disseminate Muslim doctrine and Sharia law and threaten the first amendment freedoms guaranteed by the constitution. Others claim that religious liberty applies to everyone and that therefore Muslims have a right to erect a mosque anywhere.[34]

On Saturday evening, May 1, 2010, a time bomb located on a Nissan Pathfinder was discovered in Times Square in Manhattan. The bomb failed to explode, therefore saving the lives of hundreds who were crowding into the area at that time. Shortly thereafter, Faizal Shahad, a U.S. citizen born in Pakistan, was arrested in a plane bound for Dubai. Shahad was evidently connected to the Taliban organization in Pakistan and was willing to kill Americans despite his U.S. citizenship. He was charged with the attempted use of a weapon of mass destruction.[35]

One of the consequences of the attacks on Americans was the passage of the "Patriot Act" by Congress on October 24, 2001. Accordingly, the act expands the authority of law enforcement agencies to fight terrorism by searching telephone and email communications. It also allows law enforcers to search medical, financial and other records, eases restrictions of foreign intelligence gatherings, and enhances the immigration service to deport foreigners and immigrants suspected of supporting terrorism in the United States.[36]

The terrorist attacks also had a considerable effect on air travel in the United States. Tight controls at airports force passengers to arrive early, be searched in detail, and keep numerous items from coming into any plane.

It is evident that the attack on the United States by Muslim believers continues. Other western countries and even the Philippines and the all-Muslim country of Indonesia have also been the targets of bombings and violence on the part of the so-called Islamists.

Among such Islamists are those who claim that the U.S. government itself destroyed the World Trade Center and also attacked the Pentagon. These are numerous and popular in the Muslim world, who believe or pretend to believe that the bombings were part of a plot to force the United States into a confrontation with the world of Islam. An example is a statement of General Hameed Gul, formerly head of Pakistan's Interior Services Intelligence, who claimed in an interview that the U.S. Air Force carried out the destruction at the Pentagon. He called the attacks an "inside job" organized by President Bush. According to Gul and other such conspiracy theorists, "there is a diabolical school that wants to launch an anti-Muslim crusade."[37]

ATTACKS ON EUROPEANS IN THE NETHERLANDS, SPAIN, AND ENGLAND

On November 2, 2004, the Dutch filmmaker Theodoor Van Gogh was murdered on an Amsterdam street by the son of Muslim immigrants from Morocco. Muhammed Bouyeri, a Dutch born 27 year old citizen, shot and stabbed and cut the throat of van Gogh as he bicycled near the city zoo. The killer, dressed in Muslim clothes, waited alongside van Gogh after he shot and stabbed him to make sure he was dead. Bouyeri killed van Gogh because van Gogh had produced a film, Submission, exposing the manner in which Muslims treat women. The film contends that the Koran sanctions violence against women, as confirmed by Ayaan Hirsi Ali, a Somali refugee who fled an arranged Islamic marriage and became a Dutch politician elected to parliament. She collaborated with van Gogh and, since the murder, has continued under police protection, as the film enraged Muslims. Van Gogh had received death threats. His name and picture appeared on Muslim web sites captioned "wicked infidel," a label also used to designate Hirsi Ali.[38]

Muhammad Bouyeri was sentenced to life in prison without the possibility of parole. In court he said he would kill van Gogh again, as he viewed his victim an enemy of Islam. He also left a letter on the body threatening Hirsi Ali with a similar fate.[39]

The murder of van Gogh affected not only the victim, but also Dutch society as a whole. The result was that Dutch extremists burned mosques and assaulted Muslims in revenge. The Dutch population was suddenly confronted with a homegrown terrorist, when previously it has always been thought that terrorists came from foreign lands. The murder of van Gogh also caused a decline in public confidence in the government. This came about as people had to face that their own boys and girls could turn into murderers. Moreover, the Dutch were hardly equipped to deal with the fact that a religion would motivate its followers to hate and kill. The religious aspect of the murder demonstrated the danger of mixing religion with politics, which was always remote among the Dutch population but seemed the rule among the 900,000 Muslims, or 5.8% of the population, living in the Netherlands. Many Dutch citizens asked whether Islam is compatible with democratic values, which rest on the belief that freedom of expression is sacrosanct. The evidence is that at least the radical front line of Islam rejects western democracy. Instead these jihadists seek to replace democratic government with an Islamic caliphate. For these reasons, the murder of Theo van Gogh brought an end to peaceful coexistence between the general Dutch community and the Muslim minority. The majority of the Dutch viewed the murder as an attack on freedom of speech, leading the Dutch parliament to pass a "Crimes of Terrorism Act."[40]

Spanish Trains Bombed

On March 11, 2004, ten bombs exploded near Madrid on four commuter trains during the morning rush hour, killing 194 and wounding more than 1,000 commuters. Initially it was thought that the bombers were acting on behalf of the Basque liberation movement. However, it soon turned out that the bombers were Muslims who had taped excerpts from the Koran to a van near the Madrid railroad station. This attack occurred three days before the scheduled general election. The bombs went off in quick succession shortly before 8 a.m., when the police found and detonated three additional bombs. At the main commuter station in the center of Madrid, an explosion cut a train in two, shooting pieces of metal at passengers who crawled bleeding from the wreckage. Broken bodies and body parts were hurled on the platform. The streets around the railroad station became littered with human brains and ribs, as relatives rushed to the hospitals to find family members who had been on the trains. The police found that more than 220 pounds of dynamite in backpacks had been used in the attacks.[41]

Shortly after this mass slaughter, an Arabic language newspaper in London, England received an email issued by the Brigade of Abu Hafs al-Masri in the name of al-Qaeda, saying that its death squad had penetrated one of the pillars of the crusader alliance. The message continued, "This is part of settling accounts with Spain, the crusader, and America's ally in its war against Islam" (The crusades took place between 1095 and 1291).[42]

Three days after these killings the polls opened as thirty five million people voted. The winner was the socialist candidate Luis Rodrigues Zapatero, who had condemned the war in Iraq while his opponent, Jose Maria Aznar, the prime minister, supported that war. Evidently the Spanish electorate "caved in" to the demands of the terrorists, to whom this meant that violence could influence western elections in their favor. They therefore planned to attack the United States before November 2004 in the hope of influencing the American election at that time.[43]

In 2006, an Italian court found Rabel Ahmed guilty of "masterminding" the massacre of 2004 and sentenced him to ten years in prison. Italy allows the trial of non-Italians for terrorism. Yaya Ragheh, another killer, was sent to prison for five years.

On October 3, 2007, a Spanish court convicted 21 men of the Madrid train bombing. Three of the convicted were found guilty of mass murder and sentenced from thirty-four thousand (34,000) to forty three thousand (43,000) years in prison. Two of the men are Muslim immigrants from Morocco, but Emilio Suarez Trashorras is a native Spaniard. The others received lesser sentences.[44]

On July 7, 2005, three underground explosions on the London subway occurred simultaneously at about 8:50 a.m. The devices were exploded on three different trains and a bus traveling through central London. Fifty-two people were killed at once and more than seven hundred were injured.[45]

The attacks were carried out by four men who packed explosives into backpacks and left them at several subway stations and on one bus. The leader of these attacks was an English born Muslim, Mohammed Siddique Khan. Associated with him in these killings were Hasib Hussain, Shehzad Tanweer, and Jermaine Lindsay. The four died in these bombings with the understanding that they would thereby achieve immortality.[46]

The first device exploded at 8:51 a.m. and killed seven people. The second device exploded at 8:56 a.m. and killed twenty-one people. At 9:17 a third blast killed seven, followed by the killing of seventeen bus riders at 9:47 a.m. Half of the bus was blown away as people jumped from the double-decker into the street.[47]

On July 21, 2005, four Muslim men attempted once more to kill numerous passengers traveling on the London subway system and on one bus. Because only the detonators on the bombs exploded, there was no loss of life, although one person was wounded. As a result subway stations were evacuated and traffic interrupted for hours. Cameras provided the London police with images of the would-be killers. All four were arrested and convicted. Investigations revealed that the plot was organized by al-Qaeda and carried out by Muktar Said Ibrahim, Yassin Omar, Ramzi Mohammad and Hussein Osman. The court sentenced the four terrorists to prison for life. The court held that the four defendants sought to

replicate the attacks of July 7, 2005 with the knowledge of what the consequences would be for those subject to this intended attack.[48]

London has been called Londonistan, as its Muslim population has increased thirty fold since 1980. It has been estimated that there are 2.5 million
Muslims out of a population of 59 million in the United Kingdom of England,
Scotland, Wales, and Northern Ireland. Because family planning is seldom used
in Muslim society, the population of Muslims grows faster than that of any other
religious group in the world. In Europe the fertility rate of Muslims is 8.1, while
the general European population has a fertility rate of 1.38.[49]

SOME REASONS FOR THE MUSLIM ASSAULT ON THE WEST

Between 649 and 709 all of Christian North Africa was conquered by the Muslim Arabs. Since then the assault of the Muslim world upon the western Christian world has continued, albeit with years of interruptions.[50]

It comes at a surprise to westerners that in the Muslim world the Crusades
are remembered and are a motivating force in the effort to promote violence
against European and American targets. The first crusade was preached by Pope
Urban II in 1095 at the Council of Clermont. This succeeded for a time in re-
gaining the Holy Land for Christians but ended when Sal-ad-Din, the Kurdish
ruler, captured Jerusalem in 1187, so that by 1191 Christian dominance in the
Holy Land had come to an end despite some feeble attempts by later crusaders
to reverse this outcome. The crusades had long lasting effects on the Muslim
world and are especially symbolic in Arab perceptions because the position of
Muslims substantially declined after the 12th century while the western world,
including the United States, achieved considerable ascendancy thereafter.[51]

That ascendancy is visible because it consists mostly of achievements in
science and technology. Those achievements came about because of the auton-
omy of intellectual inquiry, the creation of international scientific languages,
particularly mathematics, and the routinization of research and its diffusion
around the world.[52]

In the democracies of Europe and America, private property is sacrosanct
and is therefore protected from arbitrary decisions by dictators. In the Muslim
world the opposite is the case. Therefore, private investments suffer as it is too
risky to invest in technology or business when government can seize anything,
any time.[53]

Language became another means of bringing about the ascendancy of the
west over eastern civilizations. From the beginning of the "Middle Ages" (1453)
until the middle of the 18th century, Latin was the international language in
which the learned of all western countries corresponded. This meant that early
science and advances in the humanities were all written in Latin to the exclusion
of the Arab- speaking peoples, who had at one time dominated these intellectual

enterprises. French was the international language of diplomacy until the beginning of the 20th century, so that it too became a tool for promoting the dominance of western civilization over that of the east.[54]

From the middle of the eighteenth century until the middle of the 20th century, French was undoubtedly dominant among western scholars and diplomats. Since about 1949, English has taken the place of French, so that eighty percent of academic journal articles are now written in English, except for areas of limited national interest such as studies in "Germanistics" or Russian literature. The physical sciences make almost exclusive use of English and the world diplomatic language is also English. It has been estimated that 914 million people speak English as their native or second language, so that English has become the most widespread language to the exclusion of all others. This is viewed as a threat to their own civilization even by western countries, let alone the Arabic speaking peoples and others.[55]

The globalization process which has diffused science and technology all over the world is another cause of Arab resentment and has contributed mightily to Arab terrorism against western societies. Large segments of Arabic speaking peoples feel excluded from the globalization process. It was for that reason that Arab reaction to the September 11, 2001 attacks were welcomed in the Muslim and particularly in the Arab world. Here were 29 Arabs who had succeeded in mastering aviation technology so well that they could fly into the World Trade Center and the Pentagon with precision and competence.[56]

In the traditional non-scientific countries science is often seen as incomprehensible or even catastrophic; science undermines authority and science is dangerous as it intervenes in "the natural order." The last two anti-science sentiments are particularly applicable to the Arab\Muslim point of view.

Of course, isolation from the western, scientific world weakens the Arab position. Coupled with resentment is dependence on that scientific world for all those technological products the Arab world cannot produce itself.[57]

Since the invasion of Egypt by the French under Napoleon in 1789, a collective feeling of inferiority by the Arabs vis a vis Europe and America has become a permanent feature of Arab sentiment. There are several factors which influence this feeling of inferiority and resentment. First, the importation of capital goods from western countries into Arab lands, second, arbitrary decisions made by Arab dictators as to the nature of imports from the west, and failure of education to deal with technology and science in the Arab world.[58]

Added to this frustration are aspects of western culture which seem utterly unacceptable to Muslim and non-Muslim Arab sensibilities. Most important of these western practices is the near equality of women as practiced in the western world. The contrast between the recently achieved advances in women's participation in every aspect of western life compared to the limits placed on women in Muslim societies is remarkable. Moreover, the civil rights of woman in Muslim/Arab societies are almost nonexistent and totally at odds with the position of women in western countries. In fact, women in Muslim societies have been historically invisible, as public life is limited exclusively to men.[59]

Although there is a limited "feminism" in some Arab countries, that movement is careful not to appear to imitate western views and conduct or to demand full participation with men lest such women be labeled "traitors" to their country, religion, and family. In fact, what matters most in Arab society is that women must be silent. Women in Arab society are expected to obey men, be that their father, their brother, or their husband. In Arab societies women are always on the margin.[60]

An excellent indication of the status of women in Arab societies is the practice of honor killing. Most domestic violence in Muslim countries remains unreported because women fear retaliation. Therefore, honor killings are also not always reported to the police. Such honor killings are demanded by the Muslim community, who impose on brothers and or fathers the duty to kill any woman alleged to have been sexually active outside of marriage. Since the reputation of a family depends on the killing of any girl or woman who has been viewed as an adulteress, there are many men who kill because they feel the pressure of the community to do so. Such murders usually go unpunished, as the "authorities" agree in the concept of "honor killing." It is believed in Muslim societies that the family honor is restored only when the "deviant" has been slaughtered. In many cases, female members of a family incite men to murder the deviant woman, particularly since no penalty attaches to these murders. In Muslim societies, adultery on the part of women is punished with death by stoning or 100 lashes in public.[61]

Added to these indignities is female genital mutilation, a practice to which over 130 million women worldwide are subject. It is particularly common in Egypt and has even been practiced in the United States by immigrants from Muslim countries, although it is prohibited in all states of the union.[62]

The liberty accorded women in western societies is viewed by Muslims as immoral, sexually loose, an attack on authority, and threatening the patriarchy. It is yet another source of resentment and anger directed at everything western.

Religious bigotry also plays a large part in the terror attacks aimed at the United States and other countries by Muslims. This is well illustrated by the treatment of non-Muslims in Saudi Arabia. According to the New York Times, "At a secret location every Sunday evening a young Catholic priest does a dangerous thing. He says Mass."[63]

In Saudi Arabia, Islam is the only official religion. All subjects must be Muslims and proselytizing is a crime punishable by imprisonment. Conversion of a Muslim to another religion is punishable by death. Non-Muslims, such as American service personnel, must not exhibit worship lest they be arrested, lashed, and deported. American soldiers who are in Saudi to protect the kingdom are not allowed to wear a cross or Star of David in public.[64]

According to the U.S. State Department, there are approximately ten million Christians in Egypt, which has a Muslim population of about 73 million. The U.S. Bureau of Democracy, Human Rights and Labor reports that on June 29, 2009, government forces instigated a violent clash when they prevented Christians from praying in a local church. The government also routinely fails to prosecute crimes against Christians and harasses converts from Islam to Christianity. Physical abuse of converts to Christianity is common and Coptic (Christian) priests are imprisoned at hard labor for officiating at a wedding between a Christian and a Muslim.

Mobs have repeatedly attacked and burned Christian churches while the homes of Bahai followers have been invaded and burned. Even smaller sects within Islam are harassed by Egyptian government agencies so that a Karanist, that is a follower of Islam who recognizes only the Quran but not the Hadith or interpretations, was refused a passport so that he could travel to the United States. Innumerable other obstacles are put in the way of a normal life for Christians in Egypt.[65]

Similar treatment is given Christians in other Muslim countries, while Jews are altogether banned and satanized by a level of propaganda that comes directly from Hitler's book *Mein Kampf.*

In sum, religious bigotry is so entrenched in the Muslim - Arab mind that the terrorist attacks conducted by young Muslims are without doubt heavily influenced by the religious beliefs to which all Muslim children are constantly subject. It is also of interest in this connection that the Arabic translation of Mein Kampf is a bestseller in the Arabic speaking world.[66]

NOTES

1. No author, "Teheran Students Seize U.S. Embassy And Hold Hostages," *The New York Times,* (November 5, 1979), A1.

2. Bernard Gwetzman, "President's Trip to Canada Today Put Off Because of Teheran Crisis," *The New York Times,* (November 9, 1979), A1.

3. Mark Bowden, "Guests of the Ayatollah," *The Atlantic Monthly,* vol. 297, no. 4, (May, 2006), 62.

4. Joe Stork, " The War of the Camps, the War of the Hostages," *MERIP Reports,* no. 133, (June 1985), 3-7.

5. Patrick Cockburn, "Terry Anderson is Set Free After Seven Years," *The Independent,* (December 5, 1991), 5,

6. Don Oberdorfer, "Iran Paid for Release of Hostages," *The Washington Post,* (January 19, 1994), A1.

7. William A. Rusher, "In Reagan's Defense," *National Review,* (August 9, 1985), 41.

8. Mitchell G. Bard, *The Complete Idiot's Guide to Middle East Conflict,* (New York: Alpha Books, 2005), 386.

9. Ibid, 365.

10. Fiona Beveridge, "The Lockerbie Affair," *The International and Comparative Law Quarterly,* vol.41,no.4, (October 1992), 907.

11. Sean Kirst, "They Never Got on Flight 103, but They Can't Escape the Tragedy," *The Post Standard,* (December 21, 2008),A1.

12. Michael Settle and Brian Currie, "Defiant Salmond Tells U.S. Oil Giant BP Did not Lobby to Free Megrahi,"*Herald Scotland,* (July 22, 2010), 1.

13. Gayle Reaves, "Ex-Dallas Clerk, 2nd Man Guilty in New York Bombing," *Dallas Morning News,* (November 13, 1997), 1.

14. Divya Watal, "W.T.C. Memorial for '93 victims Unveiled," *Downtown Express,* vol. 17, no. 41, (March 4-11, 2005), 1.

15. Rebecca Grant, "Khobar Towers." *Air Force Association Magazinel,* vol. 81, no.6, (June 1998), 8

16. John T. Correll, "Fallout from Khobar Towers," *Air Force Magazine,* vol. 88, no.11, (November 2005), 2.

17. U.S. Department of State, "Report of the Accountability Review Board," (Washington, .DC: The U.S. Government Printing Office, January 1999).

18. U.S. Department of State, "Report of the Accountability Review Board," (Washington, D.C. U.S. Government Printing Office, January 1999).

19. No author, "Al-Owhali Spared Death in Embassy Bombimg," *Law Center,* (June 12, 2001), 1.

20. Benjamin Weiser, "Life and Death Questions in Embassy Bombing," *The New York Times,* (June 3, 2001), 39.

21. United States Congress, *Lessons Learned from the Attack on the USS Cole,* (Washington, DC: United States Government Printing Office, 2001), 1-3

22. U.S. Justice Department, "Terrorism," (Washington, DC: 2008), 8.

23. No author, "A Day in the Life of America," *The New York Post,* (September 12, 2001), 18.

24. No author, "Deaths in World Trade Center Terrorist Attacks," *Morbidity and Mortality Weekly Report,* (Atlanta, GA: Centers for Disease Control and Prevention, September 11, 2002), 1-4.

25. National Commission on Terrorist Attacks Upon the United States, (Washington, DC: The United States Government Printing Office, (August 21, 2004) Chapter 7, 18-19.

26. U.S. Department of Defense, "Daily Casualty Release," Icasualtes.org

27. Richard K. Betts, "Is Strategy an Illusion?" *International Security,* vol.25, no. 2, (Autumn 2000), 5.

28. Human Rights Watch, "Saudi Arabia," (New York: Human Rights Watch World Report, 2001).

29. No author, "Hams Leader Faults Israeli Sanction Plan," *The New York Times,* (February 18, 2006), 1.

30. Pamela Geller, "Sharia in New Jersey," *Atlas Shrugs,* (July 24, 2010), 1.

31. Paul Walsh, "Islamic Group Backs Service Dog Owner," *Star Tribune,* (May 14, 2008), 1.

32. Curt Brown, "Racial Tensions High After Fight at Owatonna Hgh School," *Star Tribune,* (November 20, 2009), 1.

33. No author, "Cops at Michigan Arab Fest Accused of Enforcing Shariah," *Free Republic,* (June 22, 2010), 1.

34. Clyde Haberman, "In Islamic Center Fight. Lessons in Prepositions and Fear Mongering," *The New York Times,* (July 27, 2010), A 13.

35. Mark Mazzetti , Sabrina Tavrnise and Jack Healy, "Suspect Charged, Said to Admit Role in Plot," *New York Times,* (May 5, 2010), A1.

36. HR 3162, 107th Congress, (October 24, 2001).

37. Arnaud de Borchgrave, "Pakistan's Ex-Spy Chief Blames Mossad," *United Press International,* (September 26, 2001),n.p.

38. Ayan Hirsi Ali, "Grief and anger over Theo's murder; Victim of Islamists," *The International Herald Tribune,* (November 11, 2004), 8.

39. Gregory Crouch, "World Briefing Europe; The Nethelands: Van Gogh Killer Jailed for Life," *The New York Times,* (July 27, 2005), 8.

40. H. Entzinger, "The Rise and Fall of Multiculturalism: The Case of the Netherlands," In: C. Jopke and E. Morawska, (*Toward Assimilation and Citizenship,* Basingstoke: Palgrave), 59-86.

41. No author, "Manhunt for Madrid Massacre Terrorists," *Manchester Evening News,* (March 12, 2004), 1.

42. Ibid, 1.

43. Lawrence Wright, "The Terror Web," *The New Yorker,* (August 2, 2004).

44. Sergio Perez, "21 Convicted of Madrid Train Bombing; Alleged Planner Acquitted," Reuters and USA Today, (October 31, 2007), 1.

45. Elaine Sciolino and Don Van Natta, Jr. "For a Decade London Thrived as a Busy Crossroads of Terror," *The New York Times,* (July 10, 2005), 1.

46. Mark Townsend, "Leak Reveals Offical Story of London Bombings," The Guardian, (April 9, 2006), 1.

47. Hugh Muir and Rosie Cowan, "Four Bombs in 5 Minutes," *The Guardian,* (July 8, 2005), 1.

48. Peter Walker, "Four July 21 Plotters Jailed for Life," *The Guardian,* (July 11, 2007), 1.

49. Radhasyam Brahmahari, "Dangerous Policy of Muslim Appeasement in the U.K." *Faith Freedom* , (July 04, 2010), n.p.

50. C.J. Speel, "The Disappearance of Christianity from North Africa in the Wake of the Rise of Islam," *Church History,* vol. 29, no.4, (December 1960), 379-397.

51. Carole Hildenbrand, *The Crusades: Islamic Perspectives,* (Chicago: Fitzroy Dearborn, 1999), 391-419.

52. David Landes, *The Wealth and Poverty of Nations,* (New York: Norton, 1998), 201-206.

53. Douglas C. North and Robert Thomas, *The Rise of the Western World: A New Economic History,* (Cambridge University Press, 1973), 130-133.

54. F. L. Sack, "Problems of an International Language," *The Phi Delta Kappan,* Vol. 32, no. 2, (October 1950), 49.

55. Christine Keneally, *The First Word: The Search for the Origins of Language,* The Viking Press, (2007), 58, 164, 235, 287.

56. Richard Falk, "False Universalism and the Geopolitics of Exclusion" *Third World Quarterly,* vol. 18, no.1, (March 1997), 7-23.

57. Louay Safi, "From Reform to Revoluion," *Intellectual Discourse,* vol. 3, no. 1, (1995), 26.

58. Antoine Zahlan, *"Science and Science Policy in the Arab World,"* (New York: St. Martin's Press, 1980), 18.

59. Miriam Cooke, "Women, Religion, and the Postcolonial Arab World," *Cultural Critique,* no.45, (Spring 2000), 150.

60. Ibid, 151-156.

61. Fadia Faqir, "Intrafamily Femicide In Defence of Honor," *Center for Inquiry,* (August 2000), 1-10.

62. No author, "In Depth: Razor's Edge: The Controversy of Female Genital Mutilation," *IRIN* , (March 2005), 1.

63. Elaine Sciolino, "For Outsiders in Saudi Arabia, Worship Comes With a Risk," *The New York Times,* (February 12, 2002), A15.

64. Ibid, A15.

65. No author, *Egypt: International Religious Freedom Report,* (Washington DC: U.S. Departmetn of State, October 26, 2009), 1-15.

66. Sean O,Neill and John Steele, "Mein Kampf for Sale in Arabic," *The Telegraph,* (March 19, 2002), 1.

Chapter Nine
The Causes of Assassinations — Some Theories

I.

Theory, derived from the Greek word for "viewing" refers to an effort to understand a phenomenon. Theories are tools used to explain something and to make predictions. Theories follow rational thought and logic and may be expressed mathematically or verbally. Theories explain something generally based on some assumptions which may be testable. This would be true of sociological theory but cannot be said of psychoanalytic theory. This means that some theories are based on empirical data while others are based on insight or speculation without such data.

While the word "theory" is suspect as a mere hunch or guess, scientific theory refers to "a comprehensive explanation of an important feature of nature supported by facts gathered over time." [1]

A number of theories attempt to explain assassinations of prominent people. One of these theories is differential association theory which is an explanation for crimes of any kind, but particularly violent crimes, as developed by Edwin Sutherland (1883-1950). In his influential book *Principles of Criminology*, Sutherland presents a learning theory of crime which best explains those assassinations committed by the European anarchists.

According to Sutherland, criminal behavior is learned. This means that assassins must learn how to assassinate and do so in interaction with others. That is certainly the case regarding the anarchists. Sutherland furthermore argues that the principal part of the learning of criminal behavior occurs in intimate groups. Again, this fits anarchist assassinations.

Assuming then that assassinating prominent people is learned, the assassin, according to Sutherland, must learn the techniques of committing the killing and must be able to rationalize his murderous behavior. [2]

Such rationalization consists of denying responsibility for the assassination in that the assassins blame the victim who, they claim, brought his death on himsclf by his policies or repressive acts. The assassins condemn the condemner in that they claim that the victim is to be condemned, not they. In addition, assassins often appeal to higher loyalty in that they claim to act on behalf of some cause or higher goal which justifies assassination of a prominent person.[3]

Sutherland further argued that some people are surrounded by persons who have an unfavorable view of the legal code so that they are isolated from those who favor the law. That is most certainly the case of the anarchist societies as they existed in Europe in the nineteenth and early twentieth centuries. This is the crux of Sutherland's theory of differential association. He adds that frequency, duration and intensity of association with those who reject the law and authority increases the chances of committing one or more crimes including the assassination of prominent people.[4]

It is to be expected that assassins, before they kill, will consider the effectiveness of their action. Furthermore, several studies have shown that participation in assassination depends in part of the risks of collective action. Hence, the higher the risk the greater the barrier to carrying out an assassination. It has also been shown that the behavior of the authority targeted for assassination determines in part whether or not it will be carried out. The legitimacy granted an authority is involved in that the lower the legitimacy granted the authority the greater the chances of acting against it. We also note that assassins are generally people who have a good deal of free time in which to plan and activate the assassination.[5]

Social networks are very influential in promoting assassinations and that for the same reasons that such networks are always influential in making individual choices. Such networks push people into making choices and then acting upon them. Networks also deliver an opportunity to participate and socialize some people to an issue and "shape their decision to become involved." [6]

The intensity with which one is involved in social movements such as the anarchist movement depends largely on perception. Passy and Giugni have developed hypotheses concerning involvement in a cause such as anarchy. According to their research, "the more positive an individual perceives the effectiveness of his involvement ... the higher the level of participation." It has also been shown that individual participation depends on the assessment of the risks of collective action. This means that the risks of attempting or even succeeding in an assassination have a negative impact on individual participation in an assassination. This is particularly the case in a repressive situation such as a brutal dictatorship. This largely explains why so few efforts were made to assassinate Hitler in the 1930's and 1940's.[7]

Recruitment into anarchist organizations which were responsible for numerous political assassinations in the 19th and early 20th centuries depended in part of giving those interested in joining such groups sufficient information concerning the goals and rationale for carrying out assassinations. Trust is of course critical in carrying out such deeds. Therefore, a number of the assassins were recruited from among close friends who convinced the would-be assassin that he should be a member of the anarchist group and that he should act in behalf of their ideology. [8]

"True believers" among recruiters for anarchist organizations or for any organization are more likely to succeeding in gaining new recruits and are more successful in having new recruits become "true believers" themselves. Such "true believers" are most anxious to convince others of their cause and are therefore most effective in recruiting aggressive participants.[9]

Individual perception of an issue by its supporters also influences whether or not a recruit to an organization is willing to do something about the issue. Hence, anarchists are recruited from those who have had life experiences related to the issue at hand. A person who has been victimized by a tyrannical government is more likely to participate in an assassination plot than someone to whom the assassination plot is based only on theory or remote complaints. [10]

It is reasonable to assume that those who carry out assassinations as well as those who participate only verbally in anarchist organizations are very much interested in the cause that the assassins represent. These are people who have a great interest in the issue agitating the anarchists or would-be assassins. Such people are most likely to have had real experiences with the present issue and may have been victims of the individual to be assassinated. [11]

Assassinations of a political nature are usually conducted by people who consider their killing of the victim justified. Those who commit these atrocities are seldom motivated by personal gain. Instead they are willing to accept great personal sacrifices in order to succeed. Usually the assassin holds a political opinion shared by a large number of other people. Many of the assassins claim after they killed a head of state that they had no hatred of the victim but only hate the system, which the victim represented. Assassination is always a possibility in any political system although it does not necessarily succeed.

II.

There are of course assassins who have never been associated with an organization or group of any kind. Some of these have been psychotics whose murderous impulses drove them to a deed without reason. In Europe, but not in the United States, assassinations have been well planned and carried out by political organizations.[12]

It has been speculated that the reason assassinations of presidents or other heads of state seem so shocking to many citizens is that his position, rather than his person, assures people that there is protection from outside enemies inasmuch as the first duty of any government is the protection of the citizens. Assassinations seem to remove that protection.[13]

After every assassination a number of conspiracy theories become popular. This was true after the assassinations of Lincoln, Garfield, McKinley and Kennedy. After every one of these events there were many who sought to find "the real story behind the assassination." Even now, over a hundred and forty years after the murder of Lincoln, there are still those who see a far greater conspiracy than was uncovered at the time. Likewise the killers of Garfield and McKinley were seen as part of a larger anarchist conspiracy while speculation about Kennedy's killer, Oswald, never end although non-Americans, foreigners, are more likely to see a conspiracy in Kennedy's death than is true of Americans. At that time, 1963, the so-called "cold war" between the United States and the Soviet Union convinced many Americans that somehow communism was the catalyst that brought on this murder. [14]

Terrorism is another explanation for assassinations of prominent people. This may be an attack on utterly uninvolved people in the general population who become the victims of terror because the killers want to destabilize the government, by making the government appear impotent and therefore unable to protect the citizens. There is another form of terrorism called "direct" terrorism. This consists of kidnapping or killing of a prominent person whom the terrorists may not know but who represents the target group viewed as the oppressors. An excellent example is the kidnapping and murder of the German industrialist Siegfried Buback by the Red Army Fraction in 1977.[15]

Evidently, the assassination of world leaders is the most visible terrorist act available. Examples are the attempted assassination of President Ronald Reagan and Pope John Paul II in 1981 and the successful killing of Anwar Sadat, dictator of Egypt. Assassinations were particularly common in the period 1968 to 1980 when there were 721 major assassination events in the world. [16]

Because political assassinations receive considerable media coverage the assassins are actually helped in their effort to gain the attention of the public and promote their messages, whatever these may be. Media coverage is extremely important to assassins of prominent politicians because the killers are usually of the opinion that if their views are given enough publicity they will prevail and public support will insure the achievement of their aims. [17]

Thomas Snitch has developed a table showing the frequency of assassinations based on occupation or position of the victim. He found that 10.8% of successful assassinations victimized a head of state and 9.5% victimized a foreign government official. These targets were the most frequent of all assassination victims wile medical doctors, tribal chiefs, presidential candidates, agricultural leaders and small businessmen suffered the least number of assassinations. [18]

Snitch also found that five categories of actors accounted for 98% of all successful assassinations. First were extremist political groups, followed by "unspecified" actors and military coup attempts. [19]

In 1990, Michael Gottfredson and Travis Hirschi published *A General Theory of Crime*. They claim that all crime, including assassinations, stem from the lack of self control. This, they say, results from ineffective child rearing and lasts a life time. These authors hold that people with low self control act impulsively and spontaneously, value risk and adventure and care about themselves more than they care about others. This explanation suits the activities of such assassins as Charles Guiteau who killed President Garfield and Mark Chapman who killed John Lennon.[20]

The work of Godfriedson and Hirschi leads to control theory which claims that people who are controlled in most situations in their lives are more likely to commit crimes of violence than those who do the controlling. The assumption here is that people want to be as autonomous as possible and that those who are controlled more than they can tolerate will react violently. This would mean that societies suffer from dictatorships such as the erstwhile European monarchies will have a greater change of promoting assassinations than democracies such as the United States.

The meaning of an assassination depends on the culture in which the assassination takes place. This is true in Europe and Asia while in the United States most assassinations have been carried out by people who were emotionally disturbed.

The meaning of an assassination can of course be interpreted in the light of various political opinions. This became evident after John F. Kennedy was assassinated in 1963. Numerous followers of various political views found it expedient to interpret the assassination to suit their opinions.

One frequently expressed view of the Kennedy assassination and the murder of his killer, Oswald, that these murders were the product of organized plotting and not the deeds of individuals alone. So-called "liberals" blamed extremists of both the "left" and "right" for the assassinations. Some claimed that the assassinations of Kennedy and Oswald were part of a communist plot since Oswald was known for his communist sympathies, his stay in the Soviet Union and his association with Fidel Castro, the communist dictator of Cuba. [21]

Revilo Oliver, a member of the John Birch society also claimed that Kennedy had been killed for not following orders of his communist masters and that the assassination was preparation for a "domestic takeover." [22]

The sum of these "communist conspiracy" theories was that "liberals" were responsible for the assassination of the president with particular reference to Fidel Castro.

Even as the opponents of communism blamed communists for the Kennedy assassination, the Soviet Union blamed "ultra-right wing fascists" and racists. The Soviet media claimed that the assassination was to be used to stir up "hysteria" against the Soviet Union and Cuba together with the innuendo that the F.B.I. was responsible for the death of Kennedy. [23]

The Arab press, as expected, blamed the assassination of president Kennedy on the Jews. They arrived at this conclusion by citing that Jack Ruby who killed Oswald was a Jew.[24]

Since 1835 when Richard Lawrence tried to assassinate Andrew Jackson, the seventh president of the United States, there have been twelve attempted or successful assassinations of U.S. presidents. Only four succeeded as Booth killed Lincoln in 1865, Guiteau killed Garfield in 1881, Czolgosz killed McKinley in 1901 and Oswald killed Kennedy in 1963.

Clarke and Lucente have analyzed the American assassins and would-be assassins of American presidents. According to their study, the assassins, including the failed assassins, are almost always male, are in need of acceptance by others, have been denied recognition and status, and have been rejected by employers or spouses or parents or other significant persons in their lives. The failed, would-be assassins were: Richard Lawrence, John Schrank who tried to kill Theodore Roosevelt in 1912, Guiseppe Zangara who tried to kill Franklin Roosevelt in 1933, Oscar Collazo and Griselio Torresola who tried to kill Harry Truman in 1950, Samuel Byck who tried to kill Richard Nixon in 1974, Lynette Fromme and Sara Jane Moore who tried to kill Gerald Ford in 1975, John W. Hinkley who tried to kill Ronald Reagan in 1981 and Francisco Duran who tried to kill Bill Clinton in 1994. Note that only two, Lynette Fromme and Sara Moore are women. [25]

According to Clarke assassins and would-be assassins can be classified in four categories of motivation. Clarke calls type one "rational political extremists" including John Wiles Booth, Leon Czolgosz, Oscar Collazo, Griselio Torresola and Sirhan Sirhan.[26]

III.

It is not unreasonable to assume that those who kill famous people can be partially motivated by the belief that they will become famous themselves and enter into the history books by becoming closely associated with their victim. John Wilkes Booth certainly succeeded if that was one of his motives. This need to be known in a negative manner can be found even among killers of unknown victims. For example, James Oliver Huberty killed 21 people who happened to eat at McDonald's restaurant in San Ysidro, California on July 18, 1984. Huberty viewed himself as a "loser" who wanted to be known. In that he succeeded as he was undoubtedly one of the most prolific mass murderers in American history. Without this dubious distinction, Huberty would never have received any recognition. [27]

Speaking to the Columbia Historical Society in 1947, Beall reviewed all the theories concerning the reasons for the assassination of Lincoln. He identified eight theories why Booth killed Lincoln. The first is that Booth was "crazy." That term is of course meaningless and refers to the user, not the target of this appellation. There was no evidence that Booth was unbalanced from a psychiatric point of view unless one wants to subscribe to the tautological argument that he was "crazy" because he assassinated the president.

The second argument, most popular at the time, was that Booth was part of a Confederate conspiracy to kill Lincoln. Yet, every effort to find evidence for such a conspiracy failed. "Nothing was ever found to link Confederate officials with any design on the person of Lincoln."[28]

Thirdly, it was claimed by some that Vice President Andrew Johnson conspired to kill Lincoln. This theory was also discredited because a congressional committee investigated this assumption but found nothing to confirm such a supposition. In fact, Johnson had also been slated for murder although the designated would-be assassin made no effort to do so.

A fourth theory concerning the assassination of Lincoln is the possibility that radical Republicans wanted to kill Lincoln because they disagreed with Lincoln's program to reunited the country, re-admit the Confederacy to the Union and end control of the government by the radicals. There is no evidence that Booth was associated with the radical Republicans or that they asked him to kill Lincoln.

Another theory seeking to explain the assassination of Lincoln was the belief that foreigners, in the service of the Emperor of Mexico, Maximilian were responsible for the escape of Booth and that they, the foreigners, sought to establish monarchies in the western hemisphere. This view was particularly enhanced by the imposition of the Austrian Maximilian who had become emperor of Mexico only because the French under Napoleon III installed him in that position in 1864. Maximilian did not last long. He was killed by revolutionaries in 1867 after Napoleon III had withdrawn his troops. Again, no evidence ever existed that Booth was an agent of any foreign power.

Booth was a friend of John Yates Beall, an officer in the Confederate army who was captured and murdered by the Union army while trying to establish a confederate naval presence in Lake Erie. Booth made several efforts to save the life of Beall all of wich failed. He may have killed Lincoln to avenge the death of Beall.

Finally it is possible that Booth acted "on his own recognizance" in that he viewed Lincoln as a radical republican who sought to keep the South from ever rising again by imposing a permanent military presence of the Union army on the confederate states. Possibly all or several of these motives were responsible for Booth's deed. In the end, no final determination of Booth's reasons can ever be made.

It may therefore be said that Booth sought to avoid the very revenge driven conduct, which befell the South at the hands of northerners after the civil war. Book believed Lincoln would act in a manner later attributed to the "radical Republicans" although that was by no means Lincoln's intention. In short, Booth sought revenge.[29]

The revenge motive may also be found in the actions of Francisco Duran who sought to assassinate President Clinton on October 29, 1994.

Duran is an example of a would-be assassin who sought to "get even" for a disappointing life. Anger and resentment consumed him as he sought to kill the president who symbolized to him all the frustrating experiences of his entire life. This was also the motive of David Chapman who killed John Lennon in 1980.

A closer look at Francisco Duran reveals that he had been a prisoner in the federal prison at Leavenworth, Kansas. Duran was born in 1968 into a poor family in New Mexico. He lived below the poverty level with his mother and five brothers who spoke Spanish most of the time. He did not know his father any more than his brothers all of whom had a different father. His mother worked as a "cleaning lady" and supplemented her children by means of her poor income and food stamps. [30]

"Frankie" Duran was a mediocre high school student who had no distinctions except that he joined the Junior Reserve Officer Training Corps (ROTC). Arrested for a minor infraction, Duran joined the U.S. Army and the charges against him were dropped. Duran began his army career in Hawaii where he married and had a son. [31]

Then, on August 9, 1990, Frankie Duran drove into a crowd of people with whom he had engaged in a drunken argument a few minutes earlier. He injured one woman and was arrested and court martialed on a series of charges. He served two and a half years in the Fort Leavenworth army prison and was then discharged in disgrace with a Dishonorable Discharge. [32]

Duran felt betrayed by a government he wanted to serve as a career soldier. Instead he worked as an upholsterer to support his family. Meanwhile he thought of getting even with those whom he blamed for ruining his life. His anger became focused on president Clinton so that he told several associates that he would kill Clinton if given the chance.

Duran then bought a Chinese made rifle and drove to Washington, D.C. with a view of killing the president. He also anticipated his own death and therefore wrote a suicide not to his wife and small son. Arrested and convicted he was sentenced to forty four years in prison without the possibility of parole. [33]

Duran, like Oswald, who killed President Kennedy, Byck, who sought to kill Richard Nixon, and Fromme and Moore, who sought to kill Gerald Ford, all wanted to be known. Likewise, Bremer, who shot George Wallace, and Hinckley, who shot Ronald Reagan, were all seeking "infamy" or negative fame. These killers and would-be assassins are not motivated by any political doctrine but suffer from violent fantasies accompanied by self hatred. Like Duran, Byck and Fromme and Moore all felt humiliated and unjustly treated by numerous persons in their past. The target of their rage was a symbol for all who had wronged them. The prominence of a president or major political figure or important entertainer like John Lennon motivated these assassins, not the politics the targets espoused. In addition, the assassins and would-be assassins generally seek suicide as they view their lives hopeless and without purpose.

IV.

There are also assassins who act rationally and are motivated by political considerations. Examples would be Griselio Torresola and Leon Collazo who sought to kill president Harry Truman, Sirhan Sirhan who killed Senator Robert Kennedy and Leon Czolgocz who killed William McKinely.

On November 1, 1950 Griselio Torresola was killed by Leslier W. Coffelt who shot him in front of the Blair House, the then temporary residence of President Harry S. Truman. In the course of this attempted assassination, the White House policeman Leslie W. Coffelt was also killed by a shot from the gun of Torresola. In addition, policeman Donald Birdzell was shot in both knees by Oscar Collazo, Torresola's friend and accomplice. In addition, Collazo was shot in the chest by Donald Birdzell but survived. Later sentenced to death, his sentence was commuted by President Truman to life imprisonment. He was pardoned by President Jimmy Carter and released in 1979. He died in Puerto Rico in 1994. [34]

Unlike those assassins who seek fame and attention by their deeds, Torresola and Collazo acted from political motives in an attempt to call attention to the fight for Puerto Rican independence.

The history of that effort extends to the 16th century when Puerto Rican natives in 1511 organized a revolt against Spain. Revolts against the Spaniards continued into the 19th century. All were defeated by the better armed Spanish forces who easily put down the natives, armed with spears and bows and arrows. [35]

During the Spanish-American war in 1898, Puerto Rico was invaded by U.S. forces. Thereafter several Puerto Rican nationalists proposed independence for the island but were unsuccessful in persuading the U.S. government to allow this. Failing this effort led to the development of several political parties in Puerto Rico all of whom sought to bring about independence from the United States. These smaller parties joined together into the Puerto Rican Nationalist Party in 1924. Since then the nationalist have resorted to some violent acts leading to the deaths of several politicians and others. Although the United States government has suppressed the independence movement in Puerto Rico for over a century, that movement is by no means dead. In 1946 Gilberto Concepcion de Garcia founded the Independence Party although that party has elected very few legislators and has lost most of its influence. Nevertheless there are those in Puerto Rico who still seek to achieve independence by the ballot box or by violence so that as late as 2009 eight U.S. jet planes were destroyed by dissidents at a Puerto Rican military base. [36]

Political motives as well as religious hate led Sirhan Sirhan to kill Senator Robert Kennedy in 1968. Sirhan was born in Jerusalem in 1944. When he was 12, in 1956, his family emigrated to New York and then to California. He attended school in Altadena and later at Pasadena City College. He was employed as a stable boy in 1965 at the Santa Anita race track.[37]

Sirhan was raised in an Arab community which taught him and other children that no Jew has a right to be on this planet. He was taught that Jews are pigs and monkeys and that Jews drink the blood of Arab children. These hateful lessons were taught in Arab schools which were under the jurisdiction of the Kingdom of Jordan while Sirhan lived there. Killing Jews was taught as a virtue, a lesson still taught in Arab and Muslim schools around the world. The destruction of Israel was and is taught as a moral necessity and Jews are labeled the ultimate evil. Palestinian textbooks take their contents from Nazi literature claiming Jews are wild animals, locusts and treacherous.

After moving to the United States, Sirhan continued to believe in these hate filled doctrines which were even then supported by the American Arab community. He became particularly incensed against Jew when Israel succeeded in defeating four Arab armies intent on slaughtering the entire Israeli population. The Arabs of the world had reason to hope that they could achieve another holocaust only to discover that Jews will defend their lives. He then discovered that Americans were largely happy that Israel had survived. This angered him. Then, when Robert Kennedy ran for president and participated in an Israel Independence Day celebration, Kennedy said on television, "we are committed to Israel's survival." Sirhan saw this as an unacceptable view by a contender for the presidency and feared that Kennedy, if elected, would continue the U.S. support for Israel. He therefore believed that the crime of assassinating Robert Kennedy was legitimate. He was proud of his act. Like other anarchists, Sirhan believed that he could advance his cause by "propaganda of the deed."[38]

Arthur Bremer sought to kill President Richard Nixon but was unable to reach his target when Nixon visited Ottawa, Canada on April 14, 1972 where he spoke to the members of the House of Commons. One month later, Bremer shot and paralyzed the presidential candidate, Governor George Wallace of Alabama after Wallace concluded a campaign speech in Laurel, Maryland. Bremer failed both times to assassinate famous potential victims but nevertheless succeeded in giving meaning to his otherwise failed existence.[39]

According to a scheme developed by Clarke, Bremer may be classified as a nihilist, together with Guiseppe Zangara who attempted to assassinate Franklin Roosevelt. Clarke defines nihilists as psychopaths "who believe that the conditions of their lives are so intolerably meaningless and without purpose that destruction of society and themselves is desirable for its own sake." [40]

Seeking to make himself important, Bremer pretended to be an enthusiastic supporter of Governor Wallace by shouting and whistling and otherwise making a great deal of noise at Wallace's speaking appearances. This faked enthusiasm also served to cover up Bremer's intention as he yelled "over here, over here" as the governor was about to leave a political rally. This permitted Bremer to shoot Wallace who had followed his shouts and walked directly into Bremer's fire as he, Wallace reached out to shake Bremer's hand. [41]

Bremer was the product of a dysfunctional family in the sense that his mother abandoned him and left him to a foster home; that his father was an alcoholic and that hostility and conflict were ever present among his parents during his childhood. [42]

Bremer's only success was his high school diploma. Thereafter he took some courses in a Milwaukee technical school but dropped out after one year. His effort to date and attain a girl friend failed because of his gross behavior leading to rejection and a sense of abandonment by a girl whom he could not impress and whom he elevated emotionally to an importance utterly out of proportion to reality. That rejection and an appraisal of his life as useless led Bremer to seek the assassination of Richard Nixon and later George Wallace. Not the policies of these two men, but the notoriety he would achieve by shooting them attracted Bremer. In a negative sense Bremer was right. He has become prominent in American history which otherwise would have ignored him.[43]

V.

John Schrank attempted to kill President Theodore Roosevelt during the presidential campaign of 1912. On October 14 of that year, Schrank shot Roosevelt as Roosevelt was leaving a Milwaukee hotel after a political dinner. Schrank had followed Roosevelt from New Orleans and finally had a chance of shooting him as Roosevelt was about to enter his car. Roosevelt was fortunate in that the bullet hit the steel rims of his eye glasses and then entered his chest only after traveling through a 50 page speech Roosevelt carried in his jacket pocket. Roosevelt did not cough up any blood and therefore decided to deliver his speech without going to a hospital. He spoke for ninety minutes despite his pain. The bullet was never removed but Roosevelt was so badly injured that he could not campaign effectively for the third term he sought. [44]

Schrank claimed that he was advised by the ghost of William McKinley to avenge his death. The ghost had pointed to a picture of Theodore Roosevelt. Schrank also claimed that McKinley told him to prevent Roosevelt from becoming a "third termer." Doctors declared Schrank to be insane and suffering from delusions. He was therefore sentenced to remain in the Central State Mental Hospital in Waupin, Wisconsin, where he died in 1943.[45]

On March 30, 1981, John W. Hinckley attempted to assassinate president Ronald Reagan . Hinckley fired a .22 caliber revolver six times at Reagan as he left a hotel in Washington, D.C. Hinckley also wounded press secretary James

Brady, police officer Thomas Delahanty and Secret Service agent Timothy McCarthy. [46]

John Hinckley was born in 1955 the son of a wealthy family. He grew up in North Dallas among exceptional wealth and privilege. In his community ninety percent of adults hold college degrees from prestigious and expensive universities such as Vanderbilt, the college from which his brother graduated. John also has a sister who was a beauty queen and head of the cheerleaders at football games. In this atmosphere of ambition and success, John Hinckley was left out. He failed to graduate from college, failed to find a job, failed to find a girl friend and spent his time as a "loner." When his family left Texas, John remained and enrolled at Texas Technical University in Lubbock. He made no friends there and left before graduating to visit neo-Nazi rallies in Washington and other places. He then visited New Haven, the location of Yale University where he became infatuated with a minor actress whose portrayal of a 12 year old fascinated him. He wrote letters to the actress which were not answered. Then he traveled to Denver, Colorado where his family had settled. He did not live in his families luxurious home. Instead he stood in soup lines in downtown Denver. From there he flew to Los Angeles and then took a bus to Washington D.C. where he arrived after a four day trip. Meanwhile John Hinckley had become obsessed with the movie *Taxi Driver* and its protagonist. He kept writing to her without any response. Finally John Hinckley shot President Reagan and thereby gained the attention of his parents and much notoriety across the land. Using the insanity defense, Hinckley was found "not guilty by reason of insanity" and confined to a mental hospital for an indefinite stay. He was allowed to visit his parents in 2009 and was given a drivers license that same year. [47]

Two women became prominent for their attempt to kill President Gerald Ford. In September of 1975, Lyunette Fromme attempted to assassinate President Gerald Ford in Sacramento, California.Fromme was 26 years old when she pushed through a crowd, pulled a pistol from a holster on her thigh and tried to shoot president Ford who was walking from his hotel to the state capitol. Because the gun had no bullet in the chamber, it would not fire although there were four bullets in the magazine.

Fromme was sentence to life in prison. During her trial she tried to be her own lawyer and also sought to call the mass murdered Charles Manson as a witness. Because of her violent outbursts she was removed from the courtroom. She had met Manson on the street in Los Angeles at age eighteen. She followed Manson and continued to be obsessed by him even after he and others were convicted of killing actress Sharon Tate in 1969.

Fromme was eligible for parole in 1987 but refused to apply. In 1987 she escaped from prison in an effort to reach Charles Manson in his California prison. In 2008 she was granted an automatic parole hearing and released in 2009. [48]

It is instructive to compare the sentence given Fromme for attempted murder and the average sentence for attempted murder served in California prisons. There the statute holds that "as a general matter, a person guilty of attempted murder must be punished by imprisonment for five, seven or nine years." [49]

This plainly shows that attempted murder of a president results in far more prison time than attempted murder of any other citizen, thereby creating a hierarchy of citizens in which the lives of politicians are valued more than the lives of the ordinary taxpayer. This contradicts the spirit of democracy and demonstrates how far the United States has moved from a democracy to an authoritarian community. As yet, we are not a police state.

There can be little doubt that in 1975 Lynette Fromme had become a psychiatric "case" by whatever language may be used to describe her bizarre behavior. She had used a razor blade to etch a cross into her forehead. She was utterly obsessed with the killer of Sharon Tate, Charles Manson. She had spent some time in the drug culture of the Haight-Ashbury neighborhood of San Francisco where Manson found her sitting alone at the curb and crying. He took her along with others in a bus he was driving and persuaded her to shave her head. After Manson was sent to prison for his numerous crimes she became the leader of the remnants of his hippie "family." She called herself a "nun" in the service of Manson and wore red robes. Although twenty one years old when prosecutor Vincent Bugliosi met her, she gave the impression of being retarded and having the personality of a child.

In 2009, at the age of sixty, she was released from prison in Texas. She is on parole for the rest of her life. [50]

On February 22, 1974 Samuel Byck, attempted to seize an airliner and crash it into the White House in an effort to kill President Richard Nixon. The assault by Byck began when he shot and killed George Neal Ramsburg, a police officer. Ramsburg screened passengers when Byck killed him. Byck then boarded the plane carrying a handgun and a gasoline bomb. He stormed the cockpit and demanded that the two pilots take off. When they refused he shot both, killing one of them. He then grabbed a woman passenger and demanded she fly the plane. However, a policeman on board took the fallen officers gun and shot Byck through the cabin window. That led Byck to kill himself with his own gun. [51]

In 2004, three decades after the Byck's failed effort to kill Richard Nixon, the actor Sean Penn portrayed Byck in a movie entitled *The Assassination of Richard Nixon*. The movie received poor reviews and did little to explain Byck's conduct except to show that Byck was far from normal. [52]

VI.

Although American assassinations have been principally undertaken by people who lived in an unreal world created by their psyche, an understanding of assassinations cannot only rest on the assumption that those who kill or try to kill political leaders are always psychotic or otherwise impaired. Other reasons for assassination include the wish to destabilize the government and undermine confidence in it. This means that assassination of government officials is a political phenomenon because it is a direct assault on a nation's political institution.[53]

Khachadourian has shown that the motives of most assassins are usually political in nature and are not related to personal malice as is true in most homicides.[54]

In the ancient world the killing of a tyrannical ruler was endorsed by Socrates (469-399) and Xenophon (430-354). This was also the case with the assassins of Julius Caesar, who believed that Caesar sought to become dictator of Rome. In later years, Giovanni Bocassio (1313-1375) a founder of the Renaissance and Francesco Guicciardini (1483-1540) the "father of modern history" also advocated the killing of tyrants as a legitimate means of liberating a society. Likewise, Niccolo Machiavelli, (1469-1527), the "father of political science" considered assassination as one of the strategies for gaining political power.[55]

Thomas More, (1478-1575) in his Utopoia (no place) promoted the view that a policy of assassination would quickly end hostilities between states and save many lives.[56]

Relative deprivation is an additional reason for political assassinations. This concept relies on economic inequality although it can also be attributed to power inequality. Either interpretation indicates that political repression can be expected to foster assassination or other political violence. Numerous studies have shown that "the level of political repression in a society will be positively related to the level of political violence."[57]

Evidently, the lack of regular elections and the failure to provide regular means of protesting government actions and policies give rise to assassinations of political leaders and heads of state. Assassins usually believe that they can bring about political change if they can kill the head of the government. While this may be true in tyrannies which are imposed by one man, this is hardly the case in democracies whose policies are continued even if the head of state is assassinated. This means that independently powerful executives are the most likely targets of assassinations in non-democratic states.[58]

This raises the question as to whether the assassination of tyrants is justified. There are those who hold all assassinations to be murder and in the words of the Church Committee of the U.S. Senate in 1975, "inconsistent with the moral precepts fundamental to our way of life." That committee was chaired by Senator Frank Church of Idaho and dealt with the covert operations of the Central Intelligence Agency. The committee investigated the attempts at assassination of Patrice Lumumba of the Congo, Rafael Trujillo of the Dominican Republic, the Diem brothers of Viet Nam, General Rene Schneider of Chile, and the plan to kill Fidel Castro during the John Kennedy administration.[59]

No better example of the permissibility of assassination can be found than the two attempts at assassinating Adolf Hitler which would, in retrospect, have been fully justified.

Seventeen attempts to kill Hitler have been recorded by historians. Of these, only two were carried out while the others were aborted before any action could be taken by the would-be assassins. In each of these fifteen cases, Hitler either did not arrive as planned or he left sooner than expected.

Two efforts to kill Hitler did in fact lead to a bomb explosion. The first was the bomb detonated by Johann Georg Elser in a beer hall in Munich on November 8, 1939 . Hitler was to gave a speech there but suddenly ended it and left before the bomb exploded. Eight party members were killed in the explosion after Hitler left. Elser was later killed in a concentration camp.

Claus Stauffenberg carried out the second attempt to kill Hitler with a bomb. He placed a brief case containing a bomb next to a table leg at which Hitler was reading some maps. The bomb exploded after Stauffenberg had left the room. It wounded but did not kill Hitler with the result that Stauffenberg and his co-conspirators were killed by Hitler's followers. [60]

The assassins and would-be assassins who attack a brutal tyrant are of course taking the risk that even if the tyrant is killed, he will be replaced by someone equally brutal or worse. This was the case after Czar Nicholas II (1868-1918) was dethroned and murdered by the Bolsheviks in Russia in 1917 only to be subject to the far worse tyrant, Joseph Stalin. (1878-1953) This would have been the case if Saddam Hussein of Iraq had been assassinated only to be replaced by his brutal son, Udday. Furthermore, there is also the possibility that an assassinated leader, however vicious, would become a folk hero after his death.

Experience has shown that the assassination of a political leader has different outcomes for the society in which it takes place, depending on the method of succession employed. In those countries where leadership is taken by force assassination leads to considerable instability such as strikes, demonstrations, guerilla actions and even civil war.

In societies which have an accepted means of finding another leader, such as the automatic succession of he vice president to the presidency of the United States, instability actually declines. [61]

In countries which have always had a repressive regime, the chances of foreign intervention after an assassination of the leader are far greater than in countries which operate on democratic principles. This is true because repressive, tyrannical and dictatorial governments create opponents who are frequently exiled to neighboring countries and who wish to exploit assassinations of dictators in their home land by bringing foreign armies into the country for the purpose of esablishing a different government. That new government could of course also be malignant and tyrannical.

The issue is that in a democracy the legitimacy of the state and the nation is not affected by the death of its leader. In a centralized government the opposite is the case.

SUMMARY

A number of theories explain the assassination of famous people. Among these theories is the theory of differential association as developed by Sutherland. This holds that anyone may become criminal in his actions if he associates with a reference group favoring criminal conduct over a long period of time with considerable intensity and to the exclusion of other reference groups.

1. National Academy of Sciences, Washington, D.C. *National Academies Press,* (2008).

2. Edwin H. Sutherland, *Principles of Criminology,* (Dix Hills, NY: General Hall Inc., 1992), 89.

3. Gresham M. Sykes and David Matza, "Techniques of Neutralization," *American Sociological Review,* vol. 22, (1957), 664-670.

4. Sutherland, *Principles,* 89.

5. Bert Klanderman and Dirk Oegema, "Potentialsl, networks, motivations and barriers: Steps toward participation in social movements," *American Sociological Review,* vol. 52, (1987), 519-531.

6. Doug McAdam "Specifying the relationship between social ties and activism," *American Journal of Sociology,* vol. 99 (1993), 640-667.

7. Florence Passy and Marco Giugni, "Social Networks and Individual Perceptions: Explaining Differential Participation in Social Movement," *Sociological Forum,* vol. 16, no.1, (2001), 123-153.

8. Mark Granovetter, "The Strength of Weak Ties," *American Journal of Sociology,* v, 78, (1973), 1360-1380.

9. Roger V. Gould, "Collective Action and Network Structure," *American Sociological Review,* vol. 58, (1993), 182-196.

10. Donatella della Porta, "Recruitment Policies in Clandestine Political Organizations: Italian Left Wing Terrorism," In: Bert Klandermans, Hanspeter Kriesi, and Sidney Tarrow, *From Structure to Action,* (Greenwich, CT, JAI Press, 1988), 155-172).

11. Hyoyoung Kim, and Peter S. Bearman, "The Structure and Dynamics of Movement Participation," *American Sociological Review,* vol.67. (1997), 70-93.

12. Daniel Bell, "Crime as an American wasy of life," *The Antioch Review,* XIII, (June 1953), 131-154.

13. David A. Rothstein, "Presidential Assassination Syndrome," *Archives of General Psychiatry,* vol. XI, (September 1964), 245-254.

14. Edward F. Mickolus, "Statistical Approaches to the Study of Terrorism," in: *Terrorism: Interdisciplinary Perspectives,,* (New York: John Jay, 1977), 209-269.

15. Thomas Thornton, "Terror as a Weapon of Political Agitation," in: *Internal War,* H. Eckstein, editor, (New York, Free Press, 1964), 71-99.

16. Ivo K. Feierabend and Rosalind L. Feierabend, "Political Violence and Assassinaitons: A Cross National Assessment," in: William J. Crotty, Ed., *Assassinations and the Political Order,* (New York: Harper and Row, 1971), 54-140.

17. H.H.A. Cooper, "Terrorism and the Media," in: Y. Alexander and M. Finger, *Terrorism: Interdisciplinary Perspectives,* (New York, John Jay, 1977), 144.

18. Thomas H. Smith, "Terrorism and Political Assassination: A Transnational Assessment, 1968-80," *Annals of the American Academy of Political and Social Science,* vol. 463 (September 1982), 60.

19. Ibid., 64.

20. Michael Gottfredson and Travis Hirschi, *A General Theory of Crime,* (Stanford, CA: Stanford University Press, 1990).

21. The John Birch Society, "The Time Has Come" *The New York Times,* (December 15, 1963), 175.

22. Peter Khiss, "Kennedy Target of Birch Writer," *The New York Times,* (February 11, 1964), 18.

23. No author, "Cuba Attributes Murder to "Right,"" *The New York Times,* (November 27, 1963), 17

24. No author, "Cairo Press Critical," *The New York Times,* (November 27, 1963), 19.

25. James W. Clarke and Seth Lucente, "Getting Even: Some Observations on President Clinton's Would Be Assassin, Francisco Martin Duran," *British Journal of Political Science,* vol. 33, no.1, (January 2003), 130.

26. Ibid. 131.

27. Gerhard Falk, *Murder: An Analysis of Its Forms, Conditions and Causes,* (Jefferson, NC: McFarland, 1990), 88-89.

28. Ninian Beall, "Why Booth Killed Lincoln," *Records of the Columbia Historical Society,* vol.48-49, (Washington, DC:, 1947), 130.

29. Ibid, 131.

30. Alan Gottlieb, "Duran, the Child Nobody Knew," *The Denver Post,* (November 6, 1994), 1.

31. Sara Rimer, "Few Knew of White House Suspect's Turmoil," *New York Times,* (November 7, 1994), A14.

32. Ibid., A 14.

33. Toni Locy, "Duran Convicted of Trying to Kill President Clinton," *Washington Post,* (April 5, 1995), D1.

34. Teven Hunter and John Bainbridge, *American Gunfight: The Plot to Kill Harry Truman,* (New York: Simon and Schuster, 2005), 4.

35. R. A. van Middeldyk, *The History of Puerto Rico, from the Spanish Discovery to the American Occupation,* (New York: D. Appleton and Co., 1903).

36. No author, "Eight Military Jets Destroyed at Air Base in Puerto Rico," *The New York Times,* (January 12, 1981), 2.

37. Robert Windeler, "Family Remains Silent," *The New York Times,* (June 7, 1968), 1.

38. Mel Ayton, "Why Sirhan Sirhan Assassinated Robert Kennedy," *Crime Magazine,* (September 6, 2005), part II.

39. No author, "Canadian Film Details '72 Stalking of Nixon," *The New York Times,* (April 15, 1997), A9.

40. James W. Clarke and Seth Lucente, "Emotional Deprivation and Political Deviance: Some Observations on Governor Wallace's Would-Be Assassin, Arthur H. Bremer," *Political Psychology,* (Spring-Summer 1981-1982) :88.

41. Ibid,.91.

42. Brenda Goodman, Gunman Who Shot Wallace Is to be Freed," *The New York Times,* August, 24, 2007), 1.

43. Clarke, "Emotional Deprivation."

44. Robert J. Donovan, *The Assassins,* (New York: Popular Library, 1962), 101-117.

45. No author, "Died," *Time Magazine,* (September 27, 1943), 9.

46. No author, "Agents Tracing Hinckley's Path Find a Shift to Violent Emotions," *The New York Times,* (April 5, 1981), 1

47. Neil Henry and Chip Brown, "An Aimless Road to a Place in History," *The Washington Post,* (April 5, 1981),A1.

48. James C. McKinely, Jr., "Woman who Tried to Kill Ford in '75 is Paroled," *The New York Times,* (August 15, 2009), 11.

49. In the Supreme Court of California, S094597 Ct. App, 5 No. F028940 County of Fresno Super.Ct. No. 571741-8.

50. Peter Pringle, "Squeaky Little Girl Tried to Shoot the President," *The Sunday Times,* (August 16, 2009), 23.

51. Sam MacDonald, "Hijacker Targeted President in 1974," *Insight on the News,* vol.15, no.3, (June 24, 2002), 1.

52. No author, "Hey, You Talkin' to Me?" *The New York Times,* (December 29, 2004), E5L.

53. Zaryan Iqbal and Christopher Zorn, "Sic Semper Tyrannis? Power, Repression, and Assassination Since the Second World War," *The Journal of Politics,* vol. 68, no. 3, (August 2006), 489.

54. Hiag Katchadourian, "Is Political Assassination Even Morally Justified?" In: *Assassinations,* Harold Zelner, Editor, (Cambridge, Schenkman Publishing), 41-56.

55. Kai Nielson, "On Terrorism and Political Assassination," in *Assassinaition,* Harold Zellner, Editor, (Cambridge,, Schenckman Publishing Co, 1974), 97-110.

56. Thomas More, *Utopia,*(New York: Appleton-Century-Crofts, 1949), 65.

57. Chrisitian Davenport, "Multi-Dimensional Threat Perception and State Repression," *American Journal of Political Science,* vol. 39, (August 1995), 683-713.

58. Edward M. Muller and Mitchell A. Seligson, "Inequality and Insurgency," *American Political Science Review,* vol. 81, (June 1987), 425-451.

59. Seymour Hersh, "Huge C.I.A. Operation Reported in U.S. Against Anti-war Forces , Other Dissidents in Nixon Years," *The New York Times,* (December 22, 1974), 1.

60. Roger Moorehouse, *Killing Hitler,* (New York: Bantam Books, 2007).

61. Ephraim Yuchtman-Yaar and Tamar Herman, "The Latitude of Acceptance: Israeli Attitudes Toward Political Protest Before and After the Assassination of Yitzchak Rabin," *Journal of Conflict Resolution,* vol. 42, (December 1998), 721-743.

BIBLIOGRAPHY

BOOKS

Abraham, Antoine J., *The Lebanon War*, Westport, Connecticut, (1996).

Anderson, John Lee, *Che Guevara: A Revolutionary Life*, (New York: Grove Press, 1997).

Avrich, Paul, *Anarchist Voices: An Oral History of Anarchism in America*, (Princeton, NJ: Princeton University Press, 1996).

Avrich, Paul, *The Russian Anarchists*, (Princeton, NJ: The University of Princeton Press, 1967).

Axworthy, Michael, *The Sword of Persia: Nader Shah, From Tribal Warrior to Conquering Tyrant*, (New York: Palgrave Macmillan, 2006).

Baldwin, Roger N., *Kropotkin's Revolutionary Pamphlets*, (New York: Dover Publications, 1977).

Bard, Mitchell G., *The Complete Idiot's Guide to Middle East Conflict*, (New York: Alpha Books, 2005).

Barnard, Chester I., *The Functions of the Executive*, (Cambridge, Mass.: Harvard University Press, 1938).

Belfield, Richard, *The Assassination Business,: A History of State Sponsored Murder*, (New York: Carroll and Graf, Publishers, 2005).

Beyers, C.J., "Hendrik Verwoerd," *Dictionary of South African Biography*, vol.4, (Durban, South Africa, Butterworth, 1981).

Bhana, Surendra and Goolam Vahed, *The Making of a Political Reformer: Ghandi in South Africa 1893-1914*, (New Delhi: Manohar, 1969).

Bhattacharya, Sabyasachi, *The Mahatma and the Poet*, (New Delhi: National Book Trust, 1997).

Block, Maxine, Current *Biography: Who's News and Why*, (New York: H.W. Wilson Co., 1941).

Bolt, Neville and Jaz Azari, *Propaganda of the Deed*, (London: The Royal United Services Institute, 2008).

Bowersock, G. W., "The Pontificate of Augusturs," in: Kurt A Raaflaub and Mark Toner, *Between Republic and Empire: Interpretations of Augustus and His Prncipate*, (Berkeley: University of California Press, 1990).

Brass, Paul R., *The Politics of India Since Independence*, (Cambridge, England, Cambridge University Press, 1995).

Brown, Peter, *The Rise of Christendom*, (Oxford; Oxford-Blackwell Publishers, 2003)..

Burrows, Edwin G. and Mike Wallace, *Gotham: A History of New York City to 1898*, (New York:: Oxford University Press, 1999).

Bushman, Richard L., *Joseph Smith: Rough Stone Rolling*, (New York: Alfred A. Knopf, 2005).

Canfora, Luciano, *Julius Caesar: The Life and times of the People's Dictator*, (Berkeley: The University of California Press, 2007).

Chafe, William Henry, *Never Stop Running: Allard Lowenstein and the Struggle to Save American Liberalism*, (New York: Basic Books, 1993).

Chalberg, John C., *Emma Goldman: American Individualist*, (New York: Pearson Longman 1989).

Clarkson, Jesse D., *A History of Russia*, (New York: Random House, 1961).

Clay, Catrine, *King, Kaiser, Tzar*, (London: John Murray, 2006).

Cohen, Henry, *Proudhon's Solution to the Social Problem*, (New York: Vanguard Press, 1927).

Cole, Leonard A., *The Anthrax Letters*, (Washington, D.C. The Joseph Henry Press, 2003).

Conquest, Robert, *The Great Terror: A Reassessment*, (New York: Oxford University Press, 1991).

Cooper, H.H.A. " Terrorism and the Media," in: Y. Alexander and M. Finger, *Terrorism: Interdisciplinary Perspectives*, (New York, John Jay, 1977).

Coughlin, Michael E., Charles H. Hamilton, and Mark A. Sullivan, eds.. *Benjamin R. Tucker and the Champions of Liberty: A Centenary Anthology. 1st ed.*, (St. Paul: M.E. Coughlin : M. Sullivan, 1986).

Crasweller, Robert D., *Trujillo: The Life and Times of a Caribbean Dictator*, (New York: MacMillan, 1966).

Cronin, Mike A., *History of Ireland*, (New York: Palgrave Publishing, 2002).

Cummings, Richard, *The Pied Piper: Allard K. Lownstein and the Liberal Dream*, (New York: Grove Press, 1985).

Dabashi, Hamid, *Iran: A People Interrupted*, (New York, The New Press, 2006).

Davis, John Michael, *The Image of Lincoln in the South*, (Knoxville: University of Tennessee Press, 1971).

de Witt, Ludo, *The Assassination of Lumumba*, (New York: Verso Publishing, 2001).

della Porta, Donatella, "Recrui tment policies in clandestine political organizations. Italian left wing terrorism," In: Bert Klandermans, Hanspeter Kriesi, and Sidney Tarrow, *From Structure to Action*, (Greenwich, CT: JAI Press, 1988).

Dewey, John, *Not Guilty*, (New York: Harper & Brothers, 1938).

Donald, David Cahrles, *Sumner and the Rise of Man*, (New York: Alfred A. Knopf, 1069).

Donovan, Robert J., *The Assassins*, (New York: Popular Library, 1962).

Doyle, Burton T and Homer H. Swaney, *Lives of James A. Garfield and Chester A. Arthur*, (Washington, D.C.: Darby Publishers, 1881) .

Drake, Richard, *The Aldo Moro Murder Case*, (Cambridge, Mass.: Harvard University Press, 1995).

Dupree, Louis, *Afghanistan*, (Princeton, N.J.: The Princeton Univrsity Press, (1973).

Eager, Paige W., *From Fighters to Terrorists: Women and Political Violence*, (London: Ashgate Publishing, 2008).

Eder, Walter, "Augustus and the Power of Tradition," in: *The Cambridge Companion to the Age of Augustus*, (New York: Cambridge University Press, 2005).

Edwards, David B., *Before Taliban: Generations of the Afghan Jihad* (Berkeley, CA: University of California Press, 2002).

Ellerbrock, Karl P., "Detlev Rohwedder," In: *Neue Deutsche Biographie*, (Berlin, Germany: Duncker & Humboldt, 2005).

Emerick, Geoff, *Here, There and Everywhere: My Life Recording the Music of the Beatles*, (New York: Gotham Books, 2007).

Entzinger, H. "The Rise and Fall of Multiculturalism: the Case of the Netherlands," In: C. Jopke and E. Morawska, *Toward Assimilation and Citizenship*, (Basingstoe, Palgrave, 2003).

Ewans, Martin, *Afghanistan: A Short History of its People and Politics*, (New York: Harper Collins, 1987).

Falk, Candace, *Emma Goldman: a Documentary History of the American Years*, (Urbana: The University of Illinois Press, 2008).

Falk, Gerhard, *Murder: An Analysis of Its Forms, Conditions and Causes*, (Jefferson, NC: McFarland & Co., 1990).

Falk, Gerhard, *The Jew in Christian Theology*, (Jefferson, NC and London, McFarland & Co., 1992).

Feierabend, Ivo K. and Rosalind L. Feierabend, "Political Violence and Assassinaitons: A Cross National Assessment,"in: *Assassinations and the Political Order*, William J. Crotty, Ed. (New York: Harper and Row, 1971).

Fest, Joachim, *Hitler*, (New York: Vintage Books, 1975).

Fischer, Louis, *The Essential Gandhi: An Anthology of his Writings on his Life, Work and Ideas* (New York: Vintage Books, 2002).

Foner, Philip S., *History of the Labor Movement in the United States: vol.5, The AFL in the Progressive Era, 1910-1915*, (New York: International Publishers, 1980).

Frank, Katherine, *Indira: The Life of Indira Nehru Gandhi*, (New York: Houghton Mifflin Co., 2002).

Gage, Beverly, *The Day Wall Street Exploded*, (New York: Oxford University Press, 2009).

Gandhi, Rajmohan, *Patel: A Life*, (Ahmedabad, India Navajivan Publition House, 1990).

Gibbon, Edward, *The History of the Decline and Fall of the Roman Empire*, (New York: Twayne Publishers, 1963).

Goldberg, Harvey, *The Life of Jean Jaures*, (Madison: University of Wisconsin Press, 1962).

Goldhagen, Daniel Jonah, *Hitler's Willing Executioners*, (New York: Alfred A. Knopf, 1996).

Goldman Emma, *Living My Life*, (New York: Alfred Knopf, 1931).

Gordon, Jr., Raymond G., *Ethnologue: Languages of the World, 15th Edition*, (Dallas, Texas: SIL International, 2000).

Gottfredson, Michael and Travis Hirschi, *A General Theory of Crime*, (Stanford, Cal.. Stanford University Press, 1990).

Grayzel, Solomon, *A History of the Jews*, (Philadelphia: The Jewish Publication Society of America, 1947).

Green, Peter, *Alexander to Actium: The Historical Evolution of the Hellenistic Age*, (Berkeley, The University of California Press, 1990).

Guillemin, Jeanne, "Imperial Japan's Germ Warfare, the Suppression of Evidence at the Tokyo War Crimes Trial," In: Anne L. Clunan, *Terrorism, War or Disease*, (Stanford, California, Stanford University Press, 2008).

Gumbel, Andrew, *Steal This Vote*, (New York: Nation Books, 1971).

Hammond, Thomas T., *Red Flag over Afghanistan*, (Boulder., Colorado, Westview Press, 1984).

Hancock Eleanor, *Ernst Roehm: Hitler's Chief of Staff*, (New York: Palgrave McMillan, 2008).

Hildenbrand, Carole, *The Crusades: Islamic Perspectives*, (Chicago: Fitzroy Dearborn, 1999).

Hochmeister, Lutz, *Schleyer: Eine Deutsche Geschichte*, (C.H. Beck Verlag, 2004).

Housley, Norman, *Contesting the Crusades*, (Malden, MA: Blackwell Publishers, 2006).

Human Rights Watch, "Saudi Arabia," (New York: *Human Rights Watch World Report*, 2001).

Hunter, Stephen and John Bainbridge, *American Gunfight: The Plot to Kill Harry Truman*, (New York: Simon and Schuster, 2005).

Jackson, Thomas F., *From Civil Rights to Human Rights: Martin Luther King, Jr. and the Struggle for Economic Justice*, (Philadlephia: The University of Pennsylvania Press, 2007).

Jacobs, Seth, *Cold War Mandarin: Ngo Dinh Diem and the Origins of Amerca's War in Vietnam, 1950-1963*, (Lanham, MD: Rowman and Littlefield, 2006).

Josephus, *Jewish Antiquities*, Ralph Marcus, translator, (Cambridge, MA: Harvard University Press, 1986).

Karnow, Stanley, *"Antonio Canovas" in Our Image: America's Empire in the Philippines*, (New York: Random House, 1989).

Katchadourian, Haig, "Is Political Assassination Even Morally Justified?" In: *Assassination*, Harold Zellner, Editor, (Cambridge, Schenkman Publishing, 1974).

Kauffman, Michael, *American Brutus: Jiohn Wilkes Booth and the Lincoln Conspiracies*, (New York: Random House, 2004).

Kazin, Michael, *Barons of Labor*, (Urbana, Illinois, The University of Illinois Press, 1987).

Keneally, Christine, *The First Word: The Search for the Origins of Language*, (New York: The Viking Press, 2007).

Kinzer, Stephen, *All the Shah's Men*, (Hoboken, NJ: John Wiley & Sons, Inc. 2003).

Kranzler, David, *The Man Who Stopped the Trains to Auschwitz*, (Syracuse, NY: Syracuse University Press, 2000).

Krauze, Enrique, *Mexico: Biography of Power. A History of Modern Mexico, 1810-1996*, (New York: Harper Collins, 1997).

Kropotkin, Peter, *Memoirs of a Revolutionary*, (New York: Dover Publications, 1971).

Krueger. Robert, *From Bloodshed to Hope in Burundi: Our Embassy Years During Genocide*, (Austin, University of Texas Press, 2007).

Lampert, Evgenii, *Studies in Rebellion*, (London: F. A. Preager, Publishers, 1957).

Landes, David, *The Wealth and Poverty of Nations*, (New York: Norton, 1998).

Lehrer, Steven, *Wannsee House and the Holocaust*, (Jefferson, N.C.: Mc Farldand, Pulishers, 2000).

Lewis, Bernard, *Semites and Anti-semites*, (NewYork: Norton, 1984).

Lewis, D.M., "The Fourth Century BC" in: *The Cambridge Ancient History, vol. 6* (New York: Cambridge University Press, 1994).

Mac Kenzie, David M., *Black Hand on Trial: Eastern European Monographs*, (New York: Columbia University Press, 1995).

Machtan, Lothar, *The Hidden Hitler*, (New York: Basic Books, 2002).

Malvern, Linda, *Conspiracy to Murder: The Rwandan Genocide*, (NewYork: Verso, 2004).

Manchester , William, *Portrait of a President*, (New York: Little, Brown & Co., 1967).

Maximoff, G.P., *The Political Philosophy of Bakunin: Scientific Anarchism*, (Glencoe, IL: Free Press, 1953).

McGovern, George and Leonard F. Guttridge, *The Great Coalfield War*, (Boston: Houghton Mifflin Co., 1972).

McInnis, Edgar, *Canada; A Political and Social History*, (New York,: Holt, Rinehart and Winston, 1962).

McQuarrie,, Kim, The *Last Days of the Incas*, (New York: Simon and Schuster, 2007).

Merari, A., "The Readiness to Kill and Die: Suicide Terrorism in the Middle East," In: William Reich, Editor, *Origins of Terrorism*, New York: Cambridge University Press, 1990).

Merkl, Peter H., "Approaches to the Study of Political Violence," In: Peter H. Merkl, *Political Violence and Terror*, (Berkeley: University of California Press, 1986).

Mickolus, Edward F., "Statistical Approaches to the study of terrorism," in: *Terrorism: Interdisciplinary Perspectives*, (New York: John Jay, 1977).

Miller, Martin, A., *Selected Writings on Anarchism and Revolution*, (Cambridge: MIT Press, 1970).

Moorehouse, Roger, *Killing Hitler*, (New York, Bantam Books, 2007).

More, Thomas, *Utopia*, (New York, Appleton –Century-Crofts, 1949).

Moyar, Mark, *Triumph Forsaken: The Vietnam War, 1954-1965*, (Cambridge, England, Cambridge University Press, 2006).

Mwakikagile, Godfrey, *Nyerere and Africa: End of an Era*, (New York: New Africa Press, 2006).

National Commission on Terrorist Attacks Upon the United States, (Washington, D.C. The United States Government Printing Office, (August 21, 2004).

Nelson, Eric, *The Jesuits and the Monarchy: Catholic Reform and Political Authority in France, 1590-1615*, (New York: Ashgate Publishing, 2005).

Nettlau, Max, *Errico Malatesta,: The Biography of an Anarchist*, (New York: Jewish Anarchist Federation, 1924).

Nielson, Kai, "On Terrorism and Political Assassination," in *Assassinaition*, Harold Zellner, Editor, (Cambridge: Schenckman Publishing Co., 1974).

No author, *The Pentagon Papers*, (Boston: The Beacon Press, 1971).

Nomad, Max, *Apostles of Revolution*, (Boston: Little Brown, 1939).

North , Douglas C. and Robert Thomas, The Rise of the Western World: A New Economic History, (Cambridge University Press, 1973).

Norwich, John J., *A History of Venice*, (New York: Vintage Publishing, 1989).

Omstead, Albert T., *History of the Persian Empire*, (Chicago: University of Chicago Press, 1970).

Paco, Ignacio Taibo, *Guevara, also known as Che*, (New York: St. Martin's Press, 1999).

Papanikolas, Zeese, *Buried Unsung: Louis Tikas and the Ludlow Massacre*, (Salt Lake City: University of Utah Press, 1982).

Pape, Robert, *Dying to Win*, (New York, Random House, 2006).

Pares, Bernard, *A History of Russia*, (New York: Alfred A. Knopf, 1956).

Perregree, Andrew, *Europe in the Sixteenth Century*, (Oxford, England: Blackwell Publishers, 2002).

Peters, Butz, *Tödlicher Irrtum*, (Berlin: Argon Verlag, 2004).

Pfisterer, Rudolf, *Im Schatten des Kreuzes*, (Hamburg: Evangelischer Verlag, 1966)

Porter, Anna, *Kastner's Train*, (Vancouver: Douglas & McIntyre, 2007).

Prescott, William, *History of the Conquest of Peru*, (New York: Modern Library, 2005; originally 1847).

Proudhon, Pierre Joseph, *The General Idea of the Revolution in the Nineteenth Century*, (New York: The Pluto Press, 1989).

Proudhon, Pierre Joseph, *What Is Property?* (New York: Dover Publications, 1970).

Proudhon, Pierre Joseph, *System of Economic Contradiction*, (Boston: Benjamin R. Tucker, 1888).

Pyziur, Eugene, *The Philosophy of Anarchism of M.A. Bakunin*, (Milwaukee: Marquette University Press, 1955).

Quinn, Russell Hoover, *The Constitutions of Abraham Lincoln and Jefferson Davis*, (New York: Exposition Press, 1959).

Reiterman, Tim and John Jacobs, *Raven: The Untold Story of Rev. Jim Jones and His People*, (New York: E.P. Dutton, 1982).

Robbins, Mary S., *Against the Viet Nam War: Writings by Activists*, (Lanham, MD: Rowland and Littlefield, 2007).

Roberts, Allen, *The Turning Point: The Assassination of Louis Barthou and King Alexander I of Yugoslavia*, (New York: St. Martin's Press, 1970).

Rocker, Rudolf, *Nationalism and Culture*, (Los Angeles: Rocker Publication Committee, 1937).

Rogan, Eugene L. and Avi Shlaim, *The War for Palestine*, (New York: Cambridge University Press, 2007).

Roth, Cecil, A., *History of the Jews*, (New York: Schocken Books, 1963).

Rothschild, Joseph, *The Communist Party of Bulgaria: Origins and Development*, (New York: Columbia University Press, 1959).

Sageman, Marc, *Understanding Terror Networks*, (Philadelphia: University of Pennsylvania Press, 2004).

Samuel, Maurice, Blood *Accusation: The Strange History of the Beilis Case*, (New York: Algred A. Knopf, 1966).

Scarre, Charles, *The Penguin Atlas of Ancient Rome*, (London: Penguin Books, 1995).

Schlesinger, Jr., Arthur M., *The Politics of Upheaval*, (Boston: Houghton Mifflin Co. (1960).

Schlesinger, Jr., Arthur M., *Robert Kennedy and his Times*, (Boston: Houghton Mifflin, (1978).

Schneider, Ronald M., *Latin American Political History*, (New York: Westview Press, 2006).

Seibert, Jeffrey, *I Done My Duty: The Complete Story of the Assassination of President Mc Kinley*, (Bowie, Maryland: Heritage Books, 2002).

Silbey, Joel H., *A Respectable Minority*, (New York: W.W. Norton & Co. 1977).

Sinclair, Andrew, *Viva Che! The Strange Death and Life of Che Guevara*, (New York: Sutton Publishing, (1968).

Slattery, T.P., *The Assassination of D'Arcy McGee*, (Toronto: Doubleday Canada, 1968).

Smith, J. and Andre Moncourt, *The Red Army Faction: A Documentary History*, (Oakland, CA PM Press, 2009).

Smith, Robert C., *Contemporary Controversies and the American Racial Divide*, (Lanham, MD: Rowman and Littlefield, 2000).

Stoneman, Richard, *Alexander the Great*, (London; Routledge, 2004).

Sutherland, Edwin H., *Principles of Criminology*, (Dix Hills, NY: General Hall Inc., 1992).

Takao, Tsuchiya, "Transition and Development of Economic Poicty," in: Keizo Shibusawa, *Japanese Socieity in the Meiji Era*, (Tokyo: Obunsha Publishing, 1958).

Taylor, Peter, *Loyalists: War and Peace in Northern Ireland*, (New York: TV Books, 1999).

Thornton, Thomas P., "Terror as a Weapon of Political Agitation," in: *Internal War*, H. Eckstein, editor, (New York: Free Press, 1964).

Tolstoy, Leo, *War and Peace*, (London: Heineman, 1964).

Tucker, Benjamin R., Instead of a Book, by a Man Too Busy to Write One; A Fragmentary Exposition. (New York: Arno Press, 1972).

U.S. Justice Department, *Terrorism*, (Washington, DC, 2008).

United States Congress, *Lessons Learned from the Attack on the USS Cole*, (Washington, D.C., United States Governmetn Printing Office, 2001).

van Middeldyk,, R. A., *The History of Puerto Rico, from the Spanish Discovery to the American Occupation*, (New York: D. Appleton and Co., 1903).

Vincent, K. Steven, *Pierre Joseph Proudhon and the Rise of Prench Republican Socialism*, (Oxford: Oxford University Press, 1984).

Viorst, Milton, *In the Shadow of the Prophet: The Struggle for the Soul of Islam*, (Boulder, Colorado, Westview Press, 2001).

Wexler, Alice, *Emma Goldman: an Intimate Life*, (New York: Pantheon Books, 1984)

Wexler, Alice: *Emma Goldman in Exile*, (Boston: Beacon Press, 1989).

Whiteside, James, *Regulating Danger: The Struggle for Mine Safety in the Rocky Mountains*, (Lincoln, Nebraska: The University of Nebraska Press, 1990).

Whyte, George R., *The Dreyfus Affair: A Chronological History*, (Basingstoke, England: Basingstoke Books, 2008).

Wigoder, Geoffrey, editor, *The Standard Jewish Encyclopedia, 7th Edition*, (New York: Facts on File, 1992).

Wilkinson, Paul, *Terrorism versus Democracy: The Liberal State Response*, (London: Frank Cass, Publishers, 2000).

Woodcock, George, *Anarchism*, (Cleveland: World Publishing Co. 1962).

Zahlan, Antoine, *Science and Science Policy in the Arab World*, (New York: St. Martin's Press, 1980).

JOURNAL ARTICLES

Adler, Selig, "The Operation on President McKinley," Scientific American, vol. 208, no.3, (March, 1963).

Ahmad, Irfan, "Timothy McVeighs of the Orient," Economic and Political Weekly, (April 13, 2002).

Ansari, Hamied N. "The Islamic Militants in Egyptian Politics," International Journal of Middle East Studies,vol.16, no.1, (March 1984).

Appleton, Sheldon, "The Polls-Trends; Assassinations," The Public Opinion Quarterly, vol. 64,,no 4, (Winter 2000).

Ayton, Mel, "Why Sirhan Sirhan Assassinated Robert Kennedy," Crime Magazine, (September 6, 2005).

Barker, Wharton, "The Secret of Russia's Friendship," The Independent (March 24, 1904).

Battistini, Lawrence, "The Korean Problem in the Nineteenth Century," Monumenta Nipponica, vol 8, no.1, (1952).

Beall, Ninian, "Why Booth Killed Lincoln," Records of the Columbia Historical Society, vol.48-49, (Washington, D.C. 1947).

Beasley, W.G., "Councillors of Samurai Origin in the Early Meijii Government, 186809) Bulletin of the School of Oriental and African Studies, XX (1957).

Beck, Earl R., "The Martinez Campos Government of 1879: Spain's Last Chance in Cuba," The Hispanic American Historical Review, vol.56, no.2, (May 1976):275.

Bell, Daniel, "Crime as an American Way of Life," The Antioch Review, XIII (June 1953):131-154.

Bellingham, John, "Trial and execution of John Bellingham for the willful murder of the Right Hon. Spencer Perceval in the Lobby of the House of Commons," Bristol Selected Pamphlets, http:www.jstror. org. stable/ 60241852.

Berg, Gordon, "President Garfield's Proving Ground," Civil War Times, vol. 46, no.9, (2007).

Betts, Richard K., "Is Strategy an Illusion?" Internationl Security, vol. 25, no. 2, (Autumn 2000).

Beveridge, Fiona, "The Lockerbie Affair," The International and Comparative Law Quarterly, vol.41, no.4, (October 1992).

Bilsky, Leora, "Judging Evil in the Trial of Kastner," Law and History Review, vol. 19, no. 1, (Spring 2001).

Bloom, Robert, "As the British Press Saw Lincoln," A Journal of the Liberal Arts, vol.V, (Spring 1965).

Bowden, Mark, "Guests of the Ayatolla," The Atlantic Monthly, vol. 297, no. 4, (May, 2006).

Bradford, M.E., "The Lincoln Legacy," Modern Age, vol 24, (1979-80).

Brecht, Arnold, "Walther Rathenau and the German People," The Journal of Politics, vol. 10, no. 1, (February 1948).

Brunk, Samuel, "The Sad Situation of Civilians and Soldiers: The Banditry of Zapatismo in the Mexican," The American Historical Review, Vol.101, no.2, (April 1996).

Canali, Mauro, "The Matteotti Murder and the Origin of Mussolini's Totalitarian Fascist Regime in Italy," Journal of Modern Italian Studies, vol. 14, no. 2, (2009).

Carson, Clayborne, Peter Holloran, Ralph E. Luker, Penny Russell, "Martin Luther King as Scholar: A Re-examination of his Theological Writings," The Journal of American History, vol. 78, no. 1, (June 1991).

Christenson, James A. and Ronald C. Wimberly, "Who is Civil Religious?" Sociological Analysis, vol. 39, no. 1, (1978).

Clarke, James W. and Seth Lucente, "Emotional Deprivation and Political Deviance: Some Observations on Governor Wallace's Would-Be Assassin, Arthur H. Bremer" Political Psychology, (Spring-Summer 1981-1982).

Clarke, James W. and Seth Lucente, "Getting Even: Some Observations on President Clinton's Would Be Assassin, Francisco Martin Duran," British Journal of Political Science, vol. 33, no.1, (January 2003).

Cloud, John, "People told him no openly gay man could win political office," Time, (June 14, 1999).

Connolly, Ray, "The Lost Lennon Interviews," The Sunday Times Magazine, (September 6, 2009).

Cooke, Miriam, "Women, Religion, and the Postcolonial Arab World," Cultural Critique, no.45, (Spring 2000).

Correll, John T., "Fallout from Khobar Towers," Air Force Magazine, vol. 88, no.11, (November 2005).

Crenshaw, Martha, "The Causes of Terrorism," Comparative Politics, vol. 13, no.4, (July 1981).

Dance, Amber, "Anthrax Case Ignites New Forensic Field," Nature, vol. 454, no. 7206, (2008).

Dance, Amber, "Death Renews Bio-security Debate," Nature, vol. 454, (August 2008).

Davenport, Chrisitian, "Multi-Dimensional Threat Perception and State Repression," American Journal of Political Science, vol. 39, (August 1995).

DeSilva, K.M. "The Bandernaikes in the Islands Politicis," Round Table, no.350, (1999)

Doumato, Eleanor Abdella, "Manning the Barricades: Islam According to Saudi Arabia's School Texts," Middle East Journal, vol.57, no.2, (Spirng 2003).

Drake, Richard, "The Red and the Black: Terrorism in Contemporary Italy," International Political Science Review, vol.5, no.3, (1984).

Edson, Charles, "Imperium Macedonicum: The Seleucid Empire and the Literary Evidence," Classical Philology, vol. 53, no. 3, (July 1958).

Falk, Richard, "False Universalism and the Geopolitics of Exclusion," Third World Quarterly, vol. 18, no.1, (March 1997).

Faqir, Fadia, "Intrafamily Femicide In Defence of Honor," Center for Inquiry, (August 2000).

Fine, Sidney, "Anarchism and the Assassination of McKinley," The American Historical Review, vol.60, no.4, (July 1995).

Fink, Carole, "The Murder of Walther Rathenau," Judaism, (Summer 1995).

Fitzpatrick, Laura, "Scott Roeder: The Tiller Murder Suspect," Time, (June 2, 2009).

Friedman, Isaiah, "How Trans-Jordan was Severed from the Territory of the Jewish National Home," Journal of Israeli History, vol. 27, no. 1, (March 1, 2008).

Gabai, Rafael Varon and Auke Pieter Jacobs, "Peruvian Wealth and Spanish Investment," The Hispanic American Historical Review, vol 67, no. 4, (November 1987).

Gambetta, Diego, "Heroic Impatience," The Nation, (March 22, 2010).

Geller, Pamela, "Sharia in New Jersey," Atlas Shrugs, (July 24, 2010).

Gerstenfel, Manfred, "Radical Islam in the Netherlands: A Case Study of a Failed European Policy, " Jerusalem Center for Public Affairs, vol. 4, no. 14, (January 2005).

Gitelman, H.M., "Perspectives on American Industrial Violence," The Business History Review, vol. 47, no .1, (Spring 1973).

Glaser, Jack, Jay Dixit and Donald P.Greene, "Studying Hate Crime with the Internet: What Makes Racists Advocate Racial Violence?" Journal of Social Issues, vol. 58, no.1, (2002).

Gould, Roger V., "Collective Action and Network Structure," American Sociological Review, vol. 58, (1993).

Granovetter, Mark, "The Strength of Weak Ties," American Journal of Sociology, v. 78, (1973).

Grant, Rebecca, "Khobar Towers," Air Force Association Magazine, vol. 81, no.6, (June 1998).

Grinspan, Jon, "Trying to Assassinate President Jackson," American Heritage Magazine, (January 30, 2007).

Harvey, A.D., "Austria's Diminutive Dictator," History Today, vol. 59, no. 7, (July 2009)

Hauner, Milan, "Terrorism and Heroism: the Assassination of Reinhard Heydrich," World Policy Journal, vol. 24, no.2 (Summer 2007).

Hewitt, Bill, "Massacre at Fort Hood," People, vol. 72, no. 21, (November 23, 2009).

Heykal, Mohammad Hassanein, "The Saudi Era," Journal of Palestine Studies, vol. 6, no.4, (Summer 1977).

Hirshson, Stanley P., "The Garfield Orbit," The Journal of American History, vol. 65, no. 4, (March 1979).

Inglesby, Thomas V., "Anthrax as a Biological Weapon," Journal of the American Medical Association, vol 1287, no. 17, (May 2007) :2236-2252.

Iqbal, Zaryab and Christopher Zorn, "Sic Semper Tyrannis? Power, Repression, and Assassination Since the Second World War," The Journal of Politics, vol. 68, no. 3, (August 2006).

Jaszi, Oscar, "The Stream of Political Murder," American Journal of Economics and Sociology, Vol. 3, no. 3, (April 1944).

Johnson, Ludwell H., "Civil War Military History," Civil War History, v. 17, (1971).

Kaplan, Arline, "The Fort Hood Aftermath - Army Accountability and Review and Psychiatrists," Psychiatric Times, vol. 27, no. 5, (2010).

Kim, Hyoyoung and Peter S. Bearman, "The Structure and Dynamics of Movement Participation," American Sociological Review, vol.67, (1997).

Klanderman, Bert and Dirk Oegema, "Potentials, Networks, Motivations and Barriers: Steps Toward Participation in Social Movements," American Sociological Review, vol. 52, (1987).

Kleinman, Ruth, "Changing Interpretations of the Edict of Nantes," French Histotical Studies, vol 10, no. 4, (Autumn 1978).

Lai, Vinay, "Hey Ram: The Politics of Gandhi's Last Words," Humanscape, vol.8m no. 1, (January 2001).

Landauer, Carl, "The Bavarian Problem in the Weimar Republic, 1918-1923," The Journal of Modern History, vol. 16, no.2, (June 1944).

Lang, Mabel, "The Murder of Hipparchus," Historia: Zeitschrift für Alte Geschichte, vol. 3, no. 4, (1953).

Lay, Howard G., "Beau Geste! (On the Readability of Terrorism)," Yale French Studies, no. 101, (2001).

Lichtheim, George, "Socialism and the Jews," Dissent, (July-August, 1968).

Lotchin, Roger W., "Mormons and Gentiles: A History of Salt Lake City," American Historical Review, vol. 91, no. 3, (1986).

MacDonald, Brad, "Can Israel Trust Germany?" The Trumpet, vol. 19, no. 7, (August 2008).

MacDonald, Sam, "Hijacker Targeted President in 1974," Insight on the News, vol. 15, no.3, (June 24, 2002).

Magnusson, Charlotta, "Gender, Occupaitonal Prestige and Wages," European Sociological Review, vol. 25, no. 1, (2009).

Malley, Robert, "Israel and the Arafat Question," New York Review of Books, vol. 51, no.15, (October 7, 2004).

Marrus, Michael, "The Strange Story of Herschel Grynszpan," American Scholar, vol 57, no 1, (Winter 1988).

McAdam, Doug, "Specifying the Relationship Between Social Ties and Activism," American Journal of Sociology, vol. 99 (1993).

Menkhaus, Ken, "Governance without Government in Somalia," International Security, vol.31, no.3, (2007).

Meselson., Matthew, "The Sverdlovsk Anthrax Outbreak of 1979," Science, vol. 266, (1994) :1202-1208.

Messer-Kruse, Timothy and James O. Eckert, Jr., Pannee Burkel and Jeffrey Dunn, "The Haymarket Bomb: Reassessing the Evidence," Labor, vol 2, no.2, (2005).

Middle East Policy Council, "The Hariri Tribunal: Politics and International Law" Middle East Policy, vol. 15, no. 3, (Fall 2008).

Mitchell, Stewart, "The Man Who Murdered Garfield," Proceedings of the Massachusetts Historical Society, vol. 67, (October 1941-May 1944).

Moore, Michael Scott, "Did Castro Kill Kennedy?" Der Spiegel, (January 14, 2006).

Muhammed, A. Tayyeb, "Bangladesh: The Dilemmas of Independence," Asian Affairs, vol.5, no.3, (January-February, 1978).

Muller, Edward M. and Mitchell A. Seligson, "Inequality and Insurgency," American Political Science Review, vol. 81, (June 1987).

No author, "Cops at Michigan Arab Fest Accused of Enforcing Shariah," Free Republic, (June 22, 2010).

No author, "The Assassination of the Prime Minister: John Bellingham and the Murder of Spencer Perceval," Contemporary Review, vol. 290, no. 1691, (Winter 2008).

No author, "The Brutal Murder of an Old Friend Makes Her the Dark Queen of Terrorism," People, vol.8, no.26, (December 26, 1977).

No author, "Died," Time Magazine, (September 27, 1943).

No author, "EGYPT;'War and Death," Time, (March 5, 1945).

No author, "In Depth: Razor's Edge: The Controversy of Female Genital Mutilation," IRIN, (March 2005).

No author, "Propaganda by the Deed," Workers Solidarity, No. 55, (October 1998).

No author, "A Trial of Savagery: Reflections on the death of James Byrd, Jr. in Jasper, Texas," The Journal of Blacks in Higher Education, no.20, (Summer, 1998).

Padover, Saul, "Patterns of Assassination in Occupied Territory," The Public Opinion Quarterly, vol. 7, no. 4, (Winter 1943).

Parker, Janet, "Murder in Broad Daylight," The New Criminologist, (June 30, 2005).

Passy, Florence and Marco Giugni, "Social Networks and Individual Perceptions: Explaining Differential Participation in Social Movement," Sociological Forum, vol. 16, no.1, (2001).

Persico, Joseph E., "Vendetta in New Orleans," American Heritage Magazine, (June 1973).

Pidd, Helen, "Fort Hood Massacre," The Guardian, (November 7, 2009).

Plohetski, Tony, "IRS Officials Meet with Employees as Officials Confirm Pilot's Identity," American Statesman, (February 22, 2010).

Polunov, Alexandr Jurevich, "Konstantin Petrovich Pobedonostsev –Man and Politician," Russian Studies in History, vol.39, no. 4, (Spring 2001).

Pugliese, Stanislao G., "Death in Exile: The Assassination of Carlo Rosselli," Journal of Contemporary History, vol. 32, no. 3, (1997).

Ramsdell, Charles W., "Lincoln and Fort Sumter," Journal of Soutern History, vol. III (1937).

Rewald, John, "Extracts of an unedited journal by Paul Signac," Gazette des beaux arts, vol 6. no.36, (December 1949).

Rosenfeld, Gavriel, "Monuments and the Policies of Memory: Commemorating Kurt Eisner and the Bavaria Revolution, 1918-1919." Central European History, vol. 30, no..2, (1997).

Rostovtzeff, Michael, "The Foundations of Social and Economic Life in Egypt in Hellenistic Times,"The Journal of Egyptian Archeology, vol 6., no. 3, (July 1920).

Rothstein David A., "Presidential Assassination Syndrome," Archives of General Psychatry, vol. XI, (September 1964).

Rusher, William A, "In Reagan's Defense," National Review, (August 9, 1985).

Sack F. L, "Problems of an International Language," The Phi Delta Kappan, Vol. 32, no. 2, (October 1950).

Safi, Louay, "From Reform to Revoluion," Intellectual Discourse, vol. 3, no. 1, (1995).

Samuels, Richard J., "When Leadership Failed," The American Sociologist, (Spring/Summer, 2003).

Schmeidel, John, "My Enemies'Enemy," Intelligence and National Security, (vol. 8, no.4, (October 1993).

Schmitt, Bernadotte E., "July 1914: Thirty Years After," The Journal of Modern History, vol. 16, no.3, (1944).

Scribner, Charity, "Buildings on Fire: The Situationist International and the Red Army Faction," Grey Room, Winter 2007).

Shappee, Nathan D., "Zangara's Attempted Assassination of Franklin D. Roosevelt," The Florida Historical Quarterly, vol. 37, no. 2, (October 1958).

Slosson, Edward E., "An Experiment in Anarchy," Independent, vol.15, (April 2, 1993)

Snitch, Thomas H., "Terrorism and Political Assassination: A Transnational Assessment, 1968-80" Annals of the American Academy of Political and Social Science, vol. 463 (September 1982).

Soo Cha, Myung, "Did Takahashi Korekiyo Rescue Japan from the Great Depression?" The Journal of Economic History, vol. 63, no. 1, (March 2003).

Speel, C.J., "The Disappearance of Christianity from North Africa in the Wake of the Rise of Islam," Church History, vol. 29, no.4, (December 1960).

Spiegel Staff, "Germany Revisits RAF Terrorism Verdict," Der Spiegel, (April 23, 2007).

Stern, Jessica, "The Protean Enemy," Foreign Affairs, vol.82, no. 4, (July-August 2003).

Stork, Joe, "The War of the Camps, the War of the Hostages," MERIPReports, no. 133, (June 1985).

Sykes, Gresham M. and David Matza, "Techniques of Neutralization," American Sociological Review, vol. 22, (1957).

Testi, Arnaldo, "The Gender of Reform Politics: Theodore Roosevelt and the Culture of Masculinity," Journal of American History, vol. 81, no. 4 (1995).

Thomas, Jo, "The Third Man: A Reporter Investigates the Oklahoma City Bombing," The Syracuse Law Review, vol. 59, (2008-2009).

Toher, Mark, "Octavian's Arrival in Rome," Classical Quarterly, vol 54, no. 1, (2004).

Tosti, Gustavo, "Anarchistic Crimes," Political Science Quarterly, vol. 14, (September 1899).

Tucker, Benjamin R,. "Rights and Individual Rights," Liberty, (January 7, 1882).

Tyler, Lyon G., "The South and Secession," Tyler's Quarterly Historical and Genealogical Magazine, vol. XIII, (1931-1932).

van der Spek, Bert, "New Evidence from the Babylonian Astronomical Diaries Concerning Seleucid and Arsacid History," Archiv fur Orientforschung, vol. 44/45 (1997-1998).

Walker, Peter, "Four July 21 Plotters Jailed for Life," The Guardian, (July 11, 2007).

Wakstein, Alan M. "The Origins of the Open Shop Movement, 1919-1920," Journal of American History, v.51, (1964).

Weiser, Benjamin, "Life and Death Questions in Embassy Bombing," The New York Times, (June 3, 2001).

Wendt, Alexander, "Anarchy is What States Make of It: The Social Construction of Power Politics," International Organization, vol. 46, no.2, (Spring 1992).

Wheelis, Mark, "Biological Warfare at the 1346 Siege of Caffa," Emerging Infectious Diseases, vol. 18, no. 9, (September 2002).

Wolverton II, Joe "An Officer and a Jihardist," New American, vol. 26, no.2, (2010).

Wright, Lawrence, "The Terror Web," The New Yorker, (August 2, 2004).

Yarros, Victor S., "Philosophical Anarchism: Its Rise, Decline and Eclipse," The American Journal of Sociology, vol. 41, no.4, (January 1936).

Yuchtman-Yaar, Ephraim and Tamar Hermann, "The Latitude of Acceptance: Israeli Attitudes Toward Political Protest Before and after the Assassination of Yitzhak Rabin," Journal of Conflict Resolution, vol. Vol.42, (December 1998).

Zaryab, Iqbal and Chirstopher Zorn, "The Political Consequences of Assassination," Journal of Conflict Resolution, vol. 52, no.3, (June 2008).

Zhu, Helena and Joan Delaney, "Che Guevera: Hypocritical Darling of Pop Culture," The Epoch Times, (February 23, 2009).

Newspaper Articles

Alberts, Sheldon, "Guard at U.S. Holocaust Museum Slain by Gunman; Washington D.C. Suspect Believed to be White Supremacist." National Post, (January 11, 2009).

Baker, Kevin, "Blood on the Street," The New York Times, (February 22, 2009).

Barstow, David, "An Abortion Battle Fought to the Death," The New York Times, (July 25, 2009).

Belair, Felix, "President Bids U.N. Act Today on Mideast After Pro-Nasser Coup Ousts Iraq King," The New York Times, (July 15, 1958).

Bellantoni, Christine, "Medal of Freedom for Harvey Milk," The Washington Times, (July 31, 2009).

Bigart, Homer, "Strange Was in Strange Arabia," The New York Times, (March 10, 1957).

Blumenthal, Ralph, "Bombs Used in Trade Center Blast," The New York Times, (October 28, 1993).

Bonsal, Stephen, "The Obliteration of the Kingdom of Korea," The New York Times, (July 28, 1907).

Bragg, Rick, "A Friend Is Lost and a Street is Full of Bewilderment and Pain," New York Times, (July 28, 1996).

Bragg, Rick, "2 Bomb Blasts Rock Abortion Clinic at Atlanta; 6 Are Injured," New York Times, (January 17, 1997).

Brick, Michael, "Man Crashes Plane Into Texas I.R.S. Office," The New York Times, (February 18, 2010).

Brown, Curt, "Racial Tensions High After Fight at Owatonna High School," Star Tribune, (November 20, 2009).

Bulgarian diplomat, A. "Bulgaria's Claims on Land She No Defends," The New York Times, (August 22, 1916).

Burns, John F. "The Vote, and Democracy Itself, Leave Anxious Iraqis Divided," The New York Times, (January 30, 2005).

Byas, Hugh, "Army to Stop Agitation," The New York Times, (May 16, 1932).

Caldwell, Earl, "Martin Luther King is Slain in Memphis," The New York Times, (April 5, 1968).

Cockburn, Patrick, "Terry Anderson is Set Free After Seven Years," The Independent, (December 5, 1991).

Cortes, Arnaldo, "Trotsky Dies of His Wounds," The New York Times, (August 22, 1940).

Crouch, Gregory, "World Breifing Europe; The Netherlands: Van Gogh Killer Jailed for Life," The New York Times, (July 27, 2005).

Cyphers, Luke, "Still Seeking Bomb Shelter," The Daily News, (October 1, 2000).

de Borchgrave, Arnaud, "Pakistan's Ex-Spy Chief Blames Mossad," United Press International, (September 26, 2001).

de Onis, Juan, "Motive Unknown," The New York Times, (March 26, 1975).

de Onis, Juan, "U.S. Suspends New Air to Salvador Till American Deaths Are Clarified," The New York Times, (December 6, 1980).

de Winter, Leon, "Besessen vom Leid" Die Zeit, (April 2, 2009).

Evans-Pritchard, Ambrose, 'Fortuyn killed to 'protect' Muslims," Telegraph, March 28, 2003).

Feuer, Alan, "A Worrisome Medical Puzzle, Wrapped in a Workaday Life," New York Times, (October 31, 2001).

Flint, Peter B., "Rashid Karami, Cool Persuader in a Land of Strife," The New York Times, (June 2, 1987).

Garrison, Lloyd, "Nigerian Regime Rocked by Coup; Control in Doubt," The New York Times, (January 16, 1966).

Ghattas, Sam F., "Hariri Tribunal Under Way," The Washington Times, (March 4, 2009).

Goodman, Brenda, Gunman Who Shot Wallace is to be Freed," The New York Times, August, 24, 2007).

Gottlieb, Alan, "Duran, the Child Nobody Knew," The Denver Post, (November 6, 1994).

Grieshaber, Kirsten, "World Briefing: Europe-Germany: Sentencing in 1991 Attack on Jews," The New York Times, (September 29, 2004).

Gwetzman, Bernard, "President's Trip to Canada Today Put Off Because of Teheran Crisis," The New York Times, (November 9, 1979).

Haberman, Clyde, "In Islamic Center Fight., Lessons in Prepositions and Fear Mongering," The New York Times, (July 27, 2010).

Haberman, Clyde, "Assassination in Israel," The New York Times, (November 5, 1995).

Harden, Blaine and Nina Bernstein, "Voices in His Head Muted, A Killer Rejoins the World," The New York Times, (July 31, 2000).

Henry, Neil and Chip Brown, "An Aimless Road to a Place in History," The Washington Post, (April 5, 1981).

Hersh, Seymour, "Huge C.I.A. Operation Reported in U.S. Against Anti-war Forces, Other Dissidents in Nixon Years," The New York Times, (December 22, 1974).

Hillel, "Moments in the National and Territorial Revival of the Jewish People," Das Volk or The People, (December 15, 1907).

Hirsi Ali, Ayan, "Grief and Anger Over Theo's Murder; Victim of Islamists," The International Herald Tribune, (November 11, 2004).

Hoge, Warren, "Renegade Protestants Kill Lawyer in Ulster," The New York Times, (March 16, 1999).

Hoge, Warren, "An Irish Accord: Irish Talks Produce An Accord to Stop Decades of Bloodshed" The New York Times, (April 11, 1998).

Ibrahim, Youssef M., "Algerian President Fatally Shot at Rally," The New York Times, (June 30, 1992).

Jameson, Sam, "Even in Death, Park's Authoritarian Shadow Looms Over Korea," Los Angeles Times, (November 4, 1979).

John Birch Society, "The Time Has Come" The New York Times, (December 15, 1963).

Johnston, David, "After Car Bomb Attack in Oklahoma City Wrecks 9 Story Federal Office Building," The New York Times, (April 20, 1995).

Kamm, Henry, "Sadat in Jerusalem: Day of Challenge," The New York Times, (November 21, 1977).

Khiss, Peter, "Kennedy Target of Birch Writer," The New York Times, (February 11, 1964).

Kifner, John, "Authorities Hold a Man of Extreme Right Wing Views," The New York Times, (April 22, 1995).

Kilgannon, Corey, "Most-wanted Fugitive is Arrested," New York Times, (April 1, 2001).

Kirst, Sean, "They Never Got on Flight 103, but They Can't Escape the Tragedy," The Post Standard, (December 21, 2008).

Kron, Joseph, "Extremist Hutu Officials Blamed in '94 Rwandan Assassination," *The New York Times*, January 11, 2010.

Lagos, Claudia, and Patrick J. McDonne, "Pinochet-era General is Caught," Los Angeles Times, (August 3, 2007).

Lardner, George and Lorraine Adams, "To Unabomb Victims, a Deeper Mystery," Washington Post, (April 14, 1996).

Ledbetter, Les, "Bangladesh Reports Death Of President Ziaur Rahman," The New York Times, (May 30, 1981).

Ledbetter, Les, "John Lennon of Beatles Is Killed," The New York Times, (December 9, 1980).

Locy, Toni, "Duran Cnvicted of Trying to Kill President Clinton," Washington Post, (April 5, 1995).

Mazzetti, Mark, Sabrina Tavernise and Jack Healy, "Suspect Charged, Said to Admit Role in Plot," The New York Times, (May 4, 2010).

McKinley, Jr., James C., "Woman Who Tried to Kill Ford in '75 is Paroled," The New York Times, (August 15, 2009).

McLaughlin, J. W., "Escaped Briton Tells Full Story of Afghan Plot," The New York Times, (May 29, 1919).

McQuiston, John T., "Kahane Is Killed After Giving Talk in New York Hotel," The New York Times, (November 6, 1990).

Merrill, N.O., "Torees, Ex-President of Bolivia Found Murdered in Argentina," The New York Times, (June 4, 1976).

Milloy, Ross E., "An Angry Telephone Call Signals the End of the World for Cult Members," The New York Times, (April 20, 1993).

Morris, Willy, "Kaczynski Ended Career in Math with no Explanation," The Buffalo News, (April 6, 1996).

Muir, Hugh and Rie Cowan, "Four bombs in 5 minutes," The Guardian, (July 8, 2005).

Newman, William, "Rename Triborough for RFK." The New York Times, (November 6, 2008).

No author, "Agents Tracing Hinckley's Path Find a Shift to Violent Emotions," The New York Times, (April 5, 1981).

No author, "Al-Owhali spared death in embassy bombimg," Law Center, (June 12, 2001).

No author, "Angiolillo dies bravely," The New York Times, (August 22, 1897).

No author, "Assassination: The Night Bobby Kennedy was Shot," The Independent, (January 21, 2007).

No author, "Bermuda Governor and Aide Are Killed By Shots in Capital," The New York Tines, (March 11, 1973).

No author, "Birth of a Nation," The New York Times, (December 25, 1971).

No author, "Blast Kills Iran Leaders," The Los Angeles Times, (August 31,1981).

No author, "Cairo Press Critical," The New York Times, (November 27, 1963).

No author, "Canadian Film Details '72 Stalking of Nixon," The New York Times, (April 15, 1997).

No author, "Ceylon's Premier is Killed; Assassin, a Monk, Seized," The New York Times, (September 26, 1959).

No author, "Chairman Frick Shot," The New York Times, (July 24, 1892).

No author, "Chronology of the Bombing Case," USA Today, (June 2, 2003).

No author, "Cuba Attributes Murder to "Right,"" The New York Times, (November 27, 1963).

No author, "Dallas Policeman's Wife Also Weeps for her Husband," The New York Times, (November 29, 1963).

No author, "A Day in the Life of America," The New York Post, (September 12, 2001).

No author, "Deaths in World Trade Center Terrorist Attacks," Morbidity and Mortality Weekly Report, (Atlanta, Ga. Center for Disease Control and Prevention, September 11, 2002).

No author, "Dutch Court Sentences van Gogh Killer to Life," The New York Times, (July 26, 2005).

No author, "Eight Military Jets Destroyed at Air Base in Puerto Rico," The New York Times, (January 12, 1981).

No Author, "English Lord Assassinated in Terrorist Attack While Vacationing Aboard a Fishing Boat," The New York Jewish Times, (August 27, 1979).

No author, "Fire Kills 19; Unions Accused," The New York Times, (October 2 ,1910).

No author, "Former President Executed in Congo," The New York Times, (March 26, 1977).

No author, "German Terrorist Sentenced for '77 Killing," The New York Times, (June 4, 1991).

No author, "The Guillotines Sure Work," The New York Times, (May 21, 1894).

No author, "Hamas Leader Faults Israeli Sanction Plan," The New York Times, (February 18, 2006).

No author, "Hey, you talkin' to me?" The New York Times, (December 29, 2004).

No author, "Holds Political Ruin Confronted Lincoln, New York Times, (February 9, 1932).

No author, "Japanese Premier Stabbed to Death by Korean Fanatic, The New York Times, (November 5, 1921).

No author, "Johann Most Dead After Brief Illness," The New York Times, (March 18, 1906).

No author, "Ludlow Massacre Monument Dedicated As US Landmark," Colorado and Denver News, (June 28, 2009).

No author, "Malagasy Head of State Killed Six Days After Taking Office," The New York Times, (February 12, 1965).

No author, "Malagasy Head of State Killed Six Days After Taking Office," The New York Times, (February 12, 1965).

No author, "Manhunt for Madrid Massacre Terrorists," Manchester Evening News, (March 12, 2004).

No author, "More Arrests made in Connection with Barret's Death," The Jackson News, (April 23, 2010).

No author, "Phalangists Identify Bomber of Gemaycl as Lebanese Leftist," The New York Times, (October 3, 1982, World).

No author, "Policeman Slays Somali President," The New York Times, (October 16, 1969).

No Author, "Political Killings Frequent in Japan," The New York Times, (August 18, 1935).

No author, "Premier of Iran Shot by Student," The New York Times, (January 22, 1965).

No author, "Prince Ito Assassinated," The New York Times, (October 26, 1909).

No author, "Rioting and Bloodshed in the Streets of Chicago," The New York Times, (May 5, 1886).

No author, "The Sadat Assassination," The New York Times, (October 7, 1981).

No author, "Scientists Says Report Casts Doubt on Story of Huey Long Death," The New York Times, (February 22, 1992).

No author, "Shot Down at His Door," The New York Times, (October 17, 1890).

No author, "Taraki Yields Afghan Presidency and Party Posts to Prime Minister" The New York Times, (September 17, 1979).

No author, "The Guillotine Sure Works: Details of the Execution of Vaillant the Anarchist," The New York Times, (February 6, 1894).

No author, "The Killing of Mr. Gandhi," The Times of London, (November 16, 1949).

No author, "The Sadat Assassination," The New York Times, (October 7, 1981).

No author, "Teheran Students Seize U.S. Embassy and Hold Hostages," The New York Times, (November 5, 1979).

No author, "The Trial That Wasn't," The New York Times, (February 23, 1997).

No author, "Third Defendant is Convicted in Dragging Death in Texas," New York Times, (November 19, 1999).

No author, "Tolbert of Liberia is Killed in a Coup by Sergeant," The New York Times, (April 13, 1980).

No author, "2 White Racists Convicted in Killing of Radio Host," The New York Times, (November 18, 1987).

O'Neill, Sean and John Steele, "Mein Kampf for Sale in Arabic," The Telegraph, (March 19, 2002).

Oberdorfer, Don, "Iran Paid for Release of Hostages," The Washington Post, (January 19, 1994).

Oppenheim, Carol, "RFK would OK parole, Sirhan says," Chicago Tribune, (May 11, 1982).

Perez Sergio, "21 Convicted of Madrid Train Bombing; Alleged Planner Acquitted," Reuters and USA Today, (October 31, 2007).

Pipes, Daniel, "Why Oslo's Hopes Turned to Dust," The New York Post, (September 9, 2003).

Pogash, Carol, "Myth of the Twinkie Defense," San Francisco Chronicle, (November 23, 2003).

Preston, Julia, "Word Briefing: United Nations: Syria balks at Hariri Tribunal," New York Times, (November 25, 2006).

Pringle, Peter, "Squeaky Little Girl to Tried to Shoot the President," The Sunday Times, (August 16, 2009).

Quinn, Eamon and John F. Burns, "After Killings Linked to I.R.A. Factions, Northern Ireland Defends Its Fragile Peace," The New York Times, (March 11, 2009).

Radin, Charles A., "Panel Confirms Plagiarism by King and BU," The Boston Globe, (October 11, 1991).

Reaves, Gayle, "Ex-Dallas Clerk, 2nd Man Guilty in New York Bombing," Dallas Morning News, (November 13, 1997).

Reuters, "Ngouabi Dies of His Wounds," The New York Times, (March 20, 1977).

Rimer, Sara, "Few Knew of White House Suspect's Turmoil," New York Times, (November 7, 1994).

Ring, Michael, "El Salvador Today: The Hope and the Challenge," Enemies of War, www.pbs.org.itvs.Enemies of war/perspectives3.

Russakoff, Dale and Serge F. Kovaleski, "An Ordinary Boy's Extraordinary Rage," The Washington Post, (July 2, 1995).

Sack, Kevin, "In Latest Atlanta Bombing, 5 Are Injured at a Gay Bar," New York Times, (February 23, 1997).

Sciolino, Elaine and Don Van Natta, Jr. "For a Decade London Thrived as a Busy Crossroads of Terror," The New York Times, (July 10, 2005).

Sciolino, Elaine, "For Outsiders in Saudi Arabia, Worship Comes With a Risk," The New York Times, (February 12, 2002).

Segev Tom, "Courting Hitler," The New York Times Sunday Book Review, (September 26, 2008).

Settle, Michael and Brian Currie, "Defiant Salmond tells U.S. Oil Giant BP Did Not Lobby to Free Megrahi," Herald Scotland, (July 22, 2010).

Simon, Mark, "A Trip into the Heart of Darkness," San Francisco Chronicle, (December 10, 1978).

Stanley, Allessandra, "Rome Journal: Agony Lingers, 20 Years After the Moro Killing," The New York Times, (May 9, 1998).

Sullivan, Ronald, "Judge Gives Maximum Term in Kahane Case," The New York Times, (January 30, 1992).

Talley, Tim, "After 10 Years, McVeigh Associate Leaves Prison," The Buffalo News, (January 21, 2006).

Thomas, Jo, "Terry Nichols Gets Life Term in Bombing Plot," The New York Times, (June 5, 1998).

Townsend, Mark, "Leak Reveals Official Story of London Bombings," The Guardian, (April 9, 2006).

Trbach, Bradford, "Korea-Japan Tension Is Centuries Old," The New York Times, (November 14, 1994).

Turner, Wallace, "San Francisco Mayor is Slain: City Supervisor Also Killed: Ex-offcial Gives Up to Police," The New York Times, (November 28, 1978).

Walsh, Paul, "Islamic Group Backs Service Dog Owner," Star Tribune, (May 14, 2008)

Watal, Divya, "W.T.C. Memorial for '93 Victims Unveiled," Downtown Express, vol. 17, no. 41, (March 4-11, 2005).

Weisman, Steven R., "Japanese Translator of Rushdie Book Found Slain," The New York Times, (July 13, 1991).

Windeler, Robert, "Family Remains Silent," The New York Times, (June 7, 1968).

Yellin, Emily, "Third Inquiry Confirms Others: Ray Alone Was King's Killer," The New York Times, (March 28, 1998).

Zielbauer, Paul, "Connecticut Woman, 94, Is Fifth to Die from Inhalation Anthrax," New York Times, (November 22, 2001).

DOCUMENTS

Congressional Record, 57, Cong. I sess.

HR 3162, 107th Congress, (October 24, 2001).

In the Supreme Court of California, S094597 Ct. App. 5 No. F028940 County of Fresno Super.Ct. No. 57174.

No author, Egypt: International Religious Freedom Report, Washington D.C. U.S. Departmetn of State, (October 26, 2009).

No author. Report of the President's Commission on the Assassination of President John F. Kennedy. (Washington, D.C.: The United States Government Printing Office, 1964).

Population Reference Bureau, World Population Data Sheet, (Washington D.C., 2009).

U.S. Department of Defense, "Daily Casualty Release," Icasualtes.org.

U.S. Department of Justice, Bureau of Justice Statistics, "Trends in Violent Victimization by Age," (2008).

U.S. Department of State, "Report of the Accountability Review Board," (Washington,.D.C.: The U.S. Government Printing Office, January 1999).

U.S. House of Representatives, Select Committee on Assassinations, (Washington, D.C. U.S. Government Printing Office, December 29, 1978).

United States of America vs. Lawrence John Layton, 666 F.Supp. 1369, no. CR-80-416 REP. U.S. (June 3, 1987).

Index

abortionists, 55
absolute dictator, 63
Academy of Sciences, 102
Achille Lauro, 149
affective ties, 119
Afghanistan, 59
air travel, 157
Akaska palace, 62
al Megrahi, 150
Al-Aqsa martyrs, 118
Albrecht, Suzanne, 115
Alexander II, 7
Alfred Murrah Federal Office Building,
   136
al-Qaeda terrorists, 152
American Airlines flight 11, 153
American service personnel, 162
American terrorism, 125
Americans for Democratic Action, 52
Anarchist Congress, 111
anarchist group, 169
anarchist groups, 42
anarchist newspapers, 107
anarchist organizations, 169
anarchist socialism, 112
anarchists, 110
Anarchy, 101
Anglo Iranian Oil Co., 71
anthrax attack, 138
antl-abortion activists, 54
anti-Muslim crusade, 157
anti-Semitism, 105
Arab from Jaffa, 87
Arab society, 162

Arab world, 116
Arab-Muslim SS unit, 75
Arabs, 53
Arbeiter Front, 106
architect of apartheid, 99
Arco, Anton, 18
Arentina, 87
Arlington County, Virginia, 153
Army redemption Council, 96
Ashrat, Hamdan ibn, xi
assassination of President Kennedy,
   153
Assassinations, Types of, xiii
assimilation, 106
Atilla the Hun, 38
Atlanta Constitution, 137
Atlanta North Side Family Planning
   Services, 136
Atta, Mohamed, 154
attempted murder, 179
Augustus, 5
Austin IRS attack, 141
Austria, 14
Aviation Security Act, 149
Baader, Andreas and Gudrun Ensslin,
   113
Bakunin, Michael, 103
Bangladesh, 61
Bank of America, 148
Bank of Japan, 64
Barnes, Harry Elmer, 38
Basque separatist movement, 29
Baton Rouge, 43
Battle of Hastings, 24

Battle of the Boyne, 22
Beirut International Airport, 148
Bermuda, 81
Bible, Jewish, 70
bin Laden, Osama, 118
biochemical analysis, 139
biological warfare, 139
Blair House, 175
blood brotherhoods, 64
bloody Sunday, 48
Bolivian government, 87
Bolsheviks, 181
bombing of Hanoi, 135
bombing of Wall street, 129
Book of Mormon, 37
Booth, John Wilkes, 37
Boss of all the Bosses, 45
Bouyeri, Mohammed, 29
Branch Davidian, 134
Bresci, Gaetano, 26
Brighton hotel bombing, 22
British Commonwealth of Nations, 35
British upper class, 81
Brookline, Massachusetts, 137
Brussels, 115
Buback, Siegfried, 20, 114
Buddhist clergy, 69
Buddhists, 66
Buenos Aires, 108
Bulgaria, 28
Burundi, 94
Byck, Samuel, 179
Byrd, James, murder of, 140
Caesar, Julius, xiii
California, 49
California Forestry Association, 131
California scientists, 131
Caligula, 7
Canovas, Antonio, 29
Castro, Fidel, 49
Catcher in the Rye, 53
Catholic Church, 141
Catholic priest, 162
Centennial Olympic Park, 136
center of the land, 135
Central Intelligence Agency, 181
Cermak, Antonin, 43

Chapman, Mark David, 53
Chicago police, 126
Chinese head of state, 62
Christ killer, 104
Christian North Africa, 160
Christianity, 7
Christianity is prohibited, 155
Christianity, converts, 163
Christians in Egypt, 163
Church of Jesus Christ of Latter Day
    Saints, 36
circular interaction, 52
civil disobedience, 67
civil rights, 162
Civil Service Reform Act, 39
civil war, 59
Civil War, 38
Cleopatra, 2
Clinton, William, President, 174
coal companies, 126
cofiscation of property, 107
College of William and Mary, 38
Colorado Fuel and Iron Co., 126
Columbia, 82
Columbia Historical Society, 173
Colvin, Claudette, 47
communist plot, 171
companyguard system, 127
concentration camp, 181
concentration camp prisoners, 21
condemn the condemner, 168
Confederate conspiracy, 173
Congo, 95
conspiracy theories, 44, 48
Constantinople, 1
Corpus Christi, 30
Cosa Nostra, 45
cost of production, 102
Council of Clermont, 160
country's first dictator, 39
County Hall of Records, 128
Crimes of Terrorism Act, 158
crusader alliance, 159
Crystal Night, 17
Cuban communism, 89
Cuban revolution, 86
Czech Republic, 74

Czolgosz, Leon, 41
Dallas Police Headquarters, 46
Dar-es-Salaam, 152
Daschle, Thomas, 138
death penalty, 81
Debtors' prison, 25
defeat by the Muslim Arabs, 116
defender of human rights, 86
Delasalle, Paul, 110
Delta Force, 147
Democratic nomination, 49
democratic principles, 182
Democratic Republic of the Congo, 95
Denver radio talk show host, 140
developed countries, 117
differential association, 168
Dirty War, The, 89
disorderly conduct, 109
division of labor, 102
Dollfuss, Engelbert, 14
Dominican Republic, 82
Donegan Bay, 21
Dreyfus Affair, 12, 105
Dual Monarchy, 13
Dutch population, 158
dynamiter, invention of, 130
Dynasty, Ptolomaic, 2
dysfunctional family, 177
Edict of Milan, 106
Edmund I, 24
Edward the Elder, 24
Eisenhower, Dwight, 96
Eisner, Kurt, 18
El Salvador, 85
eliminating all government, 101
embassy employees, 152
emotionally disturbed, 171
English, 161
epidemic of terrorism, 116
epistles, 6
Errico Malatesta, 108
ethnic fighting, 95
European immigrants, 130
Evian conference, 82
extremist political groups, 171
false accusations, 105
father of modern history, 180

FBI, The, 133
Federal Republic of Germany, 116
Feinstein, Diane, 51
first amendment, 126
First World War, 13
flaming tower, 153
Ford, Gerald, 174
Foreign Office, 25
Fort Benning, 135
Fort Leavenworth, 174
Fortier, Michael, 136
France, 117
Franz Ferdinand, 12
fraticide in Chechnya, 119
free communism, 107
Freiheit or Liberty, 109
French Assembly, 88
French Chamber of Deputies, 109
French military academy, 71
Frick, Henry Clay, 111
Garfield, James A., xiii, 39
Gaul, 4
General Theory of Crime, 171
Geneva Convention American Force
    Protection Act, 71
genital mutilation, 162
George Washington University, 44
German Chamber of Commerce, 114
German Embassy in Stockholm, 114
German government, 72, 115
German industrialists, 19
German Parliament, 109
Germans, 15
Ghandi, Indira, 68
Ghandi, Mohandas, 67
globalization process, 161
Goldman, Emma, 110
Good Friday Accords, 23
Gospel of St. John, 156
Grand Mufti, 74
Great Depression, 44
Grynszpan, Herschel, 17
guerilla actions, 181
Guevara, Ernesto, 86
Guiteau, Charles, xiii, 39
Gulf of Aden, 98
Gulf War, 135

Gunpowder Plot, xiv
Guyana, 51
Hadrian, 7
Haight-Ashbury, 179
Haiti, 82
Hamas, 155
Harbin National Railroad Station, 63
Harvard College, 46
Hassan, Nidal Malik, 141
Haymarket Riot, 110, 125
Heydrich, Reinhard, 19
hijackers, 154
Hindenburg, Paul, 19
Hindustan, 67
Hipparchus, xii
Hirohito, Emperor of Japan, 64
Hitler, Adolf, xiv, 181
Holocaust, 139
Holy History of Mankind, 105
homosexual politician, 50
honor killing, 162
House of Representatives, 45
Howells, Vernon, 134
Huberty, James Oliver, 172
Inca Empire, 89
Indian National Congress, 67
India-Pakistan war, 68
innocent bystanders, 129
insane, 41
Internal Macedonian Revolutionary
    Organization, 27
International Tribunal for the Genocide
    in Rwanda, 98
International Worker's People's
    Association, 42
involvement of women, 115
Iranian heads of State, 70
Iranian high priest, 62
Irish National Liberation Army, 23
Irish Republican Army, 22
iron workers' union, 128
Islam, 29, 77
Islamic Center, 156
Islamic Jihad, 148
Islamic Salvation Front, 93
Ismaili Muslims, xi
Israel, 94

Israeli Supreme Court, 73
Israeli territory, 74
Italian Chamber of Deputies, 26
Italian court, 159
Italian-American newspapers, 45
Ivins, Bruce E., 139
Jackson, Andrew, 172
Japanese nobility, 62
Japanese public, 64
Jaures, Jean, 12
Jerusalem, 6, 94
Jewell, Richard, 137
Jewish Defense League, 53
Jewish life in Russia, 9
Jewish population of Europe, 103
Jewish Problem, 105
Jewish refugees from Russia, 113
Jews, 8
Jews, German, 17
Jews, Hungarian, 73
John Birch Society, 171
Johnson, Lyndon, 46
Jonestown, 51
Josephus, 6
Junio Reserve Officer Training Corps,
    174
Kabul, 60
Kahane, Meir, 53
Kansas Court of Appeals, 54
Karami, Rashid, 76
Kastner, Rudolf, 73
Katanga, 96
Kennedy, John F., 45
Kennedy, Robert, 176
Kerensky, Alexander, 10
Khan, Mohammed Siddique, 159
Khobar Towers, 151
killing Jews, 176
King Victor Emanuel, 108
King, Martin Luther Jr., 47
Kishinev massacre, 9
Koran, 157
Korea, 63
Kropotkin, Peter, 106
Ku Klax Klan, 125
labor saving devices, 107
land monopoly, 112

Landauer, Gustav, 105
Latin, 5
Latin language, 5
League for the Defense of Religious
    Freedom, 84
Lebanese Christian Phalangist party, 75
Lebanese civil war, 76
Lebanese government, 148
Lebanon, 75
level of participation, 168
liberal rhetoric, 47
Libyan Intelligence Service, 149
Lidice, 20
life in prison, 152
Lincoln, Abraham, 37
Lockerbie, 149
London police, 159
London, England, 48
Long, Huey, 44
Los Angeles Times, 127
Louis XIII, 11
Ludlow massacre, 126
Lumpenproletariat, 103
Lumumba, Patrice, 95
lynchings, 40
Macedonian Empire, 2
Madgascar, 97
Madrid railroad station, 158
Malatesta, Errico, xiii
Manson, Charles, 179
MarieAntoinette, 11
Martinez de Peron, Isabel, 88
Marx, Karl, 12
Marxist revolution, 27
Maryknoll Order, 86
mass hysteria, 42
McGee, Tomas D'Arcy, 35
McKinley, William, 40
McVeigh, Timothy, 135
meaningless lives, 177
Medal of Freedom, 50
Mein Kampf, 163
Meinhof, Ulrike, 20
Memphis, Tennessee, 47
Mexican president, 84
Mexico, 83
Mexico City, 83

Middle Ages, 17, 160
Middle East, 75
military dictatorship, 72
military establishment, 155
Milwaukee, 177
Minister of Agriculture, 85
Mondale, Walter, 51
Monrovia, 96
Morgan bank, 129
Mormons, 36
Morocco, 159
Most, Johann, 108
Mountbatten, Louis, 22
murder of Lincoln, 170
murderous attack, 151
Muslim aggression, 68
Muslim countries, 115
Muslim suicide bombers, 142
Muslim women, 29
Muslims in the Netherlands, 28
Mussolini, Benito, 26
Nairobi, Kenya, 151
Nantes, Edict of, 11
Napoleon III, 173
Napoleon of Persia, 70
nation of parasites, 105
National Committe of Military
    Leadership, 97
National Crime Information Center,
    134
National Democratic Party, 114
National Erectors' Association, 128
National Guard, 47, 127
National Labor Relations Act, 128
national rebellion, 104
National Socialist German Workers
    Party, 18
Nationalist Movement, 141
Native Americans, 35
Nazi ideology, 16
Nazi party, 15
Nazi regime, 116
Nazi victory, 93
Nero, Roman Emperor, 38
New Deal, 130
New Era, The, 35
New Jersey judge, 156

New Orleans, 40
New Testament, 2
New York City, 52
New York Times, 134
Nguyen, Kathy, 138
Nicaragua, 87
Nicholas II, 10
Nigeria, 97
Nissan Pathfinder, 156
Nixon, Richard, 177
Nobel Peace Prize, 47
North Viet Nam, 66
Northern Ireland, 22
nuclear ballistic missiles, 87
Octavian, 4
Oklahoma City, 134
Operation Condor, 89
Operation Southern Watch, 151
Oslo Accords, 74
Oswald, Lee Harvey, 45
Otis, Harrison Gray, 128
Pacific Ocean, 85
Pakistan, 61
Palestine Liberation Organization, 113
Palestinians, 74
Pan Am Flight 103, 150
Pan American Exposition, 41
Party of God, 149
Pasadena City College, 176
Paterson, N.J. silk strike, 45
patriarchy, 162
Patriot Act, 156
Patriotic Union party, 82
peace treaty, 75
Pearl Harbor, 153
Pentagon attack, 154
Pentagon, the, 143
People's Mujahedin, 72
People's Temple, 50
Perceval, Spencer, 24
personal sacrifices, 169
Philip of Macedonia, 1
Philipines, 157
Phillipines, 65
Philosophy of Poverty, 102
Pinkerton detectives, 111
Pizarro, Francisco, 90

Planned Parenthood, 136
Pobedonostsev, Konstantin, 8
pogrom, 106
Polish Jews, 16
Polish language, 8
political assassinations, 170
political change, 180
Political Consequences of
   Assassination, xii
political extremists, 172
political opponents, 61
political repression, 180
Pompey, 4
Ponto, Jurgen, 21
population control, 61
president of Korea, 65
presidential election, 46
Prime Minister of Italy, 27
Princip, Gavrilo, 13
Principles of Criminology, 167
private property, 160
profit system, 112
propaganda of the deed, 108
Proudhon, Pierre Joseph, 101
Puerto Rican independence, 175
Puerto Rican Nationalisl Party, 175
Putin, Vladimir, 10
Queen Min, 65
Queen Victoria, 70
racial intermarriage, 140
radical Islamists, 155
radical Republicans, 173
Rathenau, Walther, 15
Ray, James Earl, 48
Red Army, 84
Red Army Faction, 20, 113
Red Hand Defenders, 23
religious hate, 49
religious leaders, 72
religious police, 155
revolution of 1848, 103
Rishon le Zion, 10
risks of collective action, 168
Rohm, Ernst, xiv
Roman Catholic clerics, 86
Roman Emperor Constantine, 106
Roman Empire, 3

Roosevelt, Theodore, 41
Roselli, Carlo and Nello, 26
Royal Ulster Constabulary, 22
Rudolph, Eric, 137
Ruhr, invasion of, 16
Russian government, 60
Russian Japanese War, 41
Russian Orthodox, 9
Russian revolution, 85, 111
Rwanda, 97
Ryan, Leo, 51
Sacramento, California, 178
Sadat, Anwar, 94
Samoza dynasty, 88
San Francisco Chronicle, 50
San Francsco, board of supervisors, 49
Satanic Verses, 62
Saudi Arabia, 77, 155
schizophrenic, 39
Schleyer, Hans Martin, 21
Schrank, John, 172
scientific world, 161
Second World War, 14
Security Council, 76
Sedition Act, 129
Seleucid Empire, 2
self-hatred, 174
semi-sacrilege, 48
Seoul, 65
separation of powers, 36
September 11, 2001, 151
Serbia, 14
shameless fiction, 104
Sharia law, 154, 156
show trials, 85
Sinai Peninsula, 94
Sinclair Oil, 26
slaughter of six million Jews, 103
Slepian MD, Barnett, 137
Smith, Joseph, 36
so-called celebrities, 53
Social Contract, 37
social networks, 168
Socratic method, 3
Soldier of Allah, 142
South Africa, 67
South Viet Nam, 66

Soviet troops, 60
Soviet Union, 60, 170, 171
Spanish conquerors, 90
Spanish electorate, 159
Spanish name Diego, 40
Spansh army, 30
spirit of democracy, 179
spontaneous order, 102
Sri Lanka, 69
SS killing commandos, 73
St. cloud State University, 156
Stanford University, 47
state control of banking, 112
Stetham, Robert Dean, 149
Sturm Abteilung, 19
Supreme Court, 42, 133
Syracuse University, 150
Taliban, 60
Taxi Driver, 178
temporary dictatorship, 104
terrorism, direct, 170
terrorist organization, 118
terrorists, American Muslim, 142
Texas Technical University, 178
theocracy, 147
Theory, 167
third termer, 177
Thompson, "Big Bill," 43
Times Square, 143
Tippit, J.D., 46
Tolstoy, Leo, xi
Tresca, Carlo, 45
triumvirate, 4
Trotsky, Leon, 84
Truman, Harry, 175
trust buster, 41
truth, the, 117
Tucker, Benjamin, 112
Tunisia, 149
Turkey, 77
Tutsi and Hutus, 98
TWA Flight 840, 149
twelfth century, 160
tyrannical govrnment, 169
U.S, Constitution, 154
U.S. Custom House, 129
U.S.S. Cole, 152

UC Berkeley, 133
Ulyanov, Vladimir, 10
Umberto I, 25
Unabomber, 130
Unabomber Manifesto, 133
undeclared war on the United States, 153
Understanding Human Behavior, 131
uninvolved civilians, 118
Union Army, 36, 173
Union Square, 111
United Airlines flight 175, 154
United Kingdom, 160
United Mine Workers, 127
United Nations, 76
United Nations Commission on Human Rights, 52
United States, 152
United States of America, 5
United States Steel, 128
University of California, 83, 131
Ustasa, 28
van Gogh,, Theo, 28
Vanderbilt University, 178
Versailles, Treaty of, 16
Verwoerd, Henrik, 98

Viet Nam, 48
violent crime, 117
vom Rath, Ernst, 16
Von Brunn, James, 140
von Ranke, Leopold, 3
Waco debacle, 135
Wallace, George, 176
Walter Reed Medical Center, 142
Warren Report, 45
Washington Post, 133
Washington, D.C., 44
waving the bloody shirt, 39
weapon of mass destruction, 143
western civilization, 161
western Europe, 117
What is Propoerty?, 101
wicked infidel, 157
Wilson, Henry Lane, 83
Wittelsbach monarchy, 18
Woman is the Nigger of the World, 53
World Trade Center, 54, 119, 150
Yemen, 77, 152
Young, Brigham, 37
Zapata, Emiliano, 83
Zionism, 105
Zorn, Christopher, xii